The Circulating Lifeblood of Ideas

Leo Steinberg's Library of Prints

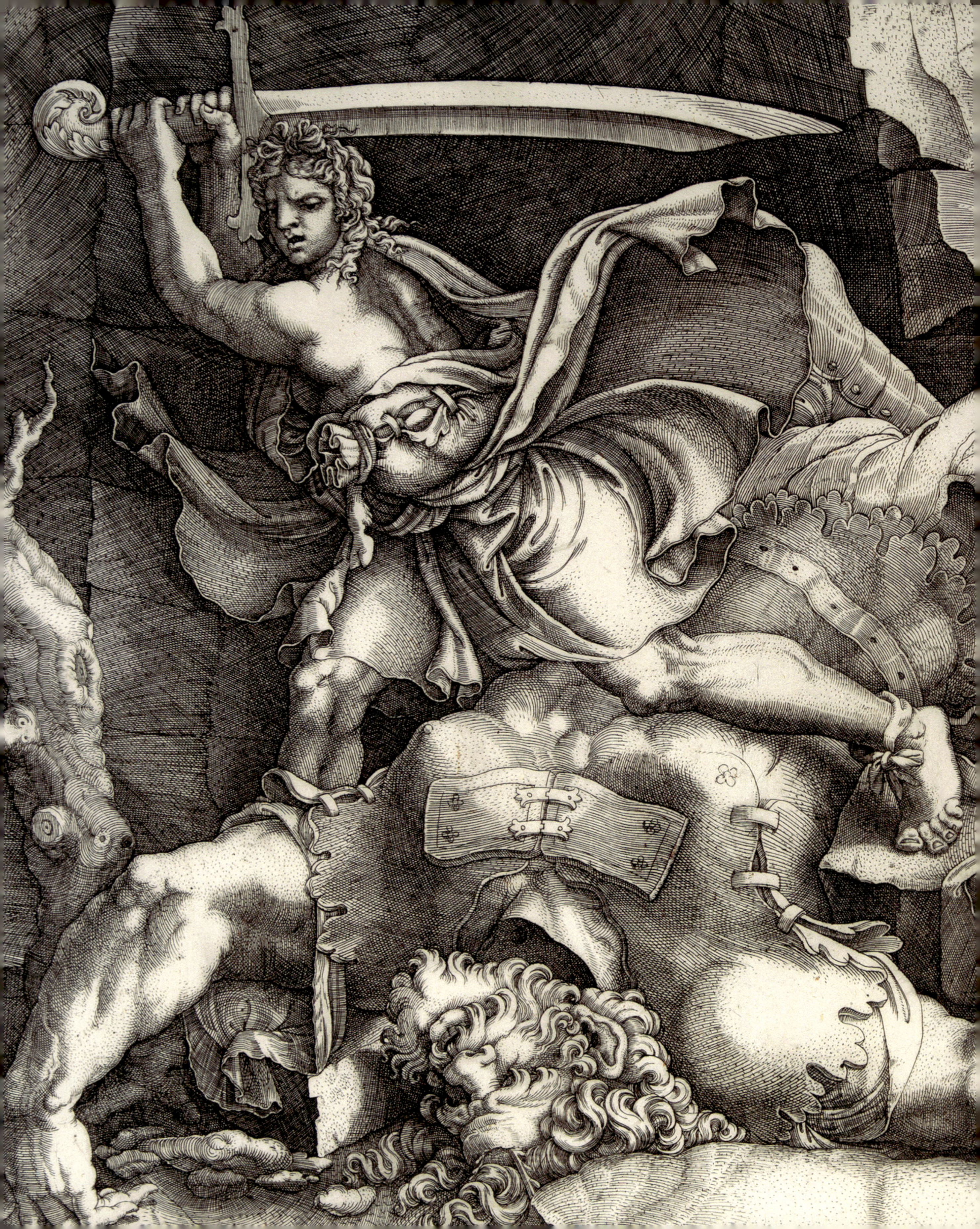

The Circulating Lifeblood of Ideas

Leo Steinberg's Library of Prints

Holly Borham

With a foreword by
Simone Wicha

and contribution by
Peter Parshall

BLANTON MUSEUM OF ART
at The University of Texas at Austin

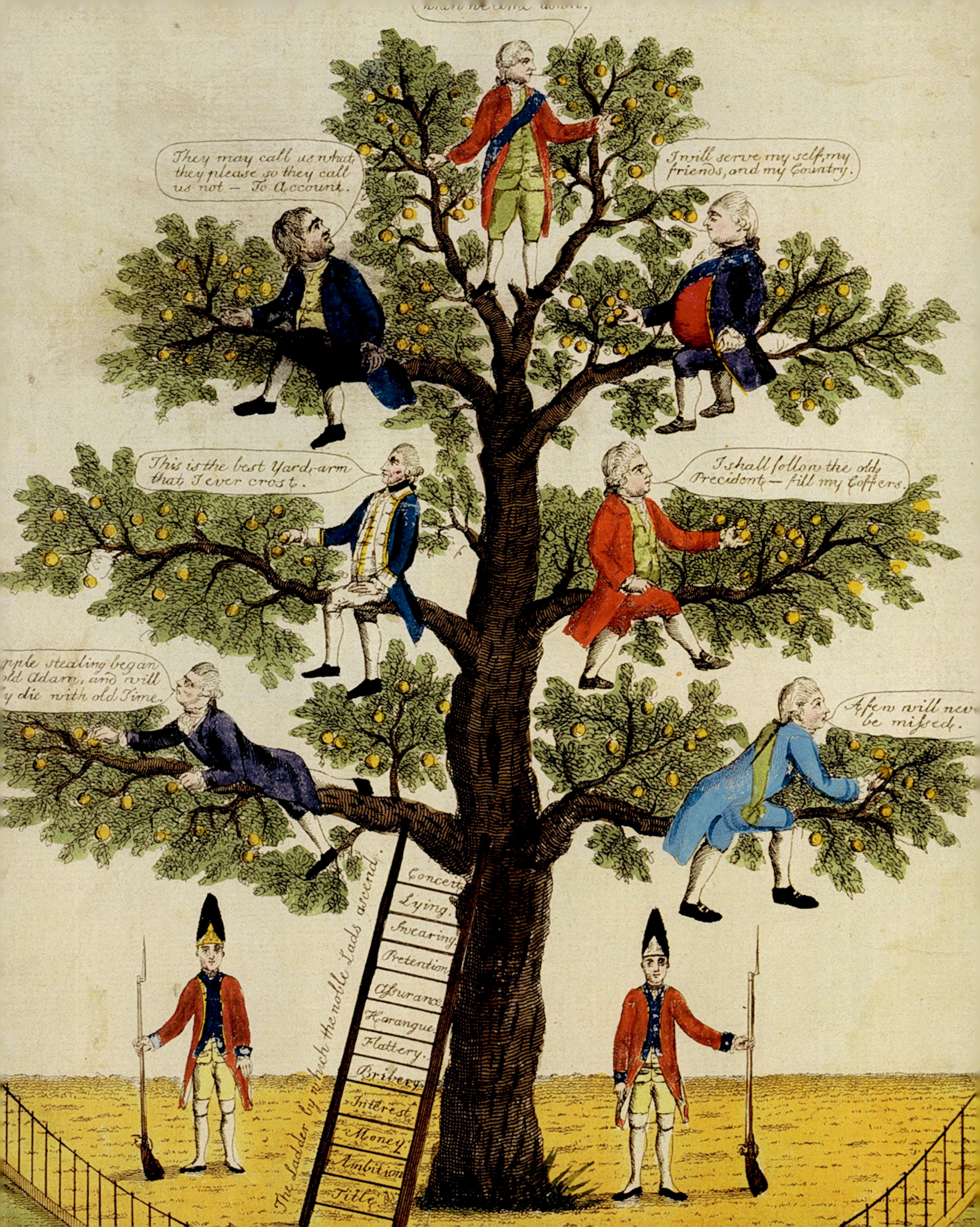

They may call us what they please so they call us not — To Account.
I will serve my self, my friends, and my Country.
This is the best Yard-arm that I ever crost.
I shall follow the old Precident — fill my Coffers.
pple stealing began
ld Adam, and will
y die with old Time.
A few will nev
be missed.
The Ladder by which the noble Lads ascend.
Conceit
Lying.
Swearing
Pretention
Assurance
Harangue
Flattery.
Bribery
Interest
Money
Ambition
Title

Contents

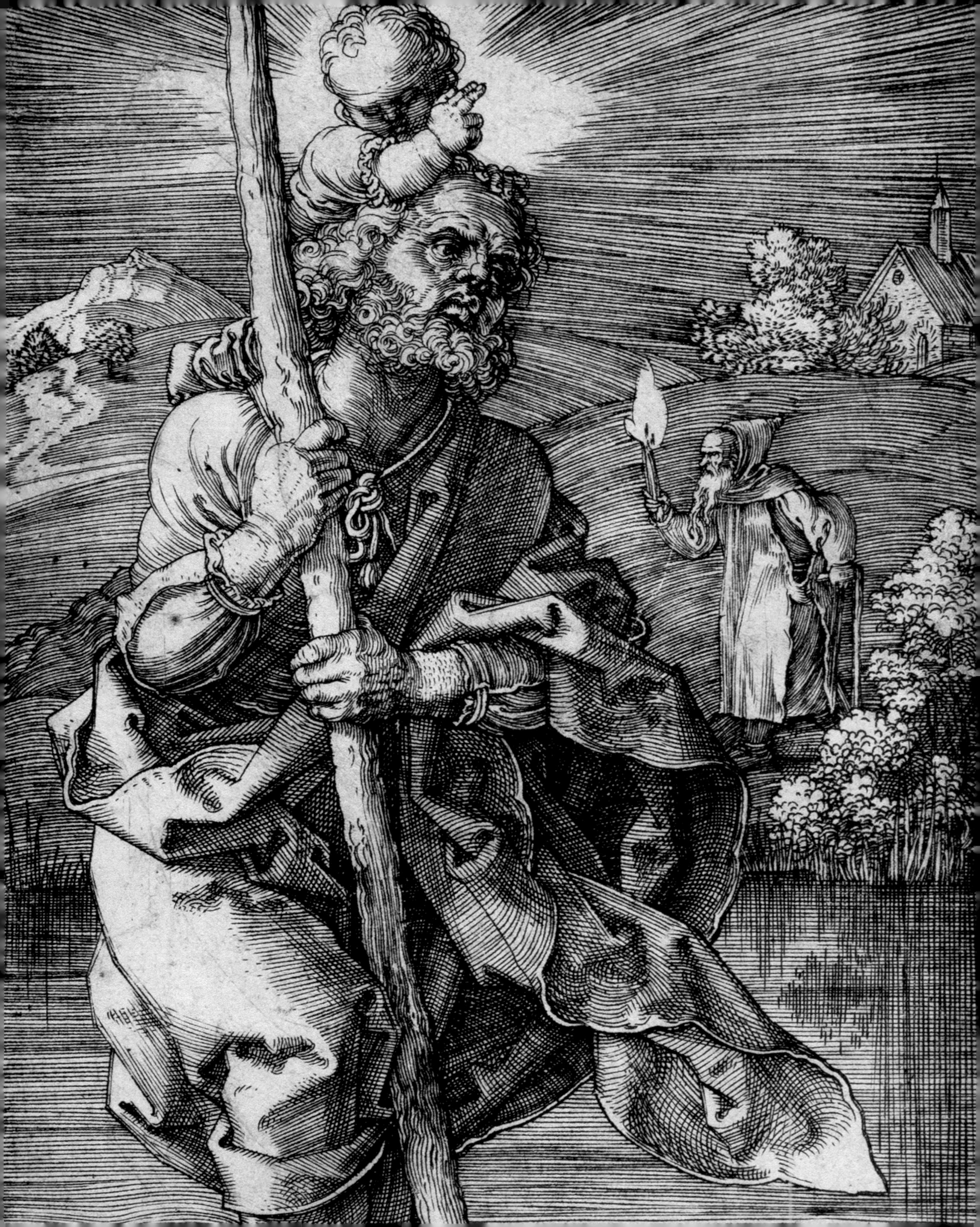

Director's Foreword

WHEN THE LEO STEINBERG COLLECTION CAME TO the Blanton in the early 2000s, it transformed the museum's print holdings. Steinberg built the collection over the course of five decades, beginning in the 1960s, and during this period also established himself as a distinguished scholar in the field of art history. The collection comprises more than 3,500 prints that span the Renaissance through the twentieth century. This wide-ranging catalogue of artworks inspired and supported Steinberg's scholarship, which was similarly ambitious in scope. In 1996, Professor Richard Shiff, currently the Effie Marie Cain Regents Chair in Art at The University of Texas at Austin, invited Steinberg to lecture at the university for the first time and this led to the formation of Steinberg's relationship with the Blanton. The museum ultimately acquired his collection in 2002, and when highlights from the acquisition were exhibited at the Blanton the following year, Steinberg returned to UT and delivered a lecture on the topic of "What I Like About Prints" before an audience of more than nine hundred people at an auditorium on campus.

A strong collection is the backbone of any exceptional museum. The Blanton develops groundbreaking scholarship and exhibitions through its collection, and activating the collection allows us to realize our mission as a laboratory for learning. In addition to serving as a classroom for graduate students at UT, tens of thousands of undergraduates and K–12 students in the community participate in educational experiences here every year. These include custom-designed lessons in the museum's galleries and classes held in the Blanton's H-E-B Study Room, where visitors can access works from the museum's extensive collections of prints and drawings. Located within the Julia Matthews Wilkinson Center for Prints and Drawings, this is one of the most active print study rooms in the country. The Leo Steinberg Collection is among the highlights of these holdings.

This collection is unique not only because of its broad scope but also for the way it allows a chronological exploration of technical developments in the history of prints. As a pedagogical tool, it enables the museum to illustrate how image-making evolved aesthetically and mechanically over the centuries. Steinberg's scholarship and collecting ranged from Michelangelo and Leonardo to Diego Velázquez and Pablo Picasso. The acquisition of the Leo Steinberg Collection added depth and elevated numerous areas of the Blanton's collection, from its European holdings to its collection of modern and contemporary art and other areas in between. The Steinberg collection also includes prints by artists of nineteen different nationalities, works that have been pivotal to the narratives the Blanton has presented in its galleries for decades.

It takes sharp curators to smartly build museum collections and create installations and exhibitions that provide contexts for great works of art. Jonathan Bober, former Curator of Prints, Drawings, and European

Paintings at the Blanton, forged a friendship with Steinberg when the latter lectured at UT in the 1990s, and Bober later suggested to Steinberg that the museum acquire his collection. Jessie Otto Hite, the museum's former director, worked with Bober to ensure that this important material came to the Blanton. This acquisition significantly expanded the museum's print collection and also resulted in further acquisitions and growth for the museum. In 2021, Holly Borham, the Blanton's Associate Curator of Prints, Drawings, and European Art, organized an illuminating exhibition showcasing the Leo Steinberg Collection—*After Michelangelo, Past Picasso: Leo Steinberg's Library of Prints*—and assembled the present volume, which represents the first published scholarship on this collection. In addition to Borham's research, this catalogue includes an insightful essay by Peter Parshall, formerly the Jane Neuberger Goodsell Professor of Art History and the Humanities at Reed College and Curator of Old Master Prints at the National Gallery of Art in Washington, DC (retired).

The Blanton is proud to steward and share the extraordinary Leo Steinberg Collection. As a museum we collect, conserve, study, and present art that highlights histories and ideas across continents, cultures, and centuries, and our collection is essential to fulfilling this mission. We could not do this work if not for the brilliance of collectors and scholars like Steinberg, whose impact on the generations that came after him is immeasurable.

Simone Jamille Wicha
Director, Blanton Museum of Art

Acknowledgments

THIS CATALOGUE AND ITS COMPANION EXHIBITION were born from a simple question: Is there any congruence between the work of Leo Steinberg (1920–2011) as a scholar and his activities as a collector? Or to put it another way: Did Steinberg's collection shape his scholarship on Renaissance and twentieth-century art to any significant degree? In sum, the answer is yes. And while Steinberg collected drawings, paintings, and sculpture, which he artfully arranged in his small Manhattan apartment, prints comprised the vast majority of his art collection and are thus the subject of the present inquiry. A trove of 3,648 of these works entered the Blanton Museum of Art's collection between 1996 and 2006 and inspired its exhibition *After Michelangelo, Past Picasso: Leo Steinberg's Library of Prints* (February 7, 2021–May 9, 2021). A digital tour and recorded talks from the accompanying symposium, *Leo Steinberg: Collector, Critic, and Scholar*, by Bernadine Barnes, Patricia Emison, Jennifer Roberts, and myself are available on the Blanton's website.

Although I never had the privilege of meeting Leo Steinberg, this project brought me into his orbit, and I am grateful to the following colleagues and friends who have generously shared their recollections and insights: Jonathan Bober, Suzanne Boorsch, Prudence Crowther, Robert Dance, Tacita Dean, Jim Goodfriend, Jessie Otto Hite, Connie McPhee, Christopher Mendez, Steve Ostrow, Peter Parshall, Richard Shiff, Alan Stone, and Roberta Waddell. Maryan Ainsworth deserves special mention for planting the seed of the idea for the exhibition. A Getty Library Research Grant gave me access to Steinberg's papers at the Getty Research Institute. And thanks to Jonathan Bober, Steinberg's ledgers recording his print purchases and related papers are now in the Blanton's collection. I am especially grateful to Heather MacDonald and the Getty Paper Project for supporting the exhibition and the catalogue. Further exhibition funding came from the International Fine Print Dealers Association (IFPDA), Leslie Shaunty and Robert Topp, the Scurlock Foundation Exhibition Endowment, Robert Dance, and Prudence Crowther.

At the Blanton Museum of Art, I would like to thank Simone Wicha, Director, and Carter Foster, Deputy Director for Curatorial Affairs, for their enthusiastic support of this project. I am grateful, too, to the IFPDA summer interns Claire Spadafora and Arianna Ray, who provided early research assistance. I also owe particular thanks to Genevra Higginson and Jana La Brasca for research and contributions to the texts in the "Highlights" section of the exhibition and catalogue, and to Lauren Rooney for similar contributions to the catalogue. For general catalogue assistance, I owe Dalia Azim and Cassandra Smith much gratitude. Annalise Gratovich brought her printmaking expertise to the physical examination of many objects. Rachel Urbano, Curatorial Assistant in the Blanton's Prints and Drawings department, and photographer Taryn Mills guided the catalogue to completion. Cassandra

Smith, our Director of Collections and Exhibitions; Matt Langland, Head of Installation and Exhibition Design; Clark Aldridge, Senior Preparator; Annalise Gratovich, Matting and Framing Preparator; and Eric Mathis, Art Preparator, ensured that the exhibition looked beautiful.

I am deeply grateful to my co-author, Peter Parshall, for his essay here and for his generous feedback on mine. Andrew Bricker, Carter Foster, Claire Howard, Britany Salsbury, Jeffrey Chipps Smith, and Hannah Yohalem were also kind enough to review and comment on sections of my texts. (Any errors are, of course, my own.) It was a privilege to work with editor Catherine Bindman and the staff at Marquand Books.

This project would have been impossible without the support of Sheila Schwartz, the go-to source for all Steinbergiana, who has graciously and extensively shared her expertise and answered my many queries with unfailing accuracy and good humor. Thank you also to my parents, Brian and Moyra Kileff, and my husband and children, Rob, Marshall, Caroline, and Henry Borham, who have accepted Leo Steinberg as a constant presence in their lives for the last several years. Finally, I owe a huge debt of gratitude to Leo Steinberg, whose collection brought me to the Blanton, whose texts were delightful companions during long pandemic quarantines, and whose prints continue to instruct, intrigue, and inspire.

Holly Borham
Associate Curator of Prints, Drawings,
and European Art, Blanton Museum of Art

The Circulating Lifeblood of Ideas
Leo Steinberg's Library of Prints

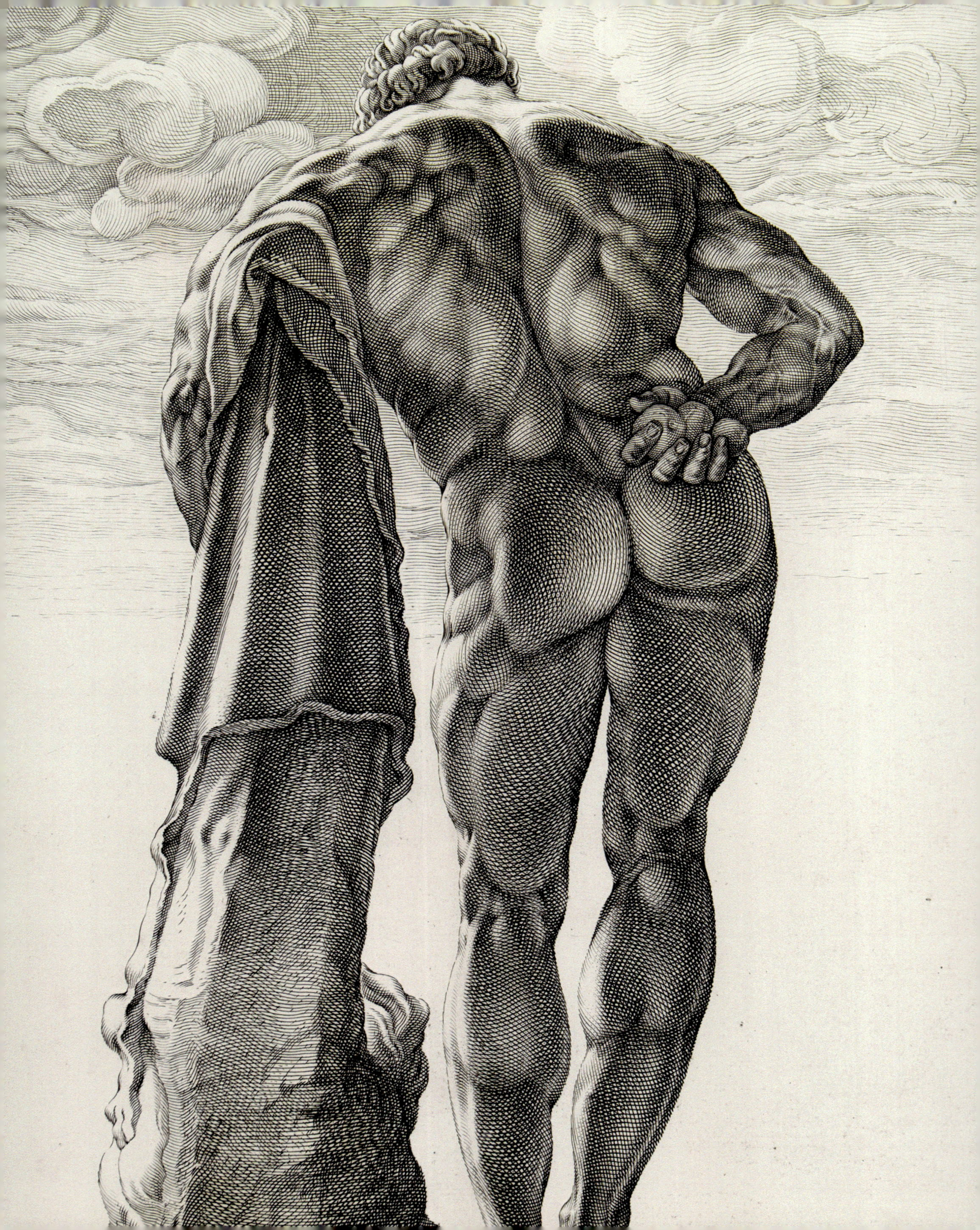

Leo Steinberg and His Library of Prints

HOLLY BORHAM

LEO STEINBERG (1920–2011) WAS THE RARE ART historian who turned his inquisitive eye and captivating prose to both Renaissance and twentieth-century art. From the late 1960s, he began publishing provocative new interpretations of Michelangelo's Pietàs and Pauline Chapel frescoes, with the Sistine Chapel frescoes soon following.[1] During the same period, he also introduced the term "post-modernist" into art criticism, first in a lecture titled "Other Criteria" at the Museum of Modern Art in New York on March 20, 1968, and later in the eponymous essay in his now-canonical anthology *Other Criteria: Confrontations with Twentieth-Century Art* (1972).[2] Here, he challenged the narrow conception of modern art propounded by the formalist critic Clement Greenberg, calling for a shift in the terminology that defined artistic invention. Steinberg's unusually wide-ranging scholarship, which addresses such major artists as Andrea Mantegna, Leonardo da Vinci, Jacopo Pontormo, Diego Velázquez, Auguste Rodin, Pablo Picasso, and Robert Rauschenberg, was grounded in his formal training at the Slade School of Fine Art in London. He approached his subjects both as an artist and as a scholar. His dictum, "the eye is part of the mind," impelled him to look first, and he frequently discovered what others had overlooked.[3]

A common motif in Steinberg's analysis of art, from any century, is the body—that of the viewer in relation to the work of art and those of the figures within the work. In a typical essay, he might observe that the face of Agnolo Bronzino's *Panciatichi Madonna*, half hidden in raking light, foreshadows Picasso's heads with double aspects, or that Michelangelo's *Medici Madonna* adopts the pose of a Hellenistic sculpture.[4] Through sustained and insatiable looking, which often included making sketches of the works under investigation, Steinberg puzzled out the relationships between the various parts of a picture and then compared both the parts and the whole to a treasury of images he had collected over decades. He often made his arguments, whether in lecture slides or in his publications, on the basis of an onslaught of visual comparisons. Although the comparing of images is fundamental to art history, Steinberg's visual repository was unusually capacious, in large part because it included his own print collection. With these resources, Steinberg constructed some of his most innovative arguments about specific works of art, theories that also confirmed the role of other artists' "corrective copies" as a form of visual criticism.[5]

Although this was not their only function, the more than 6,700 prints Steinberg acquired over the course of five decades served as primary source documents for his scholarship. They formed a private library, supplying him with information akin to that in the books on his shelf. That it was possible for him to buy so many good-quality prints with what began as the modest budget of a part-time professor speaks both to their historically low status and the fact that they

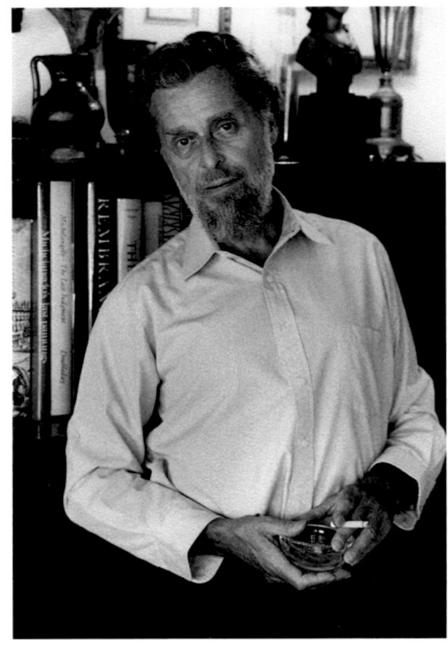

FIG. 1 Lisa Miller, *Leo Steinberg*, 1988. Photograph courtesy of Sheila Schwartz.

were still widely available in the mid-twentieth century and beyond. Among scholars and collectors of his era, Steinberg was also especially well positioned to uncover the range of interpretive clues prints could offer. He had the artistic sensibility to appreciate the stunning technical proficiency represented in such works, a quality that was unfashionable in the era of Abstract Expressionism with its robust, irreverent approach to art-making, and he was savvy enough to scoop up the many affordable fine prints then categorized outside a narrow list of acknowledged "greats." This volume examines the development of Steinberg's remarkable collection, its breadth, its role in his scholarship, and his significant contribution to the study of prints.

LEO STEINBERG: A LIFE OF THE EYE AND THE MIND

Steinberg was born into a Jewish family in Moscow in 1920, and his early life was shaped by the turbulence of the interwar decades in Europe.[6] His father, Isaac, a distinguished lawyer and a member of the Left Social Revolutionary Party, had briefly been commissar of justice in Lenin's first coalition cabinet, but resigned after four months. By 1923, the family had fled to Berlin. The seeds of Steinberg's interest in both historical and contemporary art were sown during his childhood years in Germany. He remembers his parents taking him at age eleven or twelve to meet Käthe Kollwitz, about whom he had written his first "article" for a handwritten children's magazine he had cofounded with the Jewish orphans who lived with the family.[7] His admiration for the artist would extend into adulthood, when he finally had the means to purchase several of her prints, including *Sitzender männlicher Akt* (Seated Male Nude, 1891; pl. 48). The young Steinberg's first, poignant encounter with Italian Renaissance art also took place in Berlin. As he recounts:

> My parents were Socialists, and one day in December 1932 they took me along to visit a Socialist bookshop, whose owner my father wanted to speak to. While the grown-ups talked, I browsed along the shelves and soon pulled down one of the few books in the shop that had nothing to do with politics: Richard Hamann's *The Early Renaissance of Italian Painting*, Jena 1909, in its first printing of 30,000: 50 pages of text, plus notes at the back (none of which interested me); and 200 full-page gray-and-white reproductions of paintings by artists with sonorous names, the like of which I had never heard uttered—Pollaiuolo, Ghirlandaio, Piero di Cosimo. I was enchanted, and couldn't stop looking—from that day to this. And when, after too short an hour, I was told we were leaving, I would not reshelve the book, but showed it to mother and asked timidly (for I knew we had little money)—could we buy it? Mother glanced at the price, shook her head, and looked quickly away; and all those images to vanish forever. And then a miracle happened: the bookseller turned to my father and said, "Look, any day now Hitler will be coming to power [as indeed Hitler did five weeks later, January 30, 1933], and the first thing the Nazis will do is close this shop. So why don't you just take the book for your boy."[8]

Steinberg treasured the book, inscribed on the flyleaf, "Zu Chanukka, 1932" [for Hanukkah], and it is now preserved among his papers at the Getty Research Institute.[9]

In 1933, amid rising anti-Semitism, the family moved to London, where Steinberg labored to add English to his rudimentary Russian and fluent German and Hebrew. At the age of seventeen, he discovered James Joyce and decided that English would be his language; he would quote Joyce and other great masters of English literature in scholarly writings throughout his life. Steinberg's remarkable facility in his fourth language was inevitably an asset to the presentation of his scholarly work, although a graduate-school professor reputedly chided, "I don't trust Leo Steinberg, he writes too well."[10] In 1983, he became the first art historian ever to receive the Award in Literature from the American Academy and Institute of Arts and Letters.

For Steinberg, however, proficiency in the making of art preceded writing about it. As a student at the Slade School of Fine Art in London between 1936 and 1940, he primarily produced sculptural portrait busts and drawings from live models, works that anticipate his abiding preoccupation with the human form.[11] Keenly attuned to the expressive potential of the pose, Steinberg brought his refined eye and practical training to the analysis of even the most subtle variations in facial expression, gesture, and the positioning of figures in the artworks he would later study.[12]

After wartime service as a journalist with various British government agencies, Steinberg immigrated in 1945 to New York, where he was naturalized as a U.S. citizen in 1950 and where he would spend the rest of his life. Between 1948 and 1960, he taught life drawing at Parsons School of Design, while also lecturing on art history at the 92nd Street Y, the Metropolitan Museum of Art, and elsewhere. But he had already decided that a career as a professional artist was not for him. In the meantime, his reputation as an engaging and informative speaker grew. Although he began auditing graduate courses at the Institute of Fine Arts (IFA) at New York University in 1950, he was not officially allowed to enroll until 1954, after earning a perfunctory bachelor's degree in education.[13] In graduate school, Steinberg's mental catalogue of works of art expanded radically. He remembers having to learn the full corpus of ancient art, including pottery shards.[14] Combined with his intuitive artistic understanding of the human figure, these foundational courses established him as a formidable iconographer, able to recall numerous variations on particular themes and subjects across the centuries. With the encouragement of the architectural historian Richard Krautheimer at the IFA, Steinberg began a different kind of iconographical study—a dissertation on the afterlife of Romanesque architecture. However, in 1957 a summer course in Rome with Wolfgang Lotz altered the direction of his interests and validated a method of analysis that he would employ for the next five decades. During a class visit to Santa Maria del Popolo, with its Caravaggio paintings of *The Conversion of St. Paul* and *The Crucifixion of St. Peter* in the Cerasi Chapel, Steinberg was given fifteen minutes to prepare an on-the-spot analysis. As the time ticked by, he suddenly noticed that Caravaggio had taken into account the oblique angle from which the viewer must be looking at his paintings and adjusted the perspective of the figures accordingly.[15] This way of considering the viewer's angle of address, both physically and metaphorically, became a hallmark of Steinberg's methodology.

On this same trip, Steinberg discovered the architecture of Francesco Borromini, leading him to abandon his first dissertation topic and turn to the church of San Carlino alle Quattro Fontane. Building his case from such features as the shapes of column shafts, he integrated his detailed observations into an overall analysis of the interlocking geometries of the church as fundamentally Trinitarian, centered on the worshipper's experience of the space. Although it sufficed to earn him a doctorate in 1960, Steinberg's dissertation was dismissed by his advisor as "only an interpretation" because its arguments were not primarily grounded in contemporaneous written sources.[16] This type of critique surfaced again in relation to his theory on the sexuality of Christ, to which he responded by accusing his detractors of being "textists," a line of reasoning he fleshed out in his 1995 Charles Eliot Norton Lectures at Harvard titled "The Mute Image and the Meddling Text."[17] Throughout his career, Steinberg asserted the supremacy of visual evidence over textual sources and championed the ingenuity of artists who responded to art through art, rather than producing art in response to texts.

Concurrent with his art-historical studies at the IFA, Steinberg was immersed in New York's contemporary art scene. In a monthly column for *Arts Magazine* (1955–56), his exhibition reviews of Franz Kline, Willem de Kooning, and Jackson Pollock, among others, established his critical authority and led to such opportunities as a studio visit with Mark Rothko and personal invitations to openings from artists like Josef Albers.[18] Correspondence from Philip Guston, Jasper Johns, Ray Johnson, Allan Kaprow, Ad Reinhardt, Carolee Schneemann, and Jean Tinguely also testifies to Steinberg's relevance as an interlocutor for contemporary artists.[19] Artists among his close personal friends included Paul Brach, Christo and Jeanne Claude, and Saul Steinberg.[20] Margaret Scolari ("Daisy") Barr, wife of Alfred H. Barr, Jr., founding director of the Museum of Modern Art, was an early supporter of his career. The first work to enter Steinberg's collection, Giovanni Battista Piranesi's *Veduta dell'esterno della gran Basilica di S. Pietro in Vaticano* (View of the exterior of St. Peter's Basilica in the Vatican) from the etched series the *Vedute di Roma* (Views of Rome), was a gift from Mrs. Barr in 1959, likely meant to commemorate the successful completion of his dissertation.[21] Prominent New York collectors also appreciated Steinberg's visual acuity. He encouraged Picasso collectors Victor and Sally Ganz to look at up-and-comers Jasper Johns and Robert Rauschenberg (whose works ultimately contributed to the record-breaking figure realized at the 1997 sale of their collection).[22] Dominique de Menil, founder of the Menil Collection in Houston, was another lifelong friend who purchased prints from Steinberg and brought him to Houston for a lecture series.[23] Steinberg also advised the collector Frances Leventritt on her significant purchases of late nineteenth- and twentieth-century art. Leventritt bought old master prints from Steinberg, too, which felicitously joined the rest of his collection at the Blanton by way of her estate sale and a subsequent donation.[24]

As Steinberg's academic career blossomed, his attention shifted away from the contemporary art scene to his lifelong preoccupations with Renaissance and Baroque art and Pablo Picasso. In 1961, he took up a teaching position at Hunter College, and, in 1970, went on to cofound the graduate program in art history at the City University of New York (CUNY) Graduate Center. In 1975, Steinberg accepted a prestigious appointment as Benjamin Franklin Professor of Art History at the University of Pennsylvania, which allowed him to teach only two classes in a single semester, leaving eight months a year for research, publications, and the preparation of a growing number of public lectures. His public-speaking circuit was rewarding both financially and intellectually. As he traveled the globe giving erudite and entertaining lectures in packed auditoriums—while commanding increasingly high fees—Steinberg honed his ideas, often revising a lecture repeatedly over the course of several decades; sometimes these lectures were published, but more often they were not.[25] Ever provocative, he relished eviscerating conventional opinion through sustained visual analysis followed by intelligent conjecture. Although his chosen subjects were typically the stellar works of the art-historical canon, he also seemed to delight in the challenge of rehabilitating some of the less-respected pieces by these artists. Michelangelo's Pauline Chapel frescoes at the Vatican, for example, never as highly acclaimed nor as skillfully reproduced in print as the Sistine Chapel frescoes, had either been ignored or disparaged through the early twentieth century. [26] Of the Sistine Ceiling frescoes, *The Deluge* was, according to Steinberg, "the least inviting to look at . . . the least loved and the least familiar,"[27] while the

Ancestor lunettes had long been the target of generally unsympathetic and even anti-Semitic interpretations.[28] Guercino's *St. Petronilla* altarpiece was seen as stylistically discordant,[29] and Picasso's late works were viewed as inferior to his earlier ones.[30] Steinberg convincingly refuted such entrenched perspectives through deeper looking and more incisive analysis. Perhaps his most controversial theory, however, expounded in *The Sexuality of Christ in Renaissance Art and in Modern Oblivion*, first published in a full volume of the art journal *October* in 1983 and eventually translated into three other languages, posits that Renaissance artists prominently displayed the genitals of Christ to visually express the concept of "incarnational theology" and the paradox of a Savior who was both fully God and fully man.[31]

Accolades accumulated over the course of Steinberg's career. In addition to the Award in Literature from the American Academy and Institute of Arts and Letters in 1983, he was asked to deliver the A. W. Mellon Lectures in the Fine Arts at the National Gallery of Art in 1982 and the Charles Eliot Norton Lectures at Harvard University in 1995–96. In 1984, he was given the Frank Jewett Mather Award for Distinction in Art Criticism by the College Art Association (CAA) and in 1986–91, a MacArthur Foundation Fellowship. Steinberg was also named the CAA's Samuel H. Kress Foundation Distinguished Scholar in 2002 and received no fewer than six honorary doctorates, including one from Harvard University in 2006. When he died in 2011, tributes poured in from distinguished art historians. His legacy continues to be assessed today with the publication of a five-volume series of his essays and lectures.[32] While Steinberg's significance to the field of art history is widely acknowledged, his activity as a print collector and its role in his scholarship deserve more attention.

LEO STEINBERG'S LIBRARY OF PRINTS

Steinberg's print-collecting habit had an unexpected beginning. In March 1961, as a newly minted PhD, he suffered a heart attack, months before he was due to take up his teaching position at Hunter College. Although he had already purchased or received a few prints as gifts, it was only during his enforced hiatus from academic research that Steinberg's voracious collecting practice began in earnest, and this even before he left the hospital.[33] As recorded in his ledgers, Karel van Mallery's *St. Martha* (1595–99) after Maarten de Vos was "ordered from Hospital bed out of LG Cat. sight unseen" for $2.50.[34] From the same Lucien Goldschmidt catalogue, Steinberg selected the eight engravings of Goltzius's *Roman Heroes* series (1586), a gift from his friend Phyllis Dearborn Massar. Massar was an independent art historian who would sometimes join him on print-hunting expeditions through New York's antiquarian book shops, art galleries, and frame stores in the sixties and seventies and who bequeathed her sizable collection of prints and drawings to the Metropolitan Museum of Art in 2011.[35]

Discharged from the hospital and under doctor's orders to "take it easy" during the summer of 1961, Steinberg embarked on a novel form of research: beginning to assemble a huge repository of prints that delighted the eye, expanded his iconographic library, and allowed visual and theoretical connections overlooked by those who disdained the medium as derivative or ignoble. He began making frequent visits to New York print dealers, from whom he would purchase thousands of works during the following four decades. At top-tier galleries like that of Goldschmidt as well as more modest enterprises like Rockman Prints, whose proprietor gathered castoffs from the basement stock of Colnaghi's in London, and such frame shops also dealing in prints as J. Pocker, Steinberg immersed himself in a print world that today's collectors can only regard wistfully—one in which high-quality old master prints were both plentiful and affordable. When he first began collecting, many of his sources were continental émigrés with access to old European print stocks, such as the Germans Erhard Weyhe, Walter Schatzki, and Hellmuth Wallach, and the Austrian William Schab, in addition to the Belgian Goldschmidt. Most ceased operations after the passing of their namesake founders. Kennedy Galleries, which sourced its old master prints from London auctions, had a vast stock housed in bins available for open browsing. Argosy Book Store, Pageant Print Shop, and The Old Print Shop are among the few establishments frequented by Steinberg that still exist in New York.

After devoting himself to the local market for about a year, Steinberg's print holdings stood at 746 according to his ledgers. In the summer of 1962, he made "raids on Paris and London," augmenting his bounty with five hundred more impressions.[36] In London, he established relationships with major dealers, including Colnaghi and Craddock & Barnard (eventually taken over by Christopher Mendez). Steinberg also frequented the booksellers and antique dealers at Cecil Court, a pedestrian thoroughfare near the National Gallery still lined with antiquarian bookshops, where he gravitated especially to the Jewish émigrés Ernest Seligmann and Louis Meier, as well as to Suckling & Co., with its portfolios of portraits arranged alphabetically by sitter. (Seligmann and his shop feature in R. B. Kitaj's painting of 1983–84, *Cecil Court, London W.C.2.* [*The Refugees*] in the Tate Collection). Together, Seligmann, Meier, and George Suckling would supply Steinberg with hundreds of prints over the years. He rounded out his exploration of London's ecosystem of print dealers with visits to the Portobello Road Market in Notting Hill, where he also discovered many gems. Steinberg recounts an episode that effectively characterizes the London print market of the sixties: Suckling had to leave for a lunch meeting, so he agreed that while he was out, Steinberg could be locked in the shop's dimly lit basement to browse the five-foot-high piles of prints that lined the walls. When Suckling returned two hours later, Steinberg had set aside nearly one hundred prints for further consideration. The dealer flipped through the stack and suggested a price of twenty pounds, which Steinberg immediately accepted. He was delighted to discover later that his spoils included an undescribed state of a William Blake engraving, among other treasures.[37] After establishing himself as a serious collector during that summer of 1962, Steinberg began to receive regular sales catalogues from London, though with the slow pace of transatlantic surface mail, by the time he wrote or cabled back his purchase requests, he often found his selections had been sold.[38]

In Paris, Steinberg similarly bought prints from a wide range of dealers—Maurice Baudon, Maison Ducrot, R. G. Michel, Paul Prouté, J. P. Rouillon, and Maurice Rousseau—as well as in the flea markets. His annual summer pilgrimages to London and Paris, with occasional forays to other European cities, had become more sporadic by the seventies, by which time he had expanded his domestic sources to include R. E. Lewis in San Francisco, Ferdinand Roten in Baltimore, Charles Sessler in Philadelphia, and Zeitlin & Ver Brugge in Los Angeles. Jim Goodfriend, Hill-Stone, and David Tunick in New York were among the dealers with whom he maintained regular relationships in later years.

What did Steinberg buy? Broadly speaking, his collecting focus was on European prints from the fifteenth through the early twentieth centuries, with the sixteenth and seventeenth centuries predominating. As he accumulated more and more, he realized that prints were "bursting with information."[39] Perhaps more vitally, he concluded that because the artists he was studying looked at prints, he needed to do so too. So-called reproductive prints, which replicate another artwork, were of particular interest to Steinberg because he understood their role in disseminating compositions and motifs as well as their function as visual art criticism.[40] Although his collection was broad, he was mainly interested in European fine prints, generally passing over maps, ephemera, broadsides, and illustrated books. And while he had little interest in scientific illustration, he collected a surprising number of series featuring animals, suggesting that he delighted in the free and unconstrained expressions of these

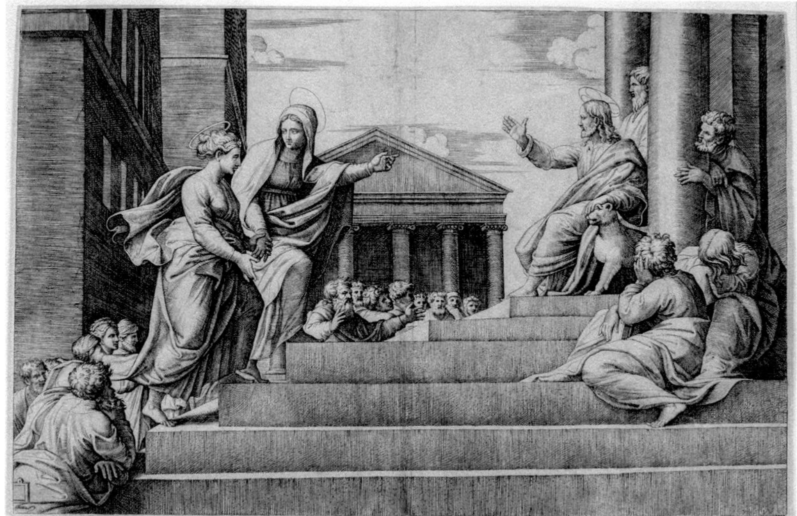

FIG. 2 Marcantonio Raimondi, *Martha Leading Mary Magdalene to Christ*, after a drawing by Giulio Romano or Raphael, ca. 1520–25. Engraving, only state, 9 × 13⅝ in. (23.3 × 34.5 cm). Bartsch XIV.51.45, Shoemaker 56 (2002.1707)

creatures. Guided as much by his curiosity and artistic instinct as by his art-historical knowledge, Steinberg's print-scavenging adventures introduced him to many artists and artworks he had certainly never encountered in graduate school.

Steinberg found conversations with curators and dealers especially instructive. He began his expansive project of self-education in the history of European printmaking by bringing armfuls of prints he had taken on approval to compare them to those in the collections of the New York Public Library and the Metropolitan Museum of Art. Once there, he would consult reference materials and seek input from the curatorial staff. The head of the print department at the Met was A. Hyatt Mayor, and Steinberg occasionally inscribed the distinguished curator's opinions in his ledgers and on the backs of his prints. The influence of Mayor, and his predecessor William Ivins, who shared a conviction that prints played a crucial social role and were indispensable documents of cultural history, surely encouraged Steinberg in his broad collecting habits.[41]

It is also noteworthy that many of the now-standard reference catalogues on prints had not yet been published when Steinberg began collecting. *The Illustrated Bartsch* (TIB) volumes, pictorial companions to Adam Bartsch's twenty-one volume *Le Peintre-Graveur* (1803–21), did not begin to appear until 1978, while the standard illustrated references on Marcantonio Raimondi and Giorgio Ghisi, artists whose prints Steinberg was particularly eager to collect, were only published in 1981 and 1985, respectively.[42] In the mid-sixties, the original, partially illustrated Dutch and Flemish Hollstein volumes extended only through "Meer–Ossenbeeck," while the German Hollstein volumes ended with Dürer. As print scholarship progressed, Steinberg revised his ledgers; an anonymous print that he had owned for twelve years finally received an attribution when TIB on Tempesta was published in 1984.

As an artist and collector, Steinberg was at home in the world of connoisseurship, highly attentive to the nuances of the medium. His query to the dealer R. E. Lewis about a Gillis Neyts etching—did he think the improperly bitten plate might have been reinforced with drypoint?—was typical of the types of conversations he enjoyed with fellow print devotees, whose opinions on impression quality he recorded, along with his own, in his ledgers.[43] Steinberg scrutinized his prints closely, perceiving that, unlike works in other mediums that might conceal their process of manufacture, finished prints reveal "the build of [their] constituent elements, the process of their fabrication."[44] He related this kind of connoisseurship to scientific investigation, asserting that looking at prints allowed him to see the artist at work "on a molecular level."[45] For instance, in Marcantonio's *Martha Leading Mary Magdalene to Christ* (ca. 1520–25; fig. 2), he counts at least seven types of marks: parallel verticals, parallel horizontals, diagonals

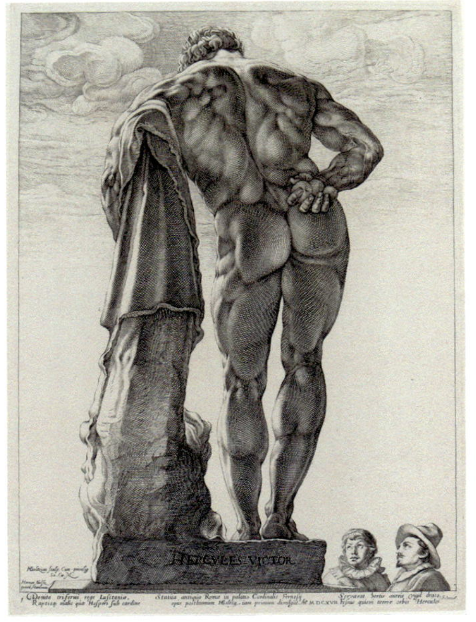

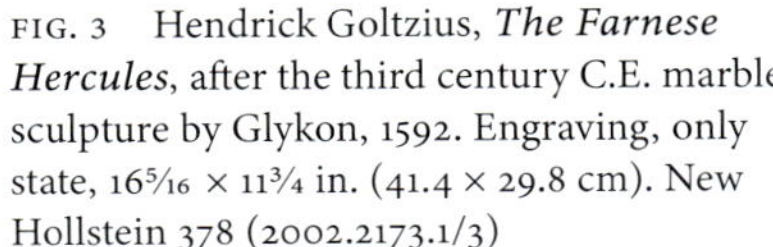

FIG. 3 Hendrick Goltzius, *The Farnese Hercules*, after the third century C.E. marble sculpture by Glykon, 1592. Engraving, only state, $16\frac{5}{16} \times 11\frac{3}{4}$ in. (41.4 × 29.8 cm). New Hollstein 378 (2002.2173.1/3)

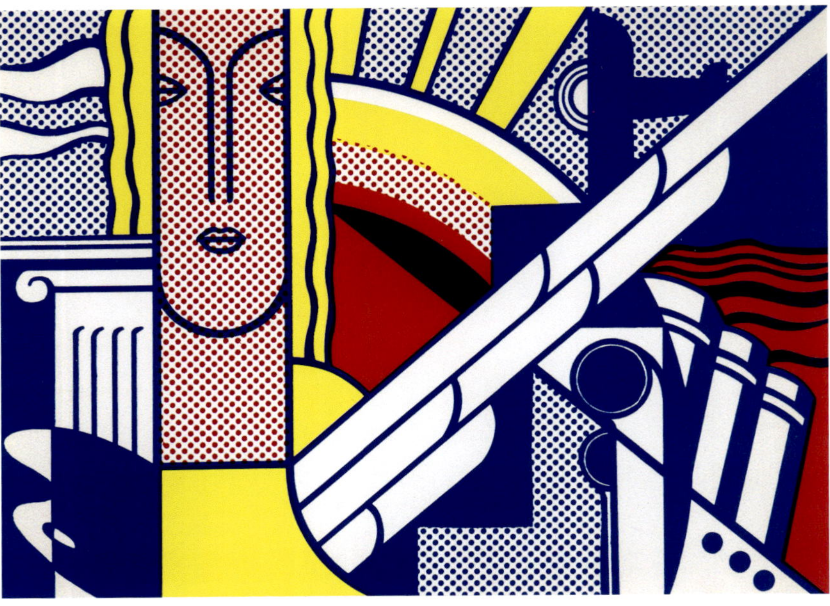

FIG. 4 Roy Lichtenstein, *Modern Art Poster*, 1967. Color screenprint, printed in three colors, unnumbered and unsigned from edition of 300, $8 \times 10\frac{7}{8}$ in. (20.3 × 27.7 cm). Corlett II.8 (2002.2780)

at the far right, curved parallels for columns and arms, cross-hatching, flicks and dots for texture and other effects, and quadrant curves at both ends of the third step.[46] As he charts the evolution of the printmaker's syntax, Steinberg delights in the swelling and tapering of Goltzius's mesh-like crosshatching in prints like the famous *Farnese Hercules* (1592; fig. 3), lines that he describes as "plow[ing] the field of the copperplate with a disciplined virtuosity" that is "ideally efficient, even poetic, like deftly rhymed verse that stays in its meter."[47] Such mechanical precision reached its apogee in the work of seventeenth-century engravers like Robert Nanteuil and Claude Mellan before falling out of favor. It was revived in the twentieth century, Steinberg argues, by Chuck Close, Roy Lichtenstein (as in his *Modern Art Poster*, 1967; fig. 4), and Agnes Martin, and lives on in pixelated digital imagery.[48] These observations not only reveal Steinberg's close engagement with the facture of his prints, but also the way his print collection, spanning centuries, facilitated comparisons fundamental to his scholarship.

Steinberg bought what he could afford. As material objects, the ledgers in which he recorded his print purchases equally reflect his frugality. Most are simple, spiral-bound notebooks that list inventory number; artist; title; purchase date; source; price (quoted, and often discounted by half); catalogue raisonné references; collectors' marks; comments on quality, rarity, and condition; subsequent valuations compared to other impressions for sale; location if deaccessioned; and final sale price, appraisal value, or tax savings if donated (fig. 5). Steinberg tallied the sum of expenditures at the bottom of each page and periodically made separate lists of his print "winners" and "losers" based on their change in value over time. In the early years, he sometimes paid as little as ten cents for a print, while a splurge on Marcantonio's *Triumph of Galatea* after Raphael (1515–16; fig. 6) cost him $125.[49] The European foray in 1962 yielded five hundred prints at a cost of approximately $2,100. This was a significant sum for Steinberg, who then earned $6,000 a year teaching part-time at Hunter College, supplemented

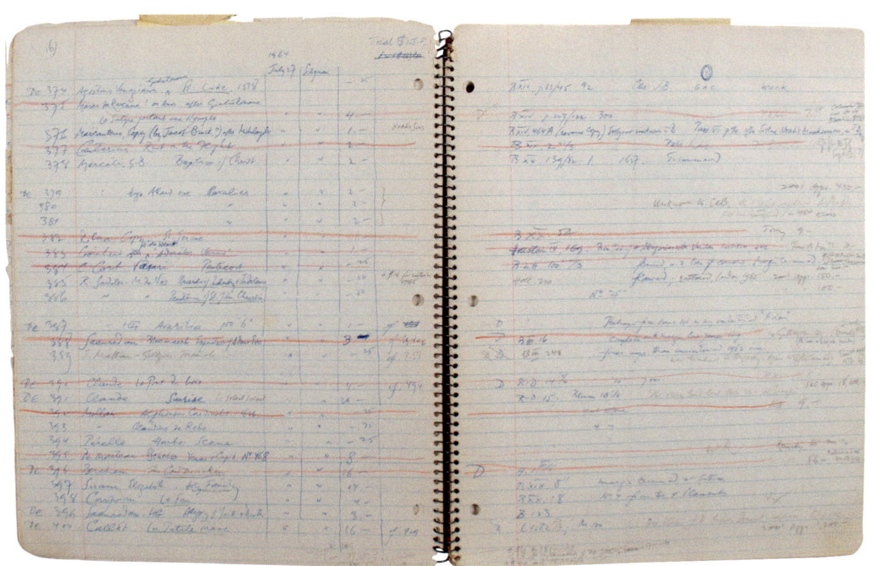

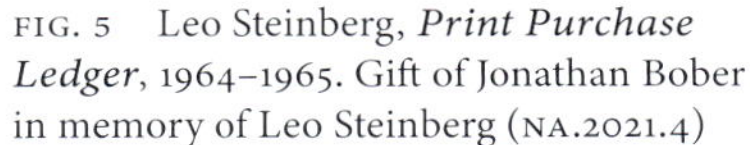

FIG. 5 Leo Steinberg, ***Print Purchase Ledger***, 1964–1965. Gift of Jonathan Bober in memory of Leo Steinberg (NA.2021.4)

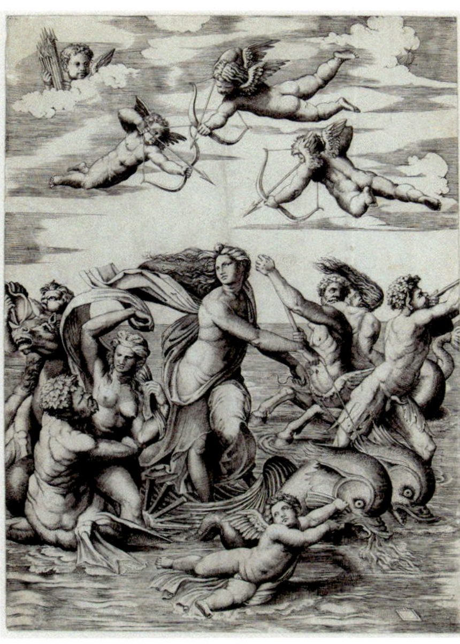

FIG. 6 Marcantonio Raimondi, ***The Triumph of Galatea***, after a fresco by Raphael, 1515–16. Engraving, only state, $15\frac{9}{16} \times 11$ in. (39.5×28 cm). Bartsch XIV.262.350, Shoemaker 33 (2002.1709)

by $100 per museum lecture and small payments for publications.[50] He did not ignore printmakers who have always been highly collectible—Dürer, Lucas van Leyden, Marcantonio, and Rembrandt—but was limited by price. When he did acquire prints by these artists, he bought good impressions that were typically much less expensive than the rare, finest impressions available on the market. Although he did manage to buy many prints by Marcantonio, an inquiry in 1964 to Craddock & Barnard received a scornful reply: "Dear Leo, You really will have to emerge from your ivory tower into the world of print prices current. A fine early Massacre of the Innocents would cost about £300 to £400; for the Grimpeurs you might have to pay £500, and a fine Judgment of Paris would be very hard to come by."[51] And in 1963, Seligmann lamented that "with artists like Canaletto or Tiepolo things are now getting pretty hopeless for the collector who has to consider his purse."[52]

While those who value quality of impression above all else may question Steinberg's credentials as a connoisseur—his collection unquestionably includes more than a few weak impressions—it is clear from his ledgers and writings that what he lacked was not sensitivity and knowledge, but rather sufficient funds and the inclination to narrowly pursue certain "greats." Steinberg's serious interest in composition and iconography meant that he was willing to purchase interesting "wrecks" and was especially drawn to prints that showed signs of use by other artists. He matted his own prints in economical one-ply mats, and, on occasion, washed them himself, a practice that was not unusual at the time even among dealers. His technique must eventually have improved, as he notes that several early purchases were "ruined by me in attempted soaking;"[53] as finances allowed, he paid for professional conservation services. Steinberg subsidized new purchases through trades and sales with other print collectors and dealers, and, beginning in the late seventies, made donations of prints to a variety of institutions for charitable and tax purposes.[54] His ledgers tell the story of growing expertise, membership in an informal and close-knit network of print devotees, and a keen awareness of the exponential rise in the value of his collection.

Between 1961 and 1969, Steinberg bought approximately eighty percent of the 6,736 prints he was to acquire during his lifetime, although due to his constant selling and trading, he never had more than 4,500 prints at any one time.[55] Escalating prices and a strategic shift to quality over quantity slowed his acquisitions to fewer than two hundred a year by the early seventies, and to the single digits by the time his collecting concluded in 2000. While many factors contributed to the rising market, Steinberg himself bore some responsibility for one of them—the fixed and dwindling supply of old master prints. Once donated to museums, of course, these works never circulate on the market again. In 1974, Lucien Goldschmidt reminisced about the market's upward trend in the years following the Korean War: "[O]ne should give credit to the professors, people like Leo Steinberg, people like Professor Gruber, who used to be at the Metropolitan Museum. They saw that it was really quite unreasonable that one could buy prints like Goltzius and other great masters for less than $50; when they were rare, and particularly in good impressions, hard to find."[56] Indeed, Goltzius and his school of engravers were among those whom Steinberg had recognized early on as being vastly undervalued relative to their aesthetic and technical achievements; consequently, he bought considerable numbers of prints not only by that Dutch master of the swelling line but also by Zacharias Dolendo, Jacques de Gheyn II, Jacob Matham, and Jan Saenredam. Sixteenth-century Italian etchings and engravings, fifteenth-century German woodcuts, and the School of Fontainebleau were subject to similarly meteoric rises in later years. Though Picasso's prints were always relatively expensive for Steinberg, he was able to translate his writing into a form of currency. In 1969, for example, he applied the proceeds from an article on Picasso for *LIFE* magazine, along with some strategic trades, toward the purchase of four Picasso prints.[57] Like the five Matisse prints he bought at around the same time, these represented shrewd investments.

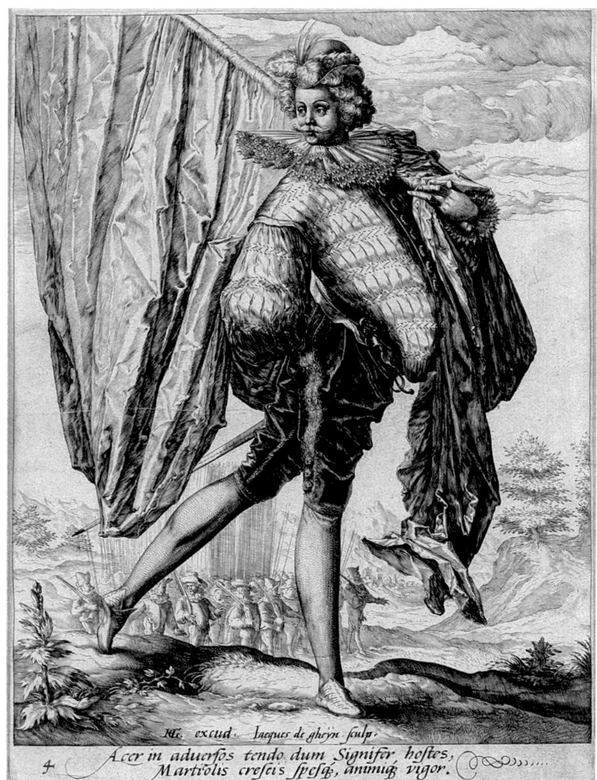

FIG. 7 Jacques de Gheyn II, *Standard Bearer*, plate 4 from *Officers and Soldiers*, after designs by Hendrick Goltzius, 1587. Engraving, second state of three, $8\frac{1}{2} \times 6\frac{3}{16}$ in. (21.6 × 15.6 cm). New Hollstein 179 (2002.2214.4/12)

While he continued to acquire whatever caught his eye, Steinberg gradually scaled back the volume in pursuit of higher-quality impressions and higher-value artists. Three German prints elucidate the varied motivations behind such later acquisitions. Pure aesthetic appreciation led to his most expensive print purchase ever—Dürer's *St. Christopher Facing Right* (1521; pl. 5)—for which he paid $4,500 in 1988. Steinberg never wrote about Dürer but was nonetheless keen to acquire such a virtuoso engraving by the great master of the medium. The last prints he ever bought were two unidentified early seventeenth-century etchings, which must have intrigued him as oddities that

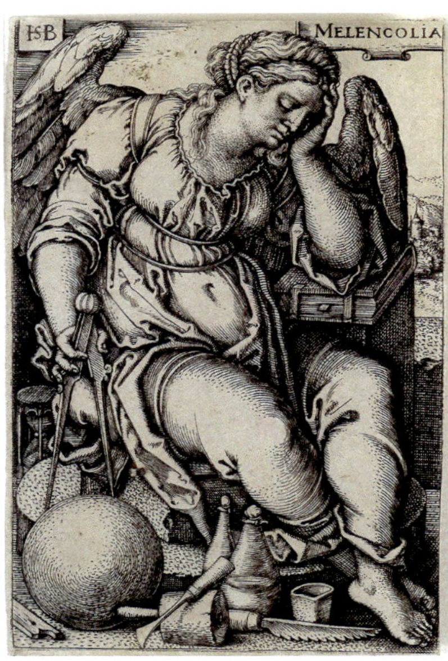

FIG. 8 Sebald Beham, *Melancholia*, 1539. Engraving, second state of five, 3⅛ × 2 1/16 in. (8 × 5.2 cm). Hollstein 145 (2002.771)

he had never encountered in forty years; they point to an intellect ever open to new discovery.[58] By the time Jonathan Bober, then Curator of Prints, Drawings, and European Paintings at the Blanton, proposed an acquisition scheme to Steinberg in the early 2000s, his collection had been refined into a highly personal, yet broad-based one, defined by the eye and mind of the artist-scholar.

Steinberg's collection is congruent with his academic interests, yet extends far beyond them. The following analysis is based on the Blanton's holdings of 3,648 prints from his collection, works representative of his overall purchasing patterns since he never systematically deaccessioned any particular part of it.[59] Divided chronologically, the collection breaks down roughly by century as follows: seventeenth (45 percent); sixteenth (25 percent); eighteenth (17 percent), nineteenth (10 percent); twentieth (2 percent); fifteenth (less than 1 percent). In geographical terms, it reflects the relative levels of production in the various centers of European printmaking through the end of the nineteenth century. Almost one-third of it is French—not unexpected since, measured by volume and quality, Paris was the leading print center of Europe by the mid-seventeenth century. Particular strengths in this category include several School of Fontainebleau rarities (pl. 11), a considerable number of Callots (pl. 26), seventeenth-century portrait engravings (pl. 28), and nineteenth-century etchings (pl. 46). Dutch prints comprise one-fifth of the collection, with many works by the circle of Goltzius (fig. 7) and notable seventeenth-century etchings (pl. 22), including those by Rembrandt (pl. 21), along with several outstanding works by Cornelis Cort (pl. 16). The many engravings after biblical narratives designed by Maarten van Heemskerck likely appealed to Steinberg's iconographic interests (fig. 28). Italian prints, more intimately tied to Steinberg's scholarship, make up slightly less than one-fifth of the collection and include many prints after Michelangelo (figs. 23, 26, 32, 35, 43, 54, pl. 14) as well as by Marcantonio (figs. 2, 6, 19, pls. 7, 9) and his followers. There are some important sixteenth- and seventeenth-century Italian etchings, with exceptional groups by Giovanni Benedetto Castiglione (pl. 31) and Stefano Della Bella (pl. 32). Flemish and German prints each constitute approximately one-tenth of the collection. Among the Flemish works, those by the circle of printmakers around Peter Paul Rubens (fig. 21, pls. 24, 25) are among the highlights. More than half of the German prints date from the sixteenth century, with many engravings by such "Little Masters," known for the diminutive size of their prints, as Heinrich Aldegrever, Sebald Beham (fig. 8), and Georg Pencz. The Germans Kollwitz (pl. 48) and George Grosz (pl. 49) are among the few twentieth-century artists in the collection.

Steinberg's British prints, which date almost entirely to the eighteenth and nineteenth centuries, make up the next largest group; among the most noteworthy are etchings by Alexander Runciman (fig. 47), John Clerk of Eldin (pl. 38), Samuel Palmer, and Francis Seymour Haden (pl. 45). Such acquisitions probably reflected both pure aesthetic appreciation and the desire to assemble a collection with representative highlights of European printmaking. A small group of Spanish prints is comprised almost entirely of examples by Jusepe de Ribera, Francisco de Goya, and Picasso (figs. 44, 45, 46, 49, 50, 51, 52), the latter the subject of many of Steinberg's lectures and essays. Finally, in descending size order, the collection includes examples of Swiss, Austrian, Bohemian/Czech, Japanese, Irish, Danish, Belgian, Swedish, and Russian prints as well as one Chilean print. Preeminent among Steinberg's small number of American prints are those by Josef Albers (pl. 51), Jasper Johns (fig. 55), and Roy Lichtenstein (fig. 4), artists whom he either knew personally or whose art he addressed in writing and lectures. If financial remuneration had been Steinberg's primary collecting purpose, he would have done well to acquire the work of those artists who captured his attention in the fifties and sixties, but not only was it already expensive then compared to the things he found in the boxes and bins of Manhattan's shops, it was also less useful to the iconographic encyclopedia he was assembling.

Innovative and unconventional in his wide-ranging and provocative scholarship, Steinberg was also an unorthodox collector, whose acquisitions went far beyond the standard group of canonical printmakers, and whose interest in so-called reproductive prints was fairly unusual at the time. Now housed at the Blanton, this collection of prints—a key component of Steinberg's visual and intellectual library—offers the next generation of scholars and artists an exceptionally broad introduction to the history of prints in its many dimensions.

NOTES

The five-volume series of Steinberg's *Selected Essays*, edited by Sheila Schwartz and published by the University of Chicago Press (2018–2023), comprises published essays, many revised for the series, as well as previously unpublished lectures and texts. It includes the following titles: *Michelangelo's Sculpture* (2018), *Michelangelo's Painting* (2019), *Renaissance and Baroque Art* (2020), *Picasso* (2022), and *Modern Art* (2023). The first endnote reference in this volume to a published essay by Steinberg cites both the republished volume and the original place(s) of publication. Subsequent references cite only the republished volume.

1 Steinberg's publications on the subjects in this period include "Michelangelo's Florentine *Pietà*: The Missing Leg," *The Art Bulletin* 50, no. 4 (December 1968): 343–353; "The Metaphors of Love and Birth in Michelangelo's *Pietàs*," in *Michelangelo's Sculpture*, 1–57. Previously published in Theodore Bowie and Cornelia V. Christenson, eds., *Studies in Erotic Art* (New York: Basic Books, 1970), 231–335; "Michelangelo's Last Paintings," in *Michelangelo's Painting*, 235–304. Previously published as *Michelangelo's Last Paintings: The Conversion of St. Paul and the Crucifixion of St. Peter in the Cappella Paolina, Vatican Palace* (New York: Oxford University Press, 1975); "The *Last Judgment* as Merciful Heresy," in *Michelangelo's Painting*, 130–159. Previously published in *Art in America* 63, no. 6 (November–December 1975): 48–63; "Eve's Idle Hand," *Art Journal* 35, no. 2 (Winter 1975–76): 130–135.

2 The Museum of Modern Art, Press Release no. 124, December 4, 1967: https://www.moma.org/momaorg/shared/pdfs/docs/press_archives/3977/releases/MOMA_1967_July-December_0059_24.pdf; Steinberg, "Other Criteria," in *Other Criteria: Confrontations with Twentieth-Century Art* (New York: Oxford University Press, 1972; 2nd edition, Chicago: University of Chicago Press, 2007), 91. Rosalind Krauss states that Steinberg invented the term; "The Slung Leg Hypothesis," *October* 136 (Spring 2011): 221.

3 Steinberg, "The Eye Is Part of the Mind," in *Other Criteria*, 280–306. Previously published in *Partisan Review* 20, no. 2 (March–April 1953): 194–212.

4 Steinberg, "The Algerian Women and Picasso at Large," in *Other Criteria*, 195–196; Steinberg, "The *Medici Madonna* and Related Works," in *Michelangelo's Sculpture*, 90–95. Previously published in *The Burlington Magazine* 113, no. 816 (March 1971): 145–149.

5 Steinberg discusses the origin of his concept of "corrective copies" in "The Line of Fate in Michelangelo's Painting," in *Michelangelo's Painting*, 213, 343–344n1. Previously published in *Critical Inquiry* 6, no. 3 (Spring 1980): 411–454. Steinberg credits Heinrich Wölfflin in his *Kunstgeschichtliche Grundbegriffe: das Problem der Stilentwickelung in der neueren Kunst* (1915), as the first scholar to cite a variant copy as an example of explicit criticism and explains that this has been his "unacknowledged methodological model" throughout his career.

6 Key events are summarized in "Leo Steinberg: Chronology," which appears at the end of each of the volumes now published in the series Leo Steinberg, *Selected Essays*. See also Sheila Schwartz, "Leo Steinberg: A Biographical Introduction," in *Leo Steinberg Now: Il pensiero attraverso gli occhi* (Rome: Campisano Editore, forthcoming). Steinberg's own account of his life can be found in "The Gestural Trace," the transcript of a 1998 interview by Richard Cándida Smith for the Art History Oral Documentation Project, Getty Research Institute, 2001, https://archive.org/details/gesturaltraceleooostei.

7 Steinberg, "The Gestural Trace," 44.

8 Steinberg, "False Starts, Loose Ends," *The Brooklyn Rail*, June 12, 2006, https://brooklynrail.org/2006/06/art/leo. Publication of a talk delivered at the CAA conference in Philadelphia in 2002, honoring Steinberg as Distinguished Scholar.

9 As the collection is only partially processed, some references are to entire boxes, while others are to specific folders. Getty Research Institute (hereafter cited as GRI), Leo Steinberg Research Papers (hereafter cited as LSRP), 930046, T63 for the Hamann book.

10 Steinberg, "The Gestural Trace," 21.

11 *The Eye Is Part of the Mind: Drawings from Life and Art by Leo Steinberg* (New York: New York Studio School of Drawing, Painting, and Sculpture, 2013).

12 Steinberg, "The Gestural Trace," 45; GRI LSRP 930046 T5 and T63. Steinberg's practice of drawing the artworks he was studying is discussed in *Leo Steinberg Now*, especially the essay by Jérémie Koering, "Dessiner voir. Steinberg et l'enquête graphique."

13 On his coursework at the IFA, see Daniele Di Cola, "Becoming Leo: Steinberg e l'Institute of Fine Arts di New York: dall'eredità dei professori tedeschi allo sviluppo di un nuovo criticism," in *Storia della critica d'arte. Annuario della S.I.S.C.A.* (Milan: Scalpendi, 2020), 65–97.

14 Steinberg, "The Gestural Trace," 81–82.

15 Steinberg, "Observations in the Cerasi Chapel," in *Renaissance and Baroque Art*, 131–143. Previously published in *The Art Bulletin*, 41, no. 2 (June 1959): 183–193. Steinberg recounts his moment of epiphany in "False Starts, Loose Ends."

16 Quoted in Steinberg's preface to the revision of his 1960 dissertation, *Borromini's San Carlo alle Quattro Fontane: A Study in Multiple Form and Architectural Symbolism* (New York: Garland, 1977), xviii.

17 For the publication history of the five lectures, see *Renaissance and Baroque Art*, 238n. See also Stephen J. Campbell's evaluation of Steinberg's approach to textual sources in his introduction to the same book, xi–xvi.

18 De Kooning, *Other Criteria*, 259–262. Previously published as "Month in Review," *Arts Magazine* 30, no. 2 (November 1955): 46–48; Pollock and Pascin, *Other Criteria*, 263–271. Previously published as "Month in Review," *Arts Magazine* 30, no. 3 (December 1955): 43–46; Kline in "Month in Review," *Arts Magazine* 30, no. 7 (April 1956): 42–45; on Rothko, see Steinberg, "The Gestural Trace," 58–60; on Albers, GRI LSRP 930046, IV.9.5.

19 Guston in GRI LSRP 930046 IV.9.5; Johns, Kaprow, Reinhardt, Tinguely in GRI LSRP 930046 T3/63; Schneemann in GRI LSRP 930046 T1 (1959) and T23/20; and mail art from Ray Johnson now in the Leo Steinberg Collection.

20 Christo and Jeanne Claude in GRI LSRP 930046 T2 (1990), T3/63, 930046ADD2 T16/63 (1991); Brach in GRI LSRP 930046 T3/63.

21 Thanked in Steinberg's dissertation as his "guardian angel," Mrs. Barr nurtured hopes that the young scholar would succeed her husband at MoMA. She had taken him under her wing, inviting him to New York art-world gatherings and advising him on his research trips to Italy. She even helped him with his dissertation research by making sketches of Borromini drawings at the Albertina when Steinberg was back in New York. Their long friendship came to a sad conclusion in 1981 when Barr received an invitation to a lecture Steinberg was giving at Columbia University (later published as *The Sexuality of Christ in Renaissance Art and in Modern Oblivion*). She found his subject "sacrilegious," GRI LSRP IV.9.8.

22 For Rauschenberg and Johns, see Steinberg, "The Gestural Trace," 70–72. Steinberg discusses his relationship with Victor and Sally Ganz and their Picassos in "In the Algerian Room," in *Picasso*, 165–169. Previously published in *A Life of Collecting: Victor and Sally Ganz*, ed. Michael Fitzgerald (New York: Christie's, 1997), 64–67.

23 GRI LSRP 930046 T4/63, T1 (1968, 1973), 930046ADD2 T16/63 (1990–91, 1992, 1997–98).

24 Steinberg, "The Gestural Trace," 68–70. One hundred and eighty-eight of Leventritt's prints from Steinberg were purchased by Lawrence and Julie Salander and given to the Blanton in 2006.

25 Some of these long-unpublished lectures are now included in the five UCP volumes.

26 See Steinberg's review of the literature in "Michelangelo's Last Paintings," in *Michelangelo's Painting*, 250–256.

27 Steinberg, "The Sistine *Deluge*," in *Michelangelo's Painting*, 20.

28 Steinberg cites previous interpretations in "Why Michelangelo Huddled Those Ancestors," in *Michelangelo's Painting*, 117–118.

29 Steinberg catalogues both adulatory and critical reviews of the painting in "Guercino's *Saint Petronilla*," in *Renaissance and Baroque Art*, 147–149. Previously published in *Studies in Italian Art and Architectural History, 15th through 18th Centuries*, ed. Henry Millon (Cambridge: MIT Press, 1980), 207–234.

30 Steinberg, "The Algerian Woman and Picasso at Large," in *Other Criteria*, 140.

31 Steinberg, "The Sexuality of Christ in Renaissance Art and in Modern Oblivion," *October* 15 (Summer 1983): 1–222.

32 In addition to individual obituaries and memorial essays, see *Source: Notes in the History of Art* 31/32, no. 4/1, Special Issue in Memory of Leo Steinberg (Summer/Fall 2012) and *Leo Steinberg Now*.

33 Steinberg kept records of his print purchases in six notebook ledgers, now in the Blanton's collection, NA.2021.1–NA.2021.6. Inventory numbers 1–20 precede his heart attack.

34 NA.2021.2, inv. 81. "LG Cat." refers to the 1961 catalogue issued by the New York dealer Lucien Goldschmidt: *Mannerism: Its Followers and Countertrends: 1530–1640: Books, Prints, Drawings*, no. 237.

35 Nadine Orenstein, "Phyllis Dearborn Massar," *Print Quarterly* 28, no. 2 (2011): 194–195.

36 NA.2021.2, 72.

37 Michael Ennis, "Prints of a Fellow," *Texas Monthly* 31, no. 6 (June 2003): 72, 80.

38 Steinberg's collection of annotated dealer catalogues, which include correspondence with dealers, is preserved at the Blanton.

39 Steinberg, "What I Like About Prints," *Art in Print* 7, no. 5 (January–February 2018): 3. This essay is adapted from a lecture Steinberg gave in April 2003 to celebrate the Blanton's acquisition of his collection.

40 The concept of the reproductive print is a contentious one; Steinberg's nuanced understanding is discussed further in the following essay. See also Susan Lambert, *The Image Multiplied: Five Centuries of Printed Reproductions of Paintings and Drawings* (New York: Abaris Books, 1987), 13–35 and Antony Griffiths, *The Print Before Photography: An Introduction to European Printmaking, 1550–1820* (London: British Museum Press, 2016), 464–465, 498–499.

41 Freyda Spira with Peter Parshall, *The Power of Prints: The Legacy of William M. Ivins and A. Hyatt Mayor* (New York: Metropolitan Museum of Art, 2016). Mayor's significant acquisitions of reproductive

prints for the Met's collection probably also encouraged Steinberg to recognize their artistic value. See Freyda Spira, "A. Hyatt Mayor's Life in Art and Letters," in *The Power of Prints*, 36–38.

42 Innis H. Shoemaker, *The Engravings of Marcantonio Raimondi* (Lawrence, KS: Spencer Museum of Art, 1981); Suzanne Boorsch, Michal Lewis, and R. E. Lewis, *The Engravings of Giorgio Ghisi* (New York: Metropolitan Museum of Art, 1985).

43 Steinberg to R. E. Lewis, May 24, 1984, Blanton Museum of Art.

44 Steinberg, "What I Like About Prints," 18.

45 Ibid.

46 Ibid., 18–19.

47 Ibid., 20.

48 Ibid., 21.

49 NA.2021.2, inv. 659, purchased May 24, 1962. When appraising the collection in 2001, Carolyn Bullard determined this impression had been minutely enhanced, with inked-over lines and toned with wash.

50 Steinberg, "The Gestural Trace," 42, 70, 129. Victor Ganz sponsored a three-part lecture series for which Steinberg was paid $1,000, anticipating the lucrative future he was to enjoy as a popular lecturer at universities and museums around the world.

51 Audrey Gibbs to Steinberg, February 28, 1964, Blanton Museum of Art.

52 Ernest Seligmann to Steinberg, November 6, 1963, Blanton Museum of Art.

53 NA.2021.4, inv. EE560; NA.2021.3, inv. D10.

54 Institutions that received or bought works from Steinberg's print collection include: the Blanton Museum of Art; Bowdoin College Museum of Art; Cantor Arts Center at Stanford University; the Clark Art Institute; the Getty Research Institute; the Kinsey Institute at Indiana University; Los Angeles County Museum of Art; the Metropolitan Museum of Art; the Jewish Museum, New York; the Museum of Art and Archaeology at the University of Missouri; the National Gallery of Art, Washington, DC; the New York Public Library; the Philadelphia Museum of Art; the Philadelphia Print Club (for fundraising auctions); the Princeton University Art Museum; RISD Museum; the University of Iowa Stanley Museum of Art; and Yale University Art Gallery. Invitations to deliver a lecture or personal connections to curators typically occasioned these gifts or sales. Since he was an inveterate smoker, Steinberg's prints often had a distinct aroma; Roberta Waddell, former Curator of Prints at the New York Public Library, recalls that this typically took two years to dissipate.

55 NA.2021.5, 24 records a total of 4,345 prints in his collection.

56 Oral history interview with Lucien Goldschmidt, 1974 May 19–June 5, transcript of an interview by Paul Cummings for the Archives of American Art, Smithsonian Institution, 10. Unpublished PDF, supplied to the author by the Archives of American Art.

57 NA.2021.3, inv. J01–J04 (2002.1987, 2002.1988, 2002.1591, 2002.1989); and Steinberg, "Picasso's Sleepwatchers," *LIFE*, December 27, 1968. Steinberg had bought two of Picasso's *Vollard Suite* prints in 1966 (NA.2021.1, inv. F100) and 1967 (NA.2021.1, inv. G92), which he traded in part to purchase *Blind Minotaur Guided by a Young Girl in the Night* (2002.1987). He made another *Vollard Suite* purchase in 1967 (NA.2021.1, inv. G1) that he later traded.

58 *Die Behaim* (2002.2334) and *Die Hirschvogel* (2002.2335) may come from a publication on Nuremberg's patrician families.

59 Steinberg's gifts and sales to the Blanton began in 1996; the bulk of his collection came in 2002; a final group was added in 2006, as explained in note 24. The tally does not include a small number of prints with the credit line "The Leo Steinberg Collection, by exchange." Those works were acquired by the trade of duplicates from Steinberg's collection.

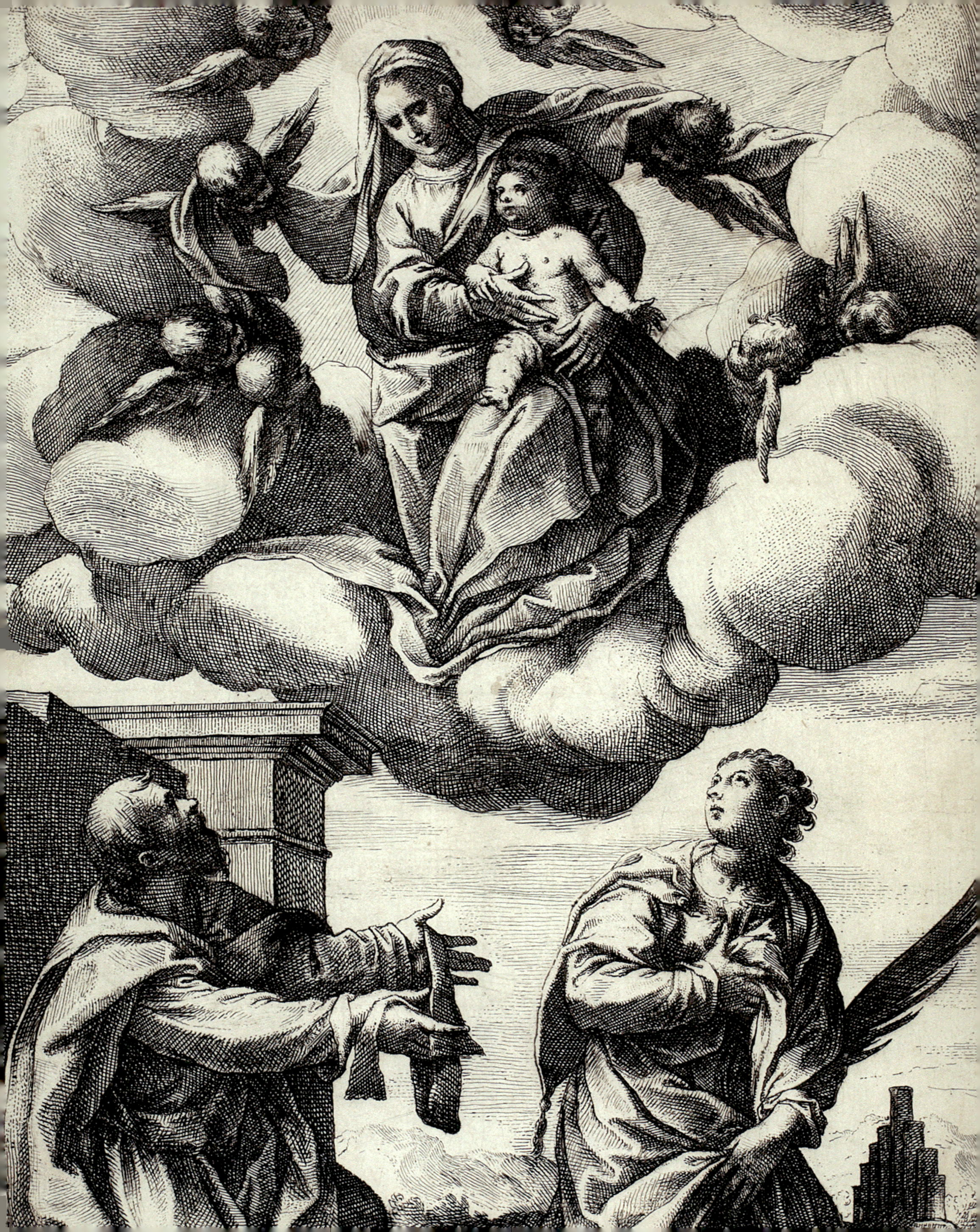

Steinberg as a Scholar

HOLLY BORHAM

THE POSTHUMOUS INVENTORY OF STEINBERG'S personal library numbered approximately six thousand volumes.[1] That even more prints passed through his collection is apposite for a scholar who privileged images over "meddling texts."[2] And if one accepts art historian Erwin Panofsky's dictum that "the one with the most [photographs] wins," then the compendium of images that Steinberg assembled in addition to his vast print collection—the voluminous file folders brimming with photographs of artworks, clipped reproductions, and newspaper advertisements—surely made him a serious candidate for the victor's crown.[3] Since many print catalogues raisonnés were not fully illustrated when Steinberg began collecting in the 1960s, his print acquisitions gave him convenient access to a large corpus of images that would have been much more difficult to retrieve through a library or museum. And just as prints circulated imagery and cultural information among artists, Steinberg's collection and study of prints provided him with a rich bank of iconography, allowed him to trace very specific chains of artistic transmission, furnished evidence of contemporaneous art criticism through "corrective copies," and even supplied him with the vocabulary and conceptual framework to challenge reigning orthodoxies about twentieth-century art. While his reputation was built on his incisive studies of art history's canonical luminaries, his expansive collection of copies and works by lesser-known artists yielded much relevant evidence for his claims about these major figures. Print scholarship thus owes Steinberg a debt, not yet sufficiently acknowledged, for the creative ways he embedded the study of prints within the larger art-historical discourse.

PRINTS IN CIRCULATION

Steinberg adduced from his collecting that prints were fundamental to early modern artistic practice and, therefore, to art history. His short articles in *The Print Collector's Newsletter*, which he helped found in 1969, invariably enmeshed prints within this larger context.[4] Steinberg's collecting habits also allowed him metaphorical entry into the studios of artists of the past, where prints were often among the tools of the trade. Through prints, Steinberg could tell a rich story, moving from the creation of a work, often in reference to another one, to its reception in its own time, and then to its afterlife in subsequent iterations. What other scholars established through historic texts and documents—that the famed collector Pierre-Jean Mariette complained that prints in Italy had been marked up and destroyed by painters in the process of mining them, for example, or that seventeenth-century theorists such as Gerard de Lairesse and Roger de Piles discussed prints as pedagogical tools for artists—Steinberg confirmed through such marks of utility on his own prints as pin pricks for transfer, squaring, and tracing on the verso.[5] A collector solely interested in owning a

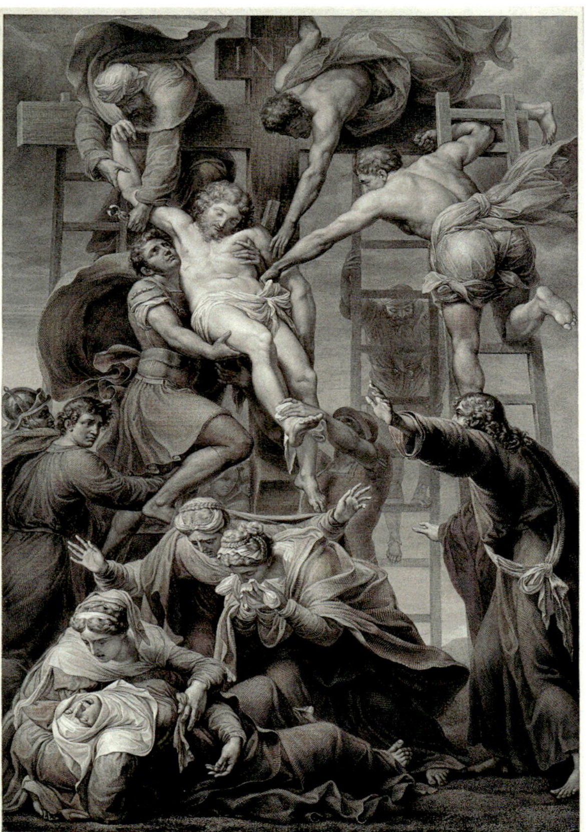

FIG. 9 Paolo Toschi, *Descent from the Cross*, after a painting by Daniele da Volterra, 1843. Etching and engraving, first state of four, 28¼ × 19⅛ in. (71.7 × 48.5 cm). LeBlanc IV.25 (2002.1674)

THE DESCENT FROM THE CROSS.
La Descente de Croix. La Bajada de la Cruz

FIG. 10 Currier and Ives, *Descent from the Cross*, after prints by Paolo Toschi and Louis Desplaces, ca. 1856. Lithograph with hand coloring, 13 × 8$\frac{7}{16}$ in. (30.5 × 21.4 cm). Gale 1691 (2002.1299)

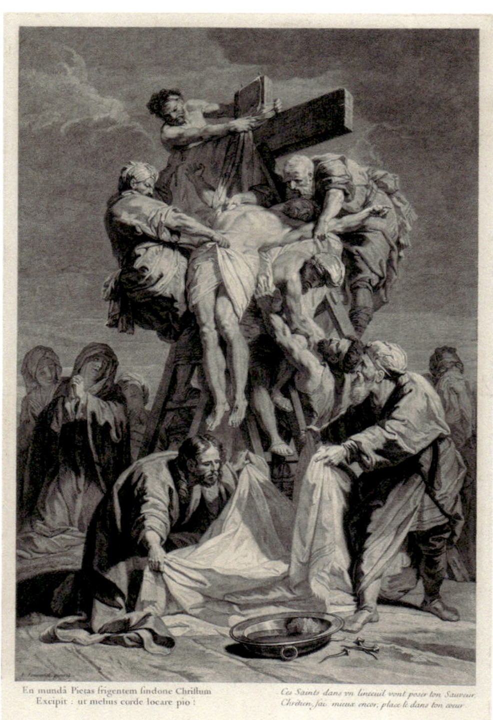

FIG. 11 Louis Desplaces, *Descent from the Cross*, after a painting by Jean Jouvenet, 1697–1739. Etching, second state of two, 22¾ × 15$\frac{5}{32}$ in. (57.8 × 38.5 cm). IFF–18 7.17. Rijksmuseum, Amsterdam. © Rijksmuseum.

pristine impression of a print might see such marks as devaluing it, whereas Steinberg prized them for their evidence of traditional artistic practice and their role in the transmission of visual information. His understanding of prints as the "circulating lifeblood of ideas" charts the various ways in which, in his words, artists actively "steal," "hijack," "raid," "import," "forage," "imitate," "transpose," "echo," "recycle," "recirculate," "quote," "plagiarize," "adopt," "appropriate," "lift," and "cannibalize" the work of their predecessors—a traffic pattern best detected by someone willing to dedicate decades to riffling through piles of bargain-basement prints, visiting collections, and reading all the relevant art-historical literature.[6]

As an artist himself, Steinberg understood that artists look to the work of others just as much as they look to nature for models, and he was thus particularly well positioned to follow chains of transmission. This was surely crucial to his perception of the "fleeting configuration" of three hands invented by Andrea Castagno for his *Last Supper* (1447) in Sant'Apollonia in Florence, adapted by Mantegna in his *A Sibyl and a Prophet* (1495), and redeployed by Leonardo in his *Last Supper* (1498).[7] By identifying the appropriation of Michelangelo's Christ figures from his Roman and Florentine *Pietàs* by Pontormo and El Greco respectively, Steinberg further mapped the migration of motifs and compositions among artists.[8]

Prints expanded and accelerated artists' access to visual material drawn from sources spanning time, place, and medium. In 1966, Steinberg purchased Paolo Toschi's *Descent from the Cross* after Daniele da Volterra (1843; fig. 9) and he must have felt a shock of recognition two years later when he encountered an image of it by the popular nineteenth-century New York lithographers Currier & Ives (ca. 1856; fig. 10). He soon recognized that Currier & Ives had created what he called a "reader's digest" version of Volterra's florid original by reducing the number of figures in the upper half and splicing the result to Louis Desplaces's etching (1697–1739; fig. 11) after Jean Jouvenet's painting of the subject; the etching shows a scene of restrained pathos in which the swooning Virgin has been relocated to a position of prayer behind the cross and replaced by two pragmatic figures who prepare to receive the body. This marriage of Italian Mannerism with French classicism results in a devotional lithograph befitting the proprieties of nineteenth-century America.[9] As his notes on mats and in his purchase ledgers indicate, Steinberg also tracked the flitting of Cupid in print from Italy to Antwerp and on to Germany via Rubens, who had seen Antonio da Correggio's *The School of Love* (ca. 1525; fig. 12) on a trip to Mantua. From there, Correggio's Cupid appears supporting a mirror in Willem Panneels's etched copy of Rubens's *Toilet of Venus* (1631; fig. 13) and surmounting a cascade of putti in *Statue of Ceres* (ca. 1615; fig. 14) by Rubens and Frans Snyders, which was later adapted for the title page of diplomat Johann Angelius von Werdenhagen's 1641 text on the history of the Hanseatic cities (fig. 15).[10] From Velázquez's importation of Dutch prints in both general and precise ways, to Sebald Beham's plucking from Marcantonio and Michelangelo, to an anonymous Italian borrowing from Jacques Callot, Steinberg's personal collection testifies to the generative nature of prints in the creative process.[11] In addition to discerning translations of prints into drawings, paintings, and sculptures, he noted their role in the ornamentation of such decorative objects as French Limoges enamels, Italian majolica (figs. 16, 17), and English Mortlake tapestries.[12] And on this basis, he argues for a broader notion of reproductive printmaking as "not so much a branch of art as the medium through which, for nearly 400 years, all branches of art interacted."[13]

CORRECTING LEONARDO

In a field that has historically disparaged reproductive engraving and prints in general, Steinberg's championing of such "copies" and the artists who made them was revolutionary. As he explains, "Copyists of paintings look harder, observe by the inch, and where they refuse

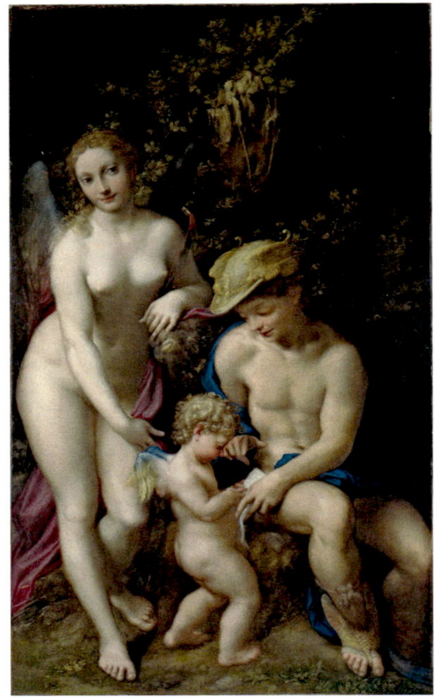

FIG. 12 Antonio da Correggio, ***Venus with Mercury and Cupid (The School of Love)***, ca. 1525. Oil on canvas, $61\frac{17}{64} \times 36$ in. (155.6 × 91.4 cm). National Gallery, London.

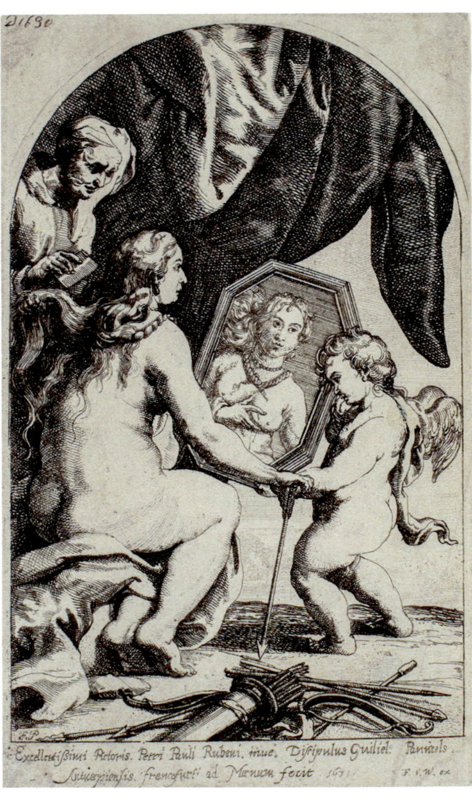

FIG. 13 Willem Panneels, ***The Toilet of Venus***, after Peter Paul Rubens, 1631. Etching, second state of two, $6\frac{9}{16} \times 3\frac{7}{8}$ in. (16.7 × 9.8 cm). Hollstein 23 (2002.1111)

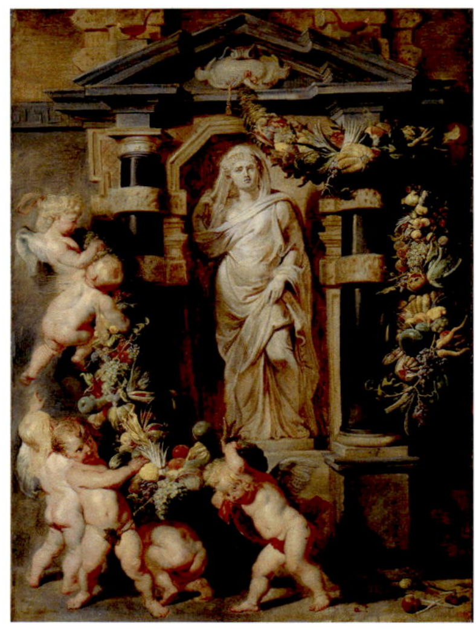

FIG. 14 Peter Paul Rubens and Frans Snyders, ***Statue of Ceres***, ca. 1615. Oil on oak panel, $35\frac{5}{8} \times 25\frac{25}{32}$ in. (90.5 × 65.5 cm). The State Hermitage Museum, St. Petersburg © The State Hermitage Museum.

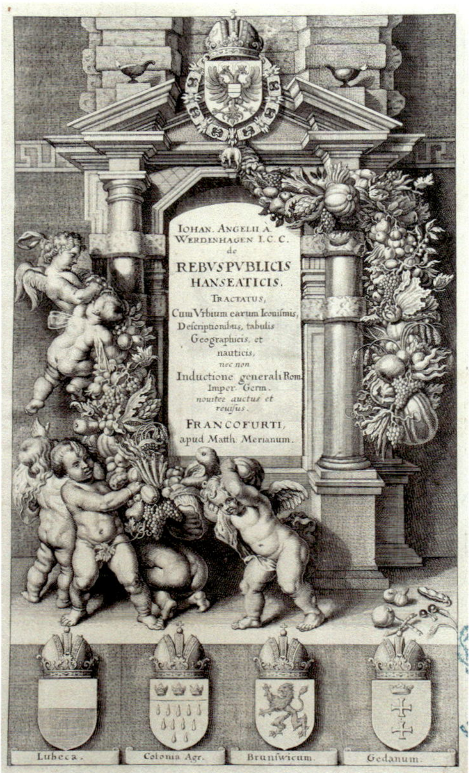

IOHAN. ANGELII A
WERDENHAGEN I.C.C.
de
REBVS PVBLICIS
HANSEATICIS.
TRACTATUS,
Cum Vrbium earum Iconismis,
Descriptionibus, tabulis
Geographicis, et
nauticis,
nec non
Inductione generali Rom.
Imper. Germ.
nouiter auctus et
reuisus.
FRANCOFURTI,
apud Matth: Merianum.

Lubeca. Colonia Agr. Brunswicum. Gedanum.

FIG. 15 Matthäus Merian I, Title page to ***De Rebus Publicis Hanseaticis***, after a painting by Peter Paul Rubens and Frans Snyders. Text by Johann Angelius Werdenhagen, Frankfurt, 1641. Etching and engraving, only state, $11\frac{9}{16} \times 6\frac{5}{8}$ in. (29.4 × 16.8 cm). Hollstein 653a (2002.2587)

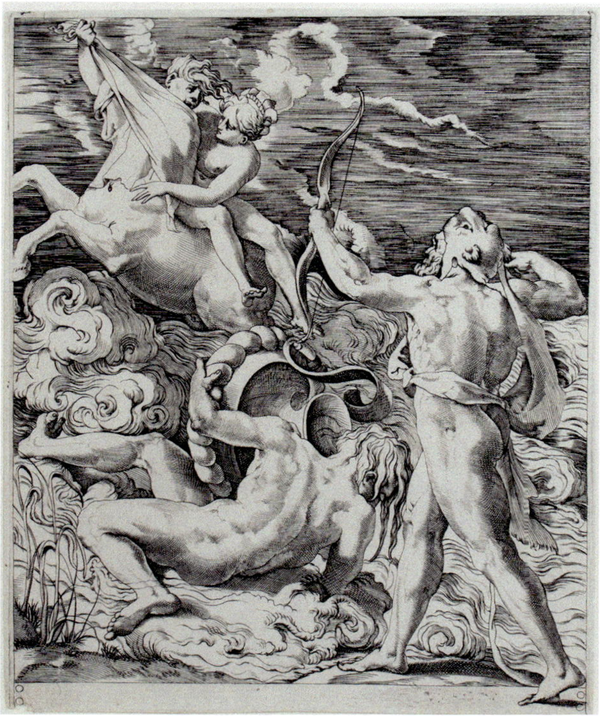

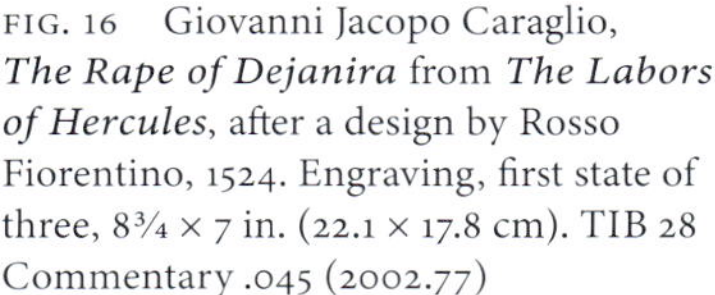

FIG. 16 Giovanni Jacopo Caraglio, *The Rape of Dejanira* from *The Labors of Hercules*, after a design by Rosso Fiorentino, 1524. Engraving, first state of three, $8\frac{3}{4} \times 7$ in. (22.1 × 17.8 cm). TIB 28 Commentary .045 (2002.77)

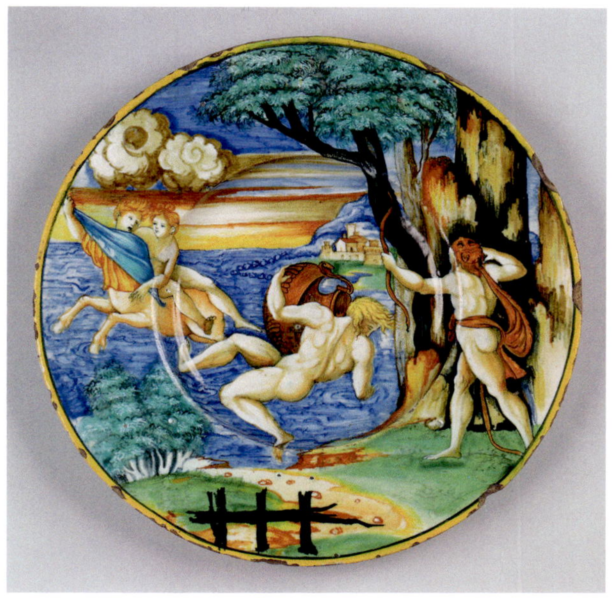

FIG. 17 Workshop of Guido Durantino, *Plate with Hercules, Nessus, and Deianira*, after a print by Giovanni Jacopo Caraglio, 1525–35. Earthenware with tin glaze (maiolica), $11\frac{5}{8} \times 1\frac{9}{16}$ in. (29.6 × 4 cm) The Walters Art Museum, Baltimore, MD.

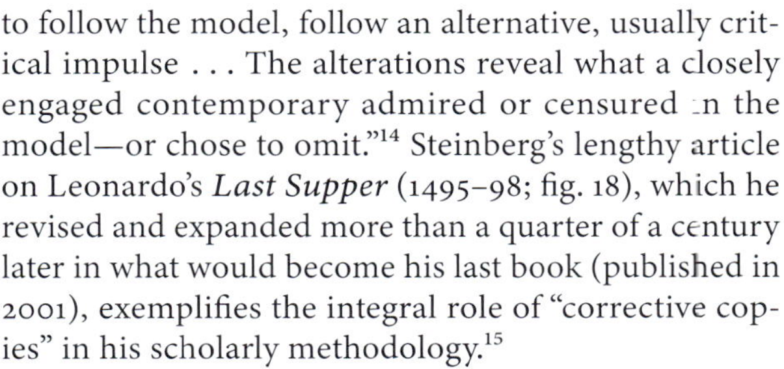

to follow the model, follow an alternative, usually critical impulse . . . The alterations reveal what a closely engaged contemporary admired or censured in the model—or chose to omit."[14] Steinberg's lengthy article on Leonardo's *Last Supper* (1495–98; fig. 18), which he revised and expanded more than a quarter of a century later in what would become his last book (published in 2001), exemplifies the integral role of "corrective copies" in his scholarly methodology.[15]

Along with the literature on the *Last Supper*, Steinberg analyzes forty-nine works of art made after it, ranging from an early sixteenth-century engraving attributed to Giovanni Pietro Birago that he describes as "inaccurate and naïve" to a nineteenth-century mosaic.[16] As a group, he considers these disparate works significant to an understanding of this complex painting, one that has been radically assailed by time, decay, and botched restorations. While copies have always played an outsize role in the study of the *Last Supper* because of its almost immediate deterioration (as well as the obliteration of its lower-central portion through the addition of a doorway in 1652), Steinberg regards the reproductions as more than mere records of lost visual information. He begins his investigations with the thorny question of precisely which narrative moment Leonardo depicts in the fresco—is it when Christ announces that one of his disciples will betray him? Or immediately after the event when the disciples wonder who the traitor is? Or is it when Christ identifies the betrayer as the one who dips his hand in the dish? Or the moment when Christ institutes the Eucharist by proffering wine and bread? He goes on to make

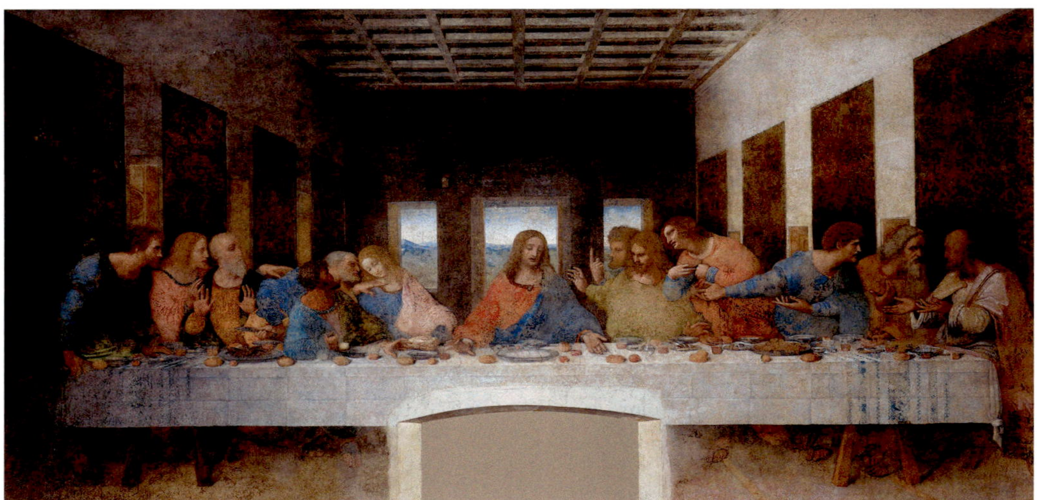

FIG. 18 Leonardo da Vinci, *Last Supper*, 1495–98. Fresco, 180 × 350 in. (70 55/64 × 137 51/64 cm). Santa Maria delle Grazie, Milan.

painstaking comparisons between Leonardo's original painting and the numerous later versions as he considers the implications of the copyists' alterations. He ultimately concludes that while Leonardo was willfully ambiguous about the subject of the painting, which is full of coincident opposites that emanate visually and conceptually from the dual divine-human nature of Christ, copyists typically reduce the painting to a single instance and a single meaning.

Among the many reproductive prints in Steinberg's collection, three contributed substantially to his analysis of Leonardo's original: Marcantonio's engraving after Raphael (ca. 1515–16), Raphael Morghen's engraving (1800), and Pieter Soutman's etching after Rubens (1636–50). Steinberg sees Raphael's design (fig. 19) as representing both homage and critique. By rotating both of Christ's palms downward and giving him an emphatically closed mouth, "the great clarifier" portrays the moment after Christ has finished speaking, though Steinberg is not sure if the terminal episode represented here is the announcement of the betrayal or the institution of the Eucharist.[17] Some three hundred years later, Morghen (fig. 20) focuses on the psychological turmoil induced by Christ's prediction of betrayal, also made explicit in the Latin caption below. Further, he removes the wine glass at Christ's right hand, thus erasing the eucharistic meaning. It was this engraving, not the original fresco, on which Goethe relied when expressing his influential view that in the *Last Supper* Leonardo presents an ethical rather than a religious drama.[18] In contrast, as Soutman's etching reveals, Rubens cleared the table entirely except for the bread and wine, thus emphasizing the sacramental aspect of the scene (fig. 21). The engraved biblical captions reference the introduction of the Eucharist, confirming that Rubens understood the disciples' agitated reactions as responses to the concept of transubstantiation.[19] Steinberg further bases his argument about the site-specific nature of Leonardo's fresco on Rubens's image; Rubens's relocation of the event to a darkened room with dramatic, billowing curtains establishes that the scale and perspective of Leonardo's background only made sense in situ, forming both the upper room described in the biblical narrative and a visual extension of the Milanese refectory in which it is painted.[20] He convincingly argues that it is only by closely examining such variant copies alongside the original that one can begin to understand the true complexity of Leonardo's remarkable painting.[21]

CORRECTING MICHELANGELO

Steinberg wrote more about Michelangelo than he did about any other artist, and despite his witty limerick —"Michelangelo Buonarroti / furnished themes convoluted and knotty / to engravers galore / whom we can't but deplore / since their work seems consistently spotty"—many of the reproductive engravings after the artist in his collection are of high quality and assisted his incisive analyses of the master's original works.[22]

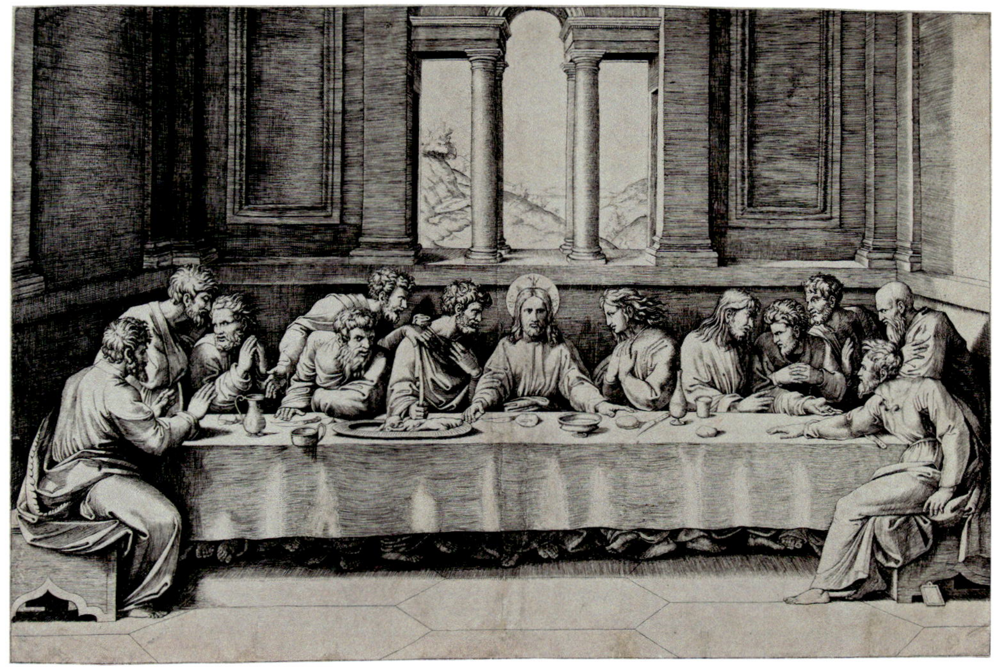

FIG. 19 Marcantonio Raimondi, ***Last Supper (La Cène aux pieds)***, after a drawing attributed to Raphael, ca. 1515–16. Engraving, only state, 11 11/16 × 16 15/16 in. (29.7 × 43 cm). Shoemaker 30 (2002.1704)

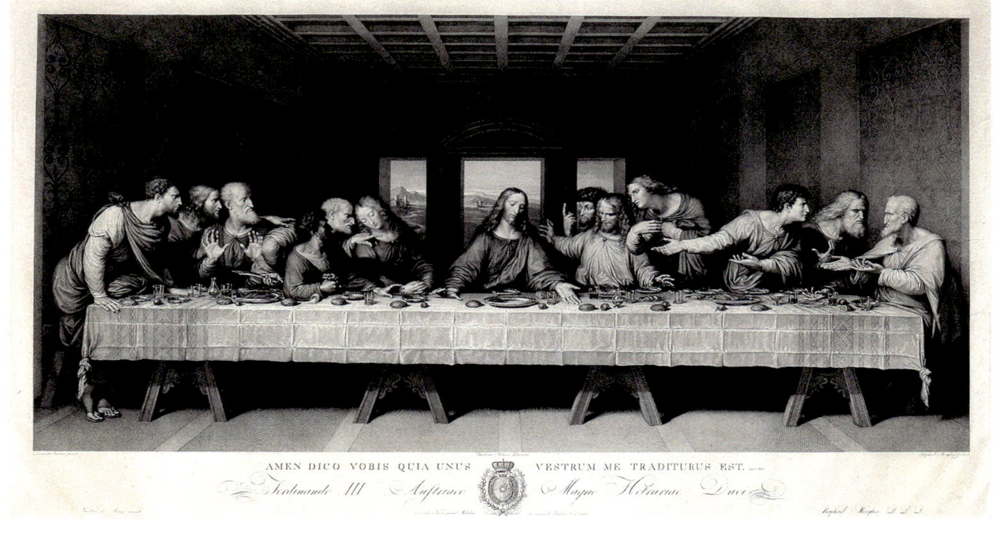

FIG. 20 Raphael Morghen, ***Last Supper***, after a fresco by Leonardo da Vinci, 1800. Etching and engraving, fourth state of six, 20 1/2 × 36 3/4 in. (52 × 93.3 cm). Le Blanc III.19 (2002.2757)

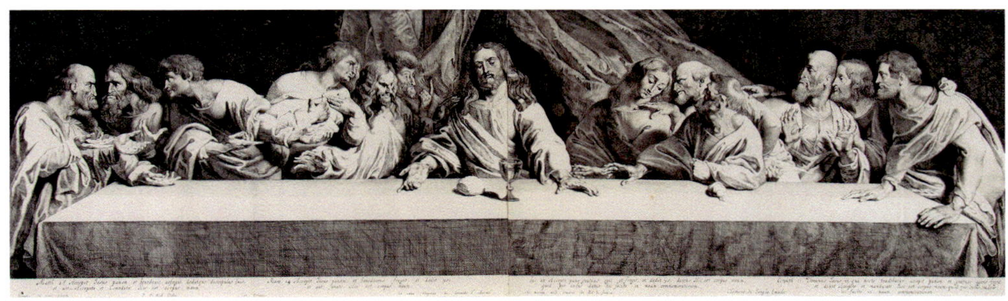

FIG. 21 Pieter Claesz Soutman, ***Last Supper***, after a drawing by Peter Paul Rubens, after a fresco by Leonardo da Vinci, 1636–50. Etching and engraving on two sheets, third state of six, 11 1/2 × 38 13/16 in. (29.2 × 98.6 cm). Hollstein 4, Barrett Pr-5 (2002.2802)

To guide his investigation of Michelangelo's Vatican frescoes, Steinberg relied heavily on engraved copies, both as records of the original compositions and as indicators of what subsequent artists misunderstood or felt compelled to correct. For the Sistine Ceiling (1508–12), corrective copies of its most famous section, the *Creation of Adam*, confirmed Steinberg's observation of hitherto overlooked figures in a corner of the veil enveloping God and his interpretation of them as the rebellious angels who revolted against God's creation of man.[23] In the *Temptation and Expulsion*, later prints revealed a bowdlerization of Eve's middle finger that obscured a phallic reference in the original, one intended to highlight the role of her womb in the Christian plan of salvation.[24]

Prints after Michelangelo's *Last Judgment* (1536–41; fig. 22) on the altar wall of the Sistine Chapel informed his interpretation of the fresco as a "merciful heresy," offering sinners reprieve from eternal punishment.[25] Steinberg argues that due to subsequent decrees by the Council of Trent affirming instead the eternal torment of sinners, copyists introduced distortions or "corrections" to bring Michelangelo's painted theology into line with Church doctrine.[26]

Steinberg sees Christ's pose in Michelangelo's composition as intentionally ambiguous. Is Christ seated, standing, rising, or striding? Is his facial expression vengeful or impassive? Is his arm raised in order to cast down, to bless, or to provide visual access to his side wound? This calculated polysemy holds in tension Christ's judgment and mercy, prominently emphasized along compositional diagonals linking heaven and hell.[27] Among the seventeen reproductions of this work in Steinberg's collection is Martino Rota's 1569 version (fig. 23), on which many subsequent copies are based, and in which Christ's straightened leg clarifies his upright posture, reflecting the artist's efforts to reduce ambiguity and establish the orthodoxy of the fresco's message.[28]

Steinberg discerns in Michelangelo's fresco a key compositional diagonal that begins at the lower right

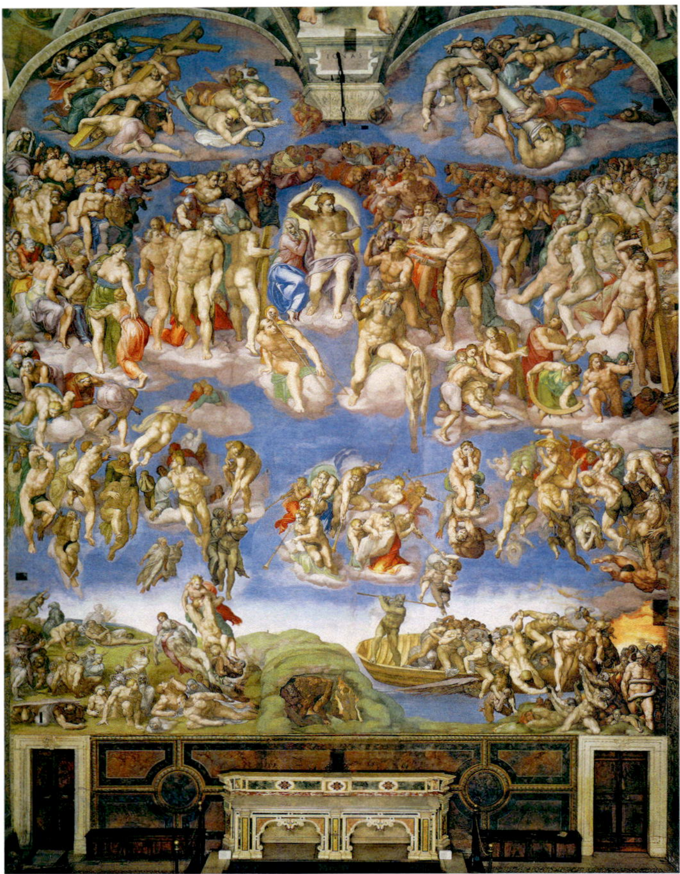

FIG. 22 Michelangelo Buonarroti, *Last Judgment*, 1536–41. Fresco, 539³⁄₁₀ × 472²⁄₅ in. (1370 × 1200 cm). The Sistine Chapel, Vatican City.

(fig. 24) with a snake-encircled figure he identifies as the Antichrist, whose loins are cradled in the mouth of the serpent, signifying his consensual, intimate relationship with sin and evil.[29] As it ascends from sin through repentance to salvation, the soul follows an upward diagonal line, from the crouching man cupping his face in shame and tugged downward by demons, to St. Bartholomew's flayed skin imprinted with Michelangelo's features and identifying the artist with all who must face judgment, to the wound of Christ who was slain for human iniquities, up to his crown of thorns and the cross that offers hope of salvation.

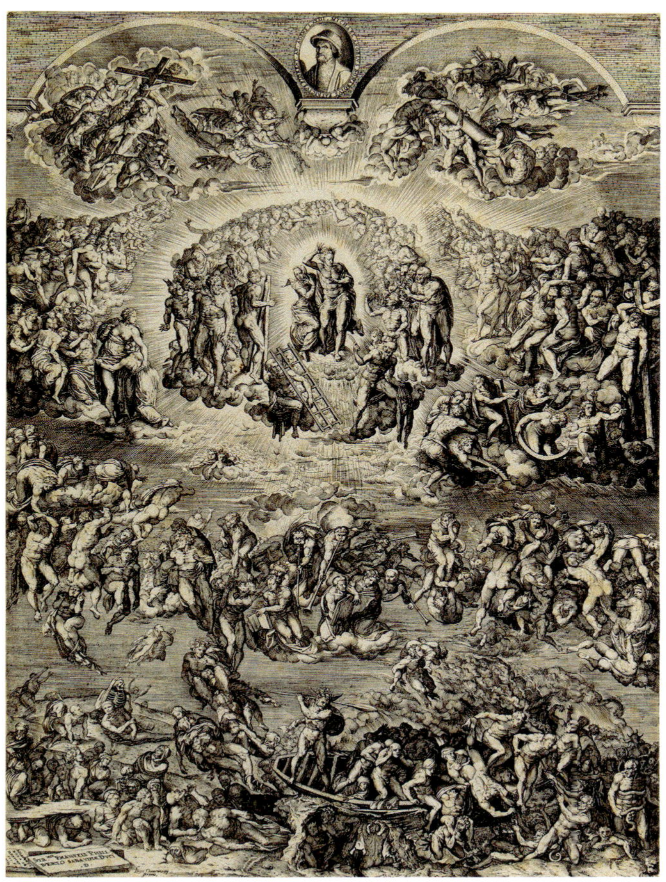

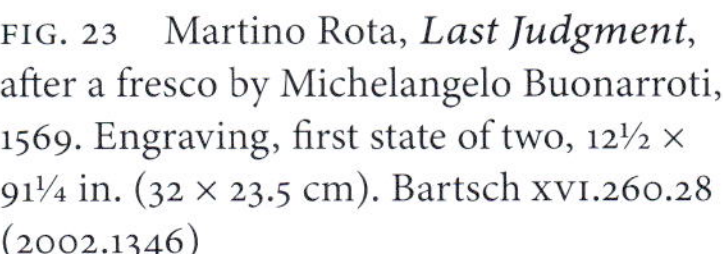

FIG. 23 Martino Rota, *Last Judgment*, after a fresco by Michelangelo Buonarroti, 1569. Engraving, first state of two, $12\frac{1}{2} \times 9\frac{1}{4}$ in. (32 × 23.5 cm). Bartsch XVI.260.28 (2002.1346)

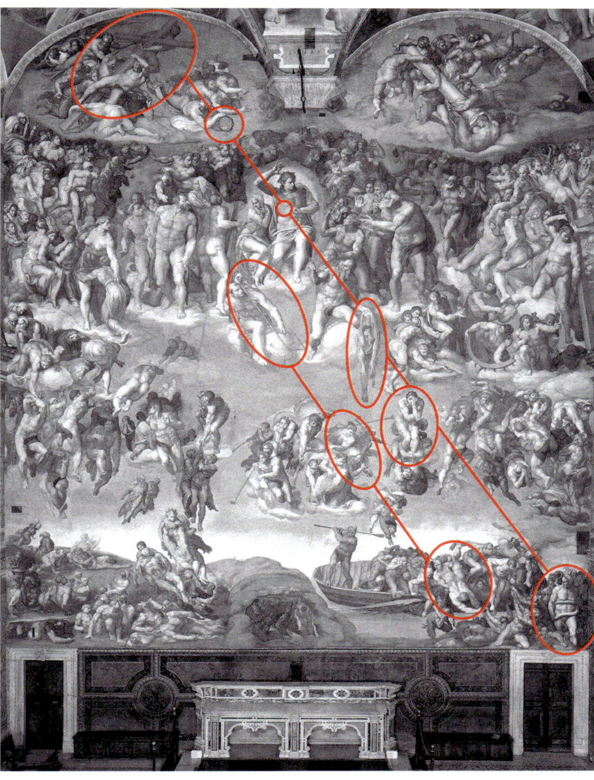

FIG. 24 Michelangelo Buonarroti, *Last Judgment* (with diagonals traced), 1536–41. Fresco, $539\frac{3}{10} \times 472\frac{2}{5}$ in. (1370 × 1200 cm). The Sistine Chapel, Vatican City.

A parallel diagonal of mercy begins with the charitable act of one figure in the boat ferried by Charon (who transported the dead souls across the rivers of the underworld). He pulls his companion, seen tumbling out of it headfirst, from the demons' grasp. Progressing diagonally upward, two angels pause the sounding of the judgments on their trumpets to allow for repentance, permitting the soul to ascend St. Lawrence's ladder (symbolizing his martyrdom on a grate over hot coals). It ultimately arrives at the foot of the Virgin, who intercedes with her son on behalf of sinners. Steinberg thus sees the lower-right corner of the image as representing a "purging fire for conscience-stricken redeemable sinners," while hell is the comparably smaller, flame-filled cave at the lower center that Christ has "overruled for humankind's redemption."[30]

Steinberg observes that reproductions like Rota's set Charon's boat on top of an enlarged central cave, effectively eliding the distinction between suffering and a permanent hell in favor of the latter. Aligned now with Christ along the central axis, Charon swells in size and dominion. Those discharged from his boat land adjacent to hell, the now-inescapable fate for all sinners, a site that Michelangelo had kept separate to

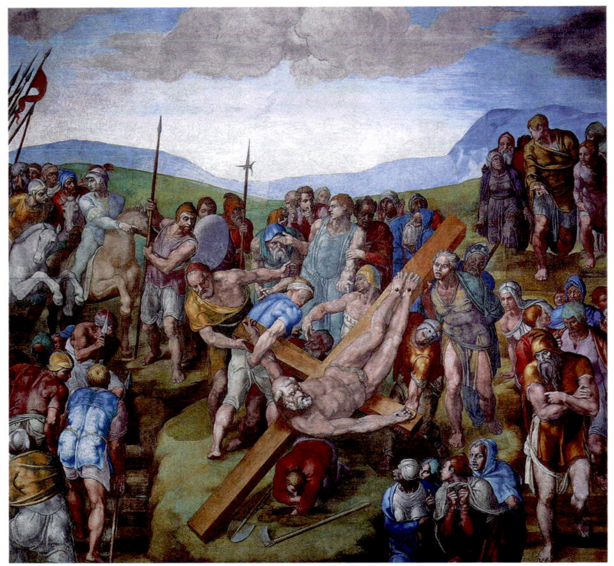

FIG. 25 Michelangelo Buonarroti, *The Crucifixion of St. Peter*, 1546–50. Fresco, 246 × 261 in. (625 × 663 cm). The Pauline Chapel, Vatican City.

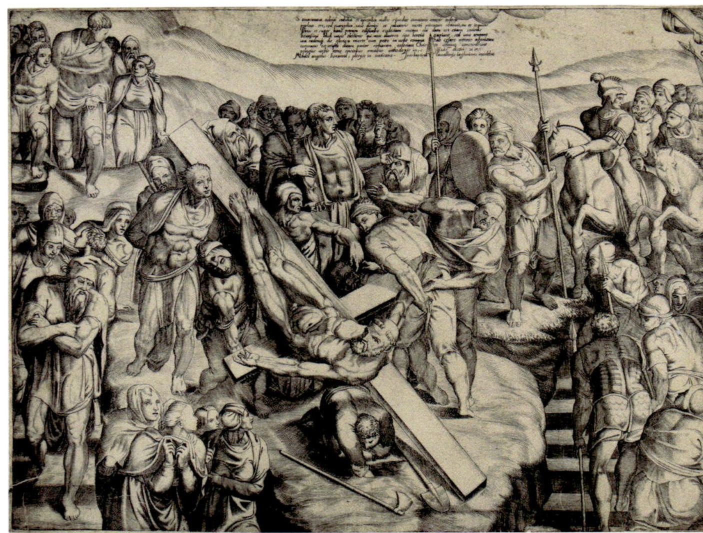

FIG. 26 Giovanni Battista de'Cavalieri, *The Crucifixion of St. Peter*, after a fresco by Michelangelo, before 1568. Engraving, second state of two, $16\frac{1}{2} \times 21\frac{9}{16}$ in. (41.9 × 54.7 cm). Scorsetti 53 (2002.1721)

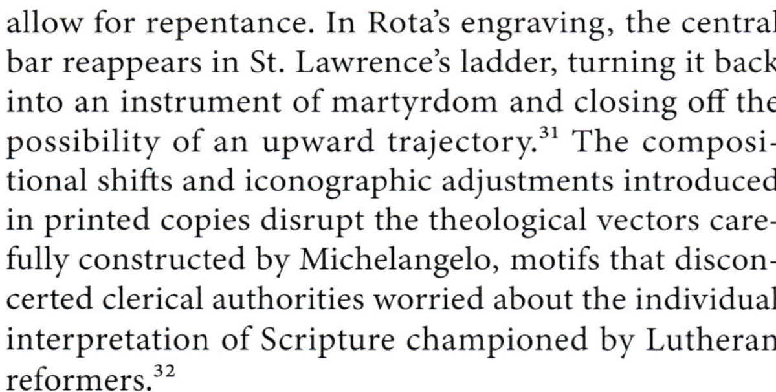

allow for repentance. In Rota's engraving, the central bar reappears in St. Lawrence's ladder, turning it back into an instrument of martyrdom and closing off the possibility of an upward trajectory.[31] The compositional shifts and iconographic adjustments introduced in printed copies disrupt the theological vectors carefully constructed by Michelangelo, motifs that disconcerted clerical authorities worried about the individual interpretation of Scripture championed by Lutheran reformers.[32]

In the same essay, Steinberg argues that copyist Giovanni Battista de'Cavalieri unwittingly disrupts a key vector in Michelangelo's Pauline fresco, *The Crucifixion of St. Peter*. After completing the *Last Judgment* in 1541, Michelangelo was commissioned by Pope Paul III to produce frescoes for a new chapel intended to serve as the site of papal conclaves for the election of popes. It was here, between 1542 and 1549, that he painted *The Conversion of St. Paul* and *The Crucifixion of St. Peter*. Both works were either ignored or disparaged by later commentators for what were seen as their discordant compositions and overall lack of grace, among other weaknesses. For Steinberg, however, the two frescoes powerfully synthesize apostolic fervor and private penance.[33]

Steinberg's analysis of the frescoes is intricate, but at least one point directly relates to his print collection. At upper left in *The Crucifixion of St. Peter* (1546–50; fig. 25), the elderly Michelangelo inserted a turbaned, younger self-portrait next to the head of a Roman captain. The portrait is the terminus of a compositional line that descends diagonally downward (or upward) through the beam of the cross to another self-portrait in the bearded man at lower right, standing with folded arms. The latter, in its echo of Barbarian prisoners on Roman sarcophagi and in Renaissance prints, suggests a captive state. In Steinberg's interpretation, the line tracks the seventy-four-year-old Michelangelo as he repents his youthful pride and love of pagan art. But the printed copies after the fresco tell a different story. In his reversed version (before 1568; fig. 26), Giovanni Battista de'Cavalieri weakens the original diagonal, interrupting its line by shifting the position of figures, truncating the beam of the cross and filling in a blank space at its crux, and removing the hand that links the heads of the young Michelangelo and the Roman captain. With these minor adjustments, surely intended as improvements, Cavalieri effectively obscures the significant autobiographical element in Michelangelo's fresco.[34] As he closely examined the fresco in the context of its copies, Steinberg disentangled a highly complex series of artistic decisions.

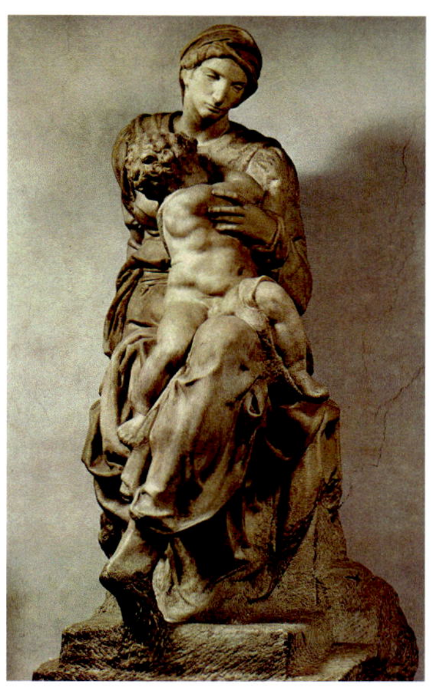

FIG. 27 Michelangelo Buonarroti, *Medici Madonna*, 1521–34. Marble, height: 89 in. (226 cm). Basilica di San Lorenzo, Florence.

MICHELANGELO AND THE THEOLOGICAL BODY

Steinberg argues that Michelangelo's deeply orthodox Catholic faith expressed itself in an intense corporeality; "in Michelangelo's hands, anatomy becomes theology."[35] He used his print collection as a sort of encyclopedia of body language as he considered the symbolism of specific poses in Michelangelo's art and the significance of adjustments made by copyists. For example, with the aid of seventeen prints in his collection that reproduce discrete vertical sections of the Sistine Chapel's lunettes and vaults, among them *Compartment of the Sistine Ceiling with the Libyan Sibyl and the Prophet Daniel* (1577, republished 1628; fig. 54), Steinberg refutes earlier interpretations of the fifty-three Ancestors in the lunettes above the chapel's windows as listless and dejected. Instead of reading the male figures as "apathetic" based on their slumped postures, he views them as engaged in waiting for the coming of Christ, some of them exhausted from generations of procreation.[36] The fecundity of these Ancestors led him to evince a crucial juxtaposition of the Active and Contemplative Lives central to medieval theology, with Christ's forebears representing the *vita activa*, while around and above them the prophets and seers who foretold Christ's coming speak for the *vita contemplativa*. Steinberg also devoted considerable attention to the artist's depictions of Christ, both as an infant on the Virgin's lap and mourned by her in various Pietàs.[37]

Steinberg identifies the cross-legged pose of the *Medici Madonna* (1521–34; fig. 27), for example, as symbolizing perpetual virginity. Michelangelo's source for the pose was a Hellenistic statue of Clio but, Steinberg argues, its significance here is related to ancient Greek images of Penelope, the wife of Odysseus, who chastely awaited the return of her husband from the Trojan War. The iconography endured and was later adapted to other women who asserted their virtue, including Susanna, falsely accused of impropriety (seen in a print after Maarten van Heemskerck, 1563; fig. 28), and the penitent Mary Magdalene, as well as such allegorical female figures by Tommaso Piroli after Raphael as Ecclesia and Pax (1797; fig. 29)—examples of which Steinberg could examine in his own print collection.[38]

In the *Medici Madonna*, the Virgin manifests her motherhood by nursing the infant Christ. In other works by the artist, her parted thighs emphasize that the child is the issue of her loins—a configuration Steinberg calls "manifest filiation."[39] Although the pose is neither unique to his work (see, for example, Léon Davent's *Holy Family with Saints* after Parmigianino (1547; fig. 30) nor to this holy pair (see also Veneziano's *Venus and Cupid* after Raphael, 1516; fig. 31), Michelangelo also employs it in the *Doni Tondo* (1505–06), where Mary sits between the thighs of Joseph in his role as God the Father, as well as in the *Bruges Madonna* (1501–04); the late *Epiphany* (1550–53) cartoon in the British Museum; and the *Pietà for Vittoria Colonna* (1540), made for a reformist Catholic friend and

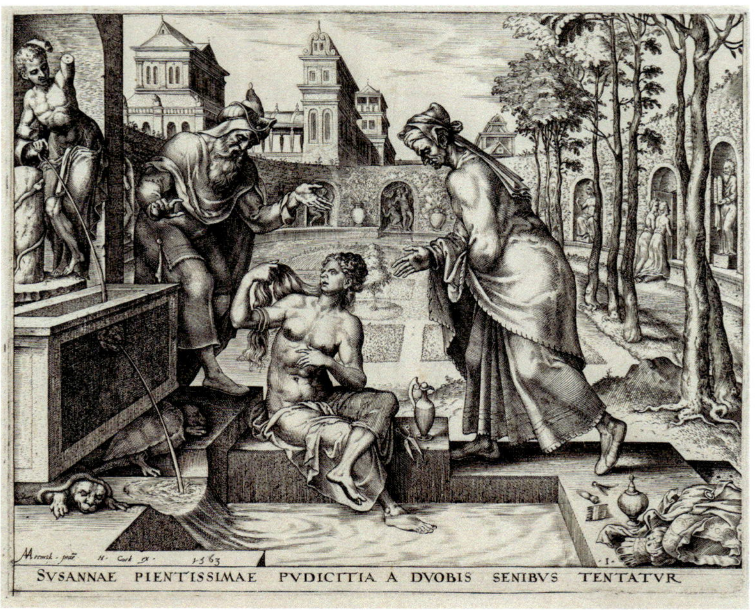

FIG. 28 After Maarten van Heemskerck, ***The Elders Trying to Seduce Susanna***, plate 1 from ***The Story of Susanna***, 1563. Engraving, first state of two, 8⅛ × 9⅞ in. (20.5 × 25 cm). New Hollstein 219 (1997.71)

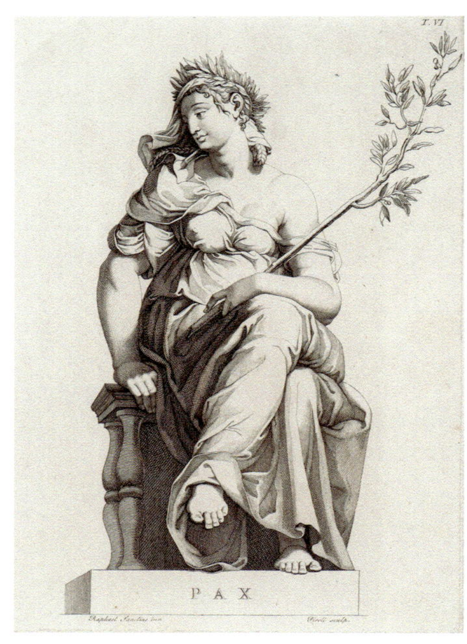

FIG. 29 Tommaso Piroli, ***Pax***, after Raphael, 1797. Engraving, 13½ × 9⅝ in. (34.4 × 24.5 cm). Höper F 25.8.6 (2002.1923)

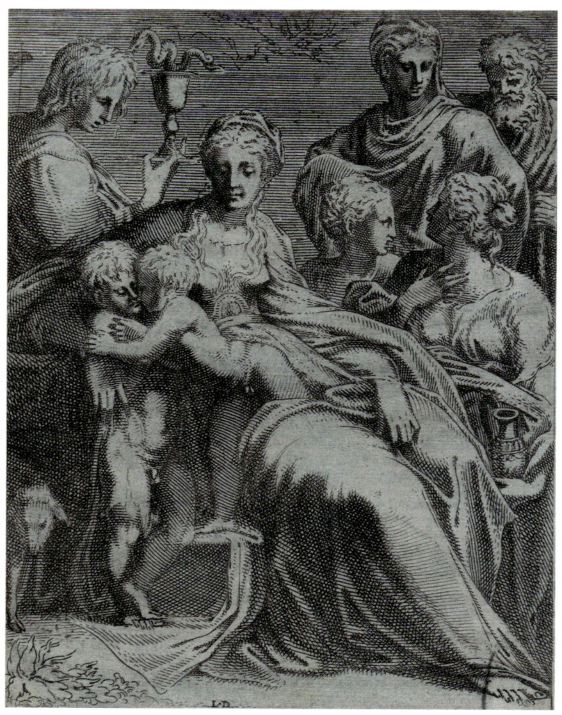

FIG. 30 Léon Davent, ***Holy Family with Saints***, after a design by Parmigianino, 1547. Etching with engraving on blue prepared paper, only state, 9⁷⁄₁₆ × 7¼ in. (24 × 18.4 cm). Jenkins LD 57 (2002.1840)

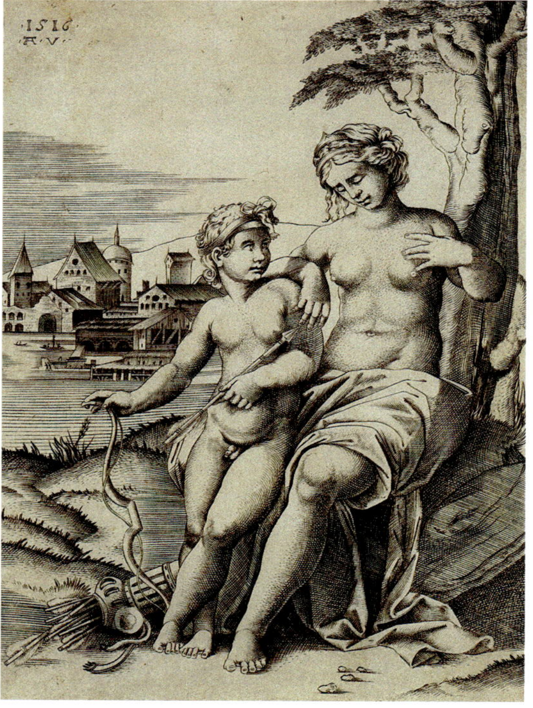

FIG. 31 Agostino dei Musi, called Agostino Veneziano, ***Venus and Cupid***, after a lost sketch by Raphael, 1516. Engraving, second state of three, 7¹⁄₁₆ × 5¼ in. (17.9 × 13.3 cm). Bartsch XIV.218.286 (2002.26)

quickly adapted and engraved, as in a print by Giulio Bonasone (1546; fig. 32).[40] In this composition, Christ's death is connected to his birth from Mary's womb, as he slumps between her parted legs in a pose reflecting the intimate connection between womb and tomb long established in theological exegesis.[41]

The Virgin's designation as the bride of Christ goes back to the early church fathers, but only Michelangelo, as Steinberg saw it, transformed this mystical concept of union through the representation of body language. His provocative description of the Roman *Pietà* (1498–99; fig. 33) as "[a] smooth marble group which, under cover of a devotional theme, displayed an exceptionally beautiful youth lying naked in the lap of a girl," likens the iconography of the Christian pair to that of Venus mourning her mortal lover, Adonis.[42] And while other artists, like Jean Mignon in an etching after Luca Penni (1530–40; fig. 34), struggled to fit a grown man onto a woman's lap, Michelangelo ingeniously contorted Christ's body into a serpentine crescent around Mary, fusing the two figures in a single pyramidal structure that visually reinforces the mystical concept of union. Moreover, Steinberg argues that although Mary's youthful appearance may be symbolic of perpetual virginity, it is also intended to denote her as a bride.[43] Sculpted and printed copies of the work undermine its eroticism by aging Mary and adjusting the interlocking figures to make them less unified. Beatrizet's 1547 engraving, for example, rotates and props up Christ's torso as if to approximate a Man of Sorrows (fig. 35).[44] Michelangelo's sculpture may be devoutly Christian, but later artists, as Steinberg realized from studying the copies, retreated from its unintended secular implications.

Steinberg also defined Michelangelo's bodily motif of the "slung leg," where one figure extends a leg over the thigh of another.[45] As he assembled images from antiquity onward, he tracked this element in its application to both carnal and spiritual unions: a prostitute's leg slung over that of the Prodigal Son in a print by Theodoor van Thulden, for example, leaves his arousal in no doubt (ca. 1633; fig. 36); in an engraving

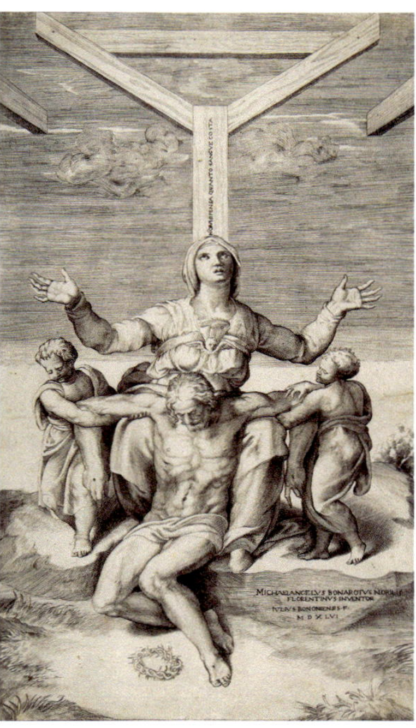

FIG. 32 Giulio Bonasone, *Pietà for Vittoria Colonna*, after a drawing by Michelangelo, 1546. Engraving, only state, 14³⁄₁₆ × 8⅛ in. (36 × 20.6 cm). Massari (1983) 77. The Metropolitan Museum of Art, Harris Brisbane Dick Fund, 1953. (Another impression is in The Leo Steinberg Collection, 2002.1323)

by Schelte Adams Bolswert showing *The Virgin Adoring Jesus* (1605–59; fig. 37), Christ's left leg slung over the Virgin's and his hand on her shoulder signify male appropriation in the mystical, proleptic sense of the heavenly Bride and Bridegroom.[46] The infant Christ of the *Medici Madonna*, straddling his mother's thigh and grasping her shoulder, is a "divine lover electing his spouse."[47] Steinberg's investigation into the motif began with the Florentine *Pietà* (1547–55; fig. 38), on which Christ's left leg is now missing. Steinberg posits that it was originally slung over Mary's thigh and that Michelangelo, in the puritanical, reformist atmosphere of 1540s Rome, smashed the leg, fearing that the vulgarization of the motif in other artworks would render his own work unacceptable.[48]

By contrast, Steinberg faced the inevitable controversy as he introduced his theory about Christ's genitals.

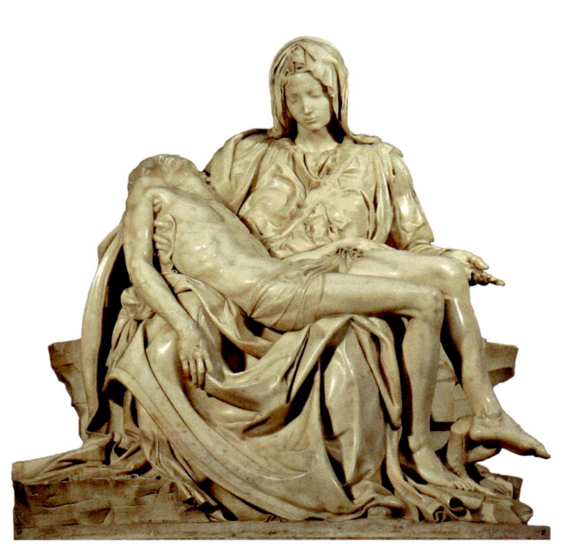

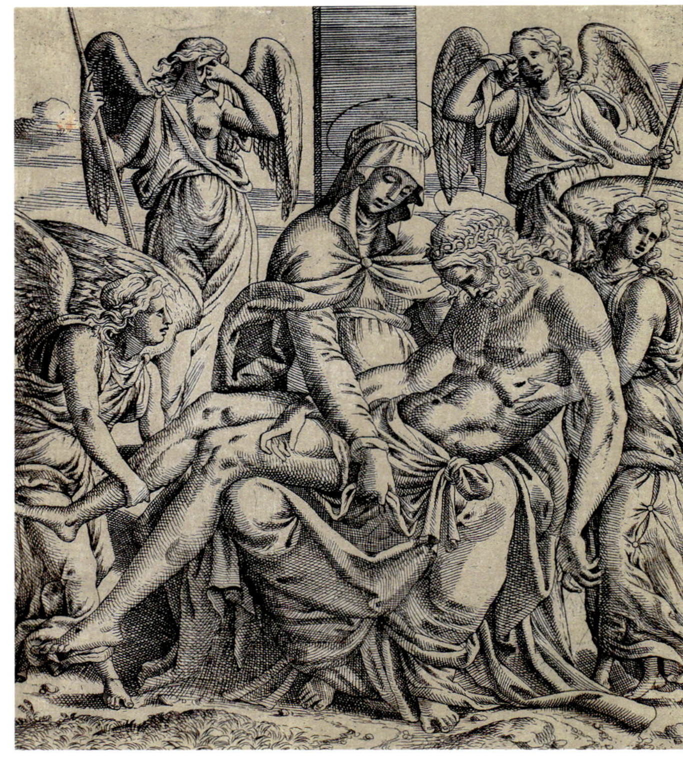

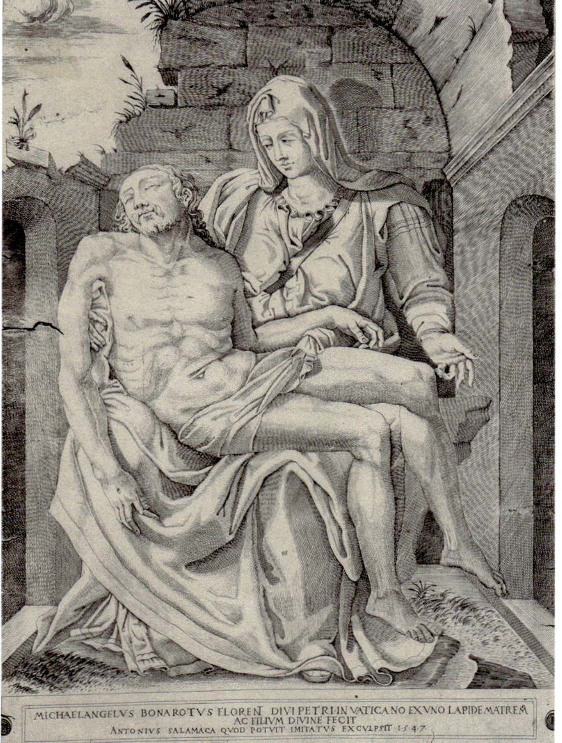

FIG. 33 Michelangelo Buonarroti, *Pietà*, 1498–99. Marble, 68½ × 76⅘ in. (174 × 195 cm). St. Peter's Basilica, Vatican City.

FIG. 34 Jean Mignon, *Pietà*, after a design by Luca Penni, 1530–40. Etching, only state, 9¹⁄₁₆ × 8 in. (23 × 20.4 cm, trimmed). Jenkins JM30 (2002.1842)

FIG. 35 Nicolas Beatrizet, *Pietà*, after the sculpture by Michelangelo, 1547. Engraving, first state of two, 14⁹⁄₁₆ × 10⅜ in. (37 × 26.4 cm). Bianchi 18 (2002.1345)

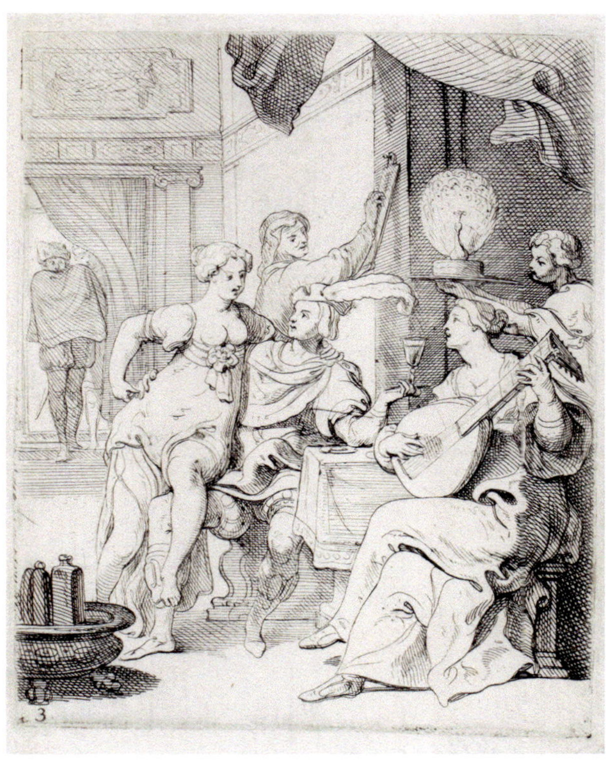

FIG. 36 Theodoor van Thulden, ***The Prodigal Son in a Brothel***, plate 3 from ***The Prodigal Son***, ca. 1633. Etching, only state, $5\frac{7}{16} \times 4\frac{5}{16}$ in. (13.8 × 11 cm). Hollstein 4. Philadelphia Museum of Art, The Muriel and Philip Berman Gift, acquired from the John S. Phillips bequest of 1876 to the Pennsylvania Academy of the Fine Arts, with funds contributed by Muriel and Philip Berman, gifts (by exchange) of Lisa Norris Elkins, Bryant W. Langston, Samuel S. White 3rd and Vera White, with additional funds contributed by John Howard McFadden, Jr., Thomas Skelton Harrison, and the Philip H. and A. S. W. Rosenbach Foundation, 1985, 1985-52-3157. (Another impression is in The Leo Steinberg Collection, 2002.2931)

FIG. 37 Schelte Adams Bolswert, ***The Virgin Adoring Jesus, with a vase***, 1605–59. Engraving and etching, first state of two, $10\frac{1}{16} \times 7\frac{1}{16}$ in. (25.6 × 18 cm). Hollstein 170, Mussini 438 (2002.53)

FIG. 38 Michelangelo Buonarroti, ***Pietà***, 1547–55. Marble, height: 89 in. (226 cm). Museo dell'Opera del Duomo, Florence.

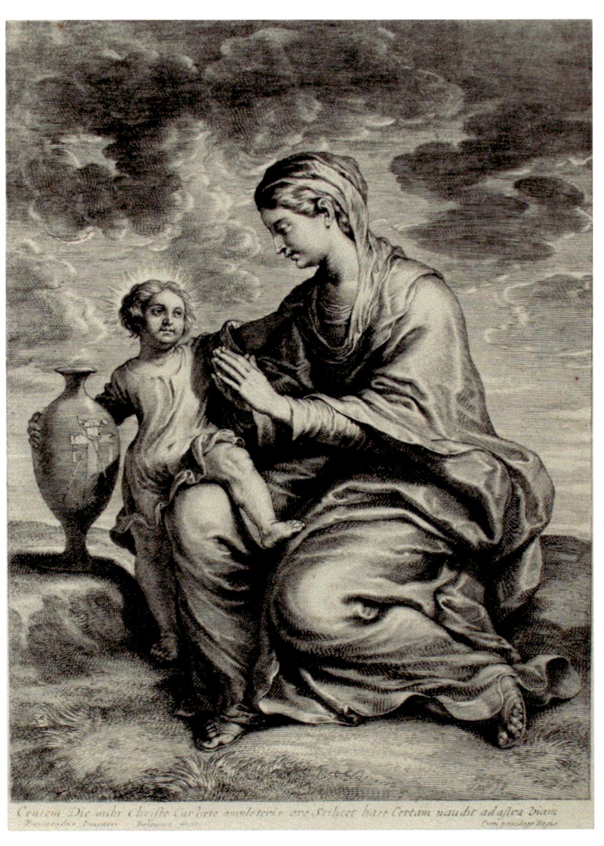

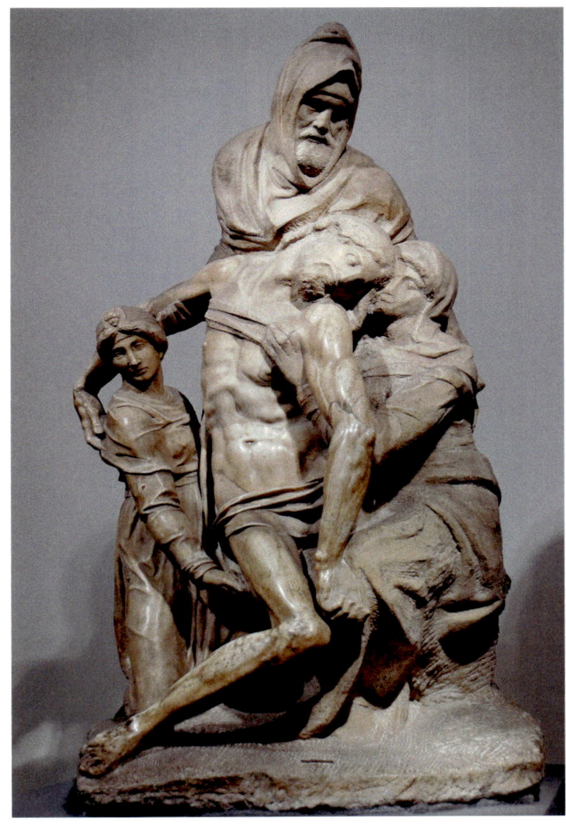

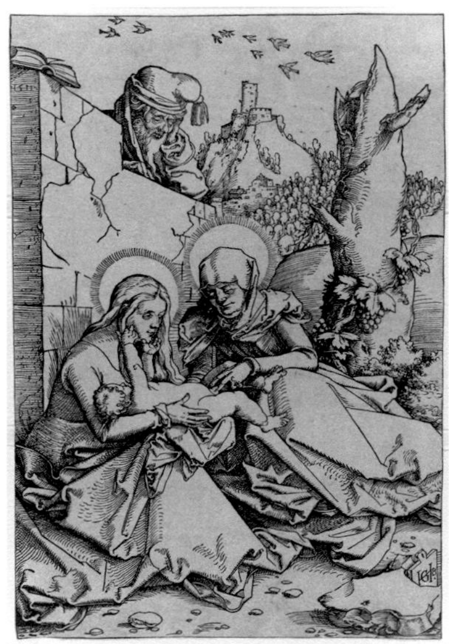

FIG. 39 Hans Baldung Grien, *Holy Family with St. Anne*, 1511. Woodcut, 14⅞ × 9¹³⁄₁₆ in. (37.6 × 24.9 cm). Hollstein 59 © The Trustees of the British Museum, London.

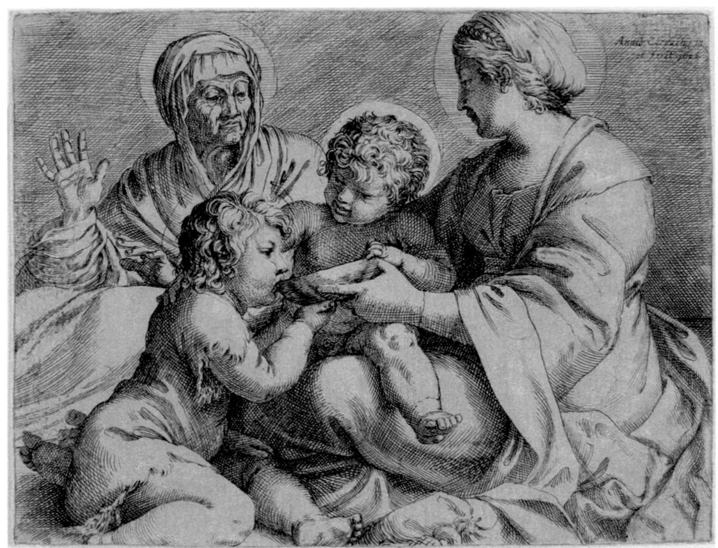

FIG. 40 Annibale Carracci, *Madonna and Child with the Young St. John the Baptist and St. Elizabeth (Madonna della Scodella)*, 1606. Etching and engraving, second state of three, 4⅞ × 6¼ in. (12.5 × 16 cm). DeGrazia Bohlin 20 (2002.157)

THE SEXUALITY OF CHRIST IN RENAISSANCE ART AND IN MODERN OBLIVION

In his best-known and most contentious book, Steinberg asserted that art historians had routinely ignored a deeply significant and pervasive theme in Renaissance art: the response to a new theological emphasis on the Incarnation, to the human aspect of Christ's dual nature. This response took the form of a pictorial emphasis on Christ's genitals in images of his infancy and of the Passion.[49] What others had taken for mere naturalism, Steinberg understood as an authentication of Christ's manhood, a proposition underpinned by numerous visual sources and exegetical texts. Although most of his supporting images are paintings, Hans Baldung Grien's woodcut, *Holy Family with St. Anne* (1511; fig. 39), in which the saint subjects her grandson to "genital manipulation," is one of his most compelling examples.[50] Many of the prints in Steinberg's collection similarly reinforce his thesis. Whether they are presented at the center of a composition and canopied by converging gestures, as in Annibale Carracci's *Madonna and Child with the Young St. John the Baptist and St. Elizabeth* (1606; fig. 40), or protectively touched by a mother with foreknowledge of her son's corporeal suffering as in Raffaello Schiaminossi's *Madonna and Child with St. Vincent and St. Cecilia* after Veronese (ca. 1601; fig. 41), or exposed and echoed by a multitude of pointing fingers as in the *Holy Family with St. John* after Goltzius (ca. 1589; fig. 42), Christ's genitals effectively become a guarantee of his humanation. Images of the Passion emphasizing Christ's genitals indicate the fulfillment of the Incarnation and are a cipher for his complete bodily resurrection. Steinberg further notes that, unlike Adam and Eve who hid their nudity after the Fall, Christ was without sin, so his genitals could be displayed without shame. In his marble sculpture of the *Risen Christ* (1521) in the church of Santa Maria sopra Minerva in Rome, Michelangelo presents him as entirely nude, although some copyists, like Jacob Matham in around 1602, fearing censorship, added drapery (fig. 43).[51] In defense of his highly

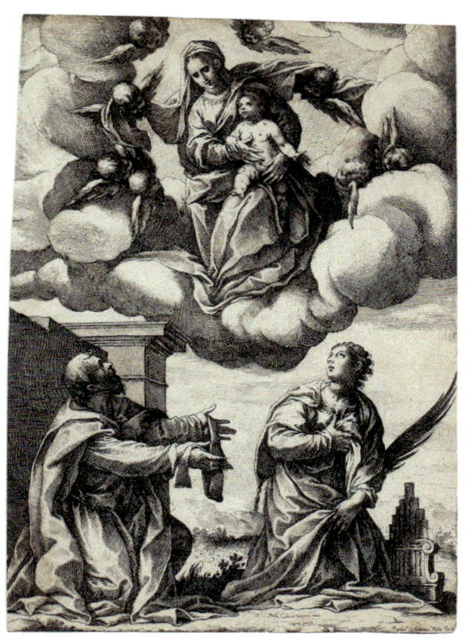

FIG. 41 Raffaello Schiaminossi, ***Madonna and Child with St. Vincent and St. Cecilia***, after a lost painting by Paolo Veronese, ca. 1601. Etching and engraving, only state, 14⅛ × 10 in. (36 × 25.3 cm, trimmed). Bartsch XVII.234.97 (2002.1699)

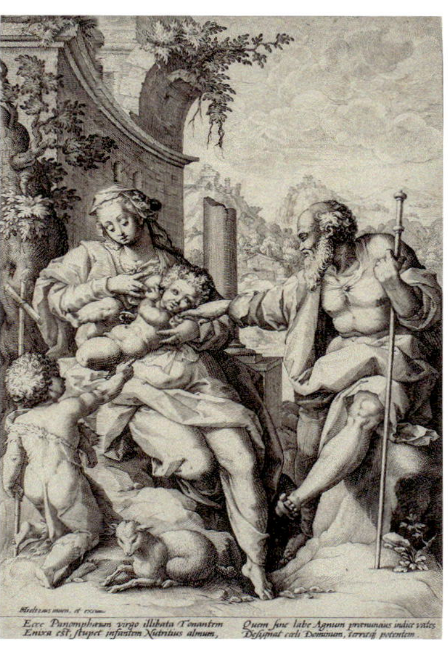

FIG. 42 Workshop of Hendrick Goltzius, ***Holy Family with St. John***, ca. 1589. Engraving, only state, 11¼ × 7¹¹⁄₁₆ in. (28.5 × 19.5 cm). New Hollstein 446 (2002.2920)

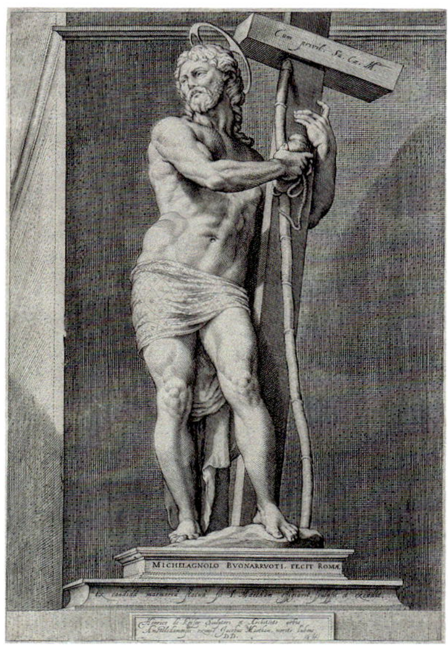

FIG. 43 Jacob Matham, ***The Savior with the Cross, Standing***, after a sculpture by Michelangelo, ca. 1602. Engraving, first state of two, 14³⁄₁₆ × 9⅝ in. (36 × 24.4 cm). New Hollstein 63 (2002.1737)

provocative theory in the face of critics who referred to the absence of textual evidence, Steinberg claimed that images alone can serve as primary texts, a conviction that equally characterized his approach to modern and contemporary art.[52]

PICASSO

Steinberg declared his allegiance to Picasso the printmaker in one of his earliest pieces of art criticism, a 1955 review of an exhibition at Carstairs Gallery in New York featuring ninety-seven (by his count) of the one hundred etchings comprising the artist's *Vollard Suite* (1930–37). In this set, Picasso explores the artist's studio as a creative space. Steinberg introduced some of his chief scholarly leitmotifs as he praised Picasso's prints as "experiments . . . in every sort of virtuosity," and noted evidence of the artist's deep engagement with the Western art-historical tradition in themes from classical antiquity to reflections on the artistic process.[53] Ever devoted to the charged iconographic potential of the body, he further effused that "Picasso is almost the only man today for whom the human gesture still remains a vehicle of revelation. May there be many more of him."[54] Steinberg made his first Picasso purchase in 1966, an etching from the *Vollard Suite*, followed by two others from the same series in 1967. Further Picasso purchases in 1969 were partially funded by the proceeds from his first Picasso article, published the year before.[55] In the seventies, while producing a spate of seminal essays on the artist, he acquired several more of his prints. As a group, they illustrate some of the key junctures and themes that he traces in Picasso's career.

Steinberg saw Picasso's work as reflecting a lifelong quest to overcome the limits of classical representation with its single point of view, "to possess the full knowledge of what is depicted, [a] refusal to be confined to an aspect."[56] In his first sustained essay on the subject, "The Algerian Women and Picasso at Large," he identified the many different pictorial means by which Picasso sought to represent this broader understanding, describing him as having "the most uncompromising three-dimensional imagination that ever possessed a great painter."[57] Among the Picasso prints in Steinberg's collection is the *Flutist and Three Nude Women* from the *Vollard Suite* (1932; fig. 44); he proposes that the two sleeping women depicted in it may, in fact, be one figure, shown in duplicate.[58] What he divides, Picasso also sutures, like a face whose nose marks the juncture between frontal and profile views in *Head of a Woman* (1925; fig. 45) or the figure in *Seated Woman in a Suit: Geneviève Laporte* (1951; fig. 46), whose genitals, buttocks, and stomach, depicted frontally, are joined to her chest, head, and legs depicted in profile. Steinberg viewed such stylistic choices as intended to serve expressive psychic and narrative content, not mere formalist or "cubist" experimentation.[59]

These unlikely juxtapositions in Picasso's work also extend to such states as sleep and wakefulness. Steinberg's essay on Picasso's recurrent theme of sleepers being watched, as in the *Flutist and Three Nude Women*, contextualizes a visual tradition in which sleep is "the opportunity of the intruder."[60] Steinberg's own prints furnish support for this history: the decapitation of Medusa is occasioned by slumber, as shown, for example, in Alexander Runciman's *Perseus Slaying Medusa* (1774; fig. 47), as is the vulnerable nymph approached by a satyr in Agostino Carracci's engraving of 1590–95 (fig. 48).[61] But in Picasso's conception, the sleeper experiences a contentment unavailable to the excluded watcher. In their opposite states of being, as Steinberg describes it, sleepers and watchers "nourish and infect" one another, and represent "twin phases of a single existence."[62]

Picasso also experimented with perspective by referencing other senses. Steinberg sees him uniting three ways of knowing (thought, sight, and touch) through the theme of sexual possession.[63] Carnal knowledge gained through touch, he suggests, occurs precisely at the moment when bodies are too close to see, shifting the balance between these simultaneous forms of knowing (see *The Rape beneath the Window* from the *Vollard Suite*; 1933; fig. 49).[64] Creation and love, vision and tactility, come together harmoniously at times, as in *Sculptor, Crouching Model, and Sculpted Head* from the same suite (1933; fig. 50), while at others, Picasso explores his inability to achieve what Steinberg described as "omnivision." The fact that the man with the "most penetrant sight of his century" should represent himself as a blind minotaur led by a small girl (1934; fig. 51) conveys the artist's struggle with the limits of his vision.[65]

Three decades later, the specter of old age threatened even the most confident consummations, as Steinberg proposed in his article on the theme of lovemaking and the artistic process in Picasso's *347* series, named for the number of prints the artist produced during an eight-month spurt of creativity on the project in 1968.[66] In *Fat Courtesan with an Old Man and a Spectator in Costume* from this ambitious etching series, a diminutive and aged Picasso stands opposite a voluptuous young woman whose nude body is depicted from multiple angles (fig. 52). Picasso's scratching out of his own phallus—a symbol Steinberg interprets as representing the artist's creative life—suggests his fear of diminishing sexual and creative potency in his ninth decade.[67] Although *Fat Courtesan* was Steinberg's last Picasso purchase, he continued publishing on the artist until he was eighty-seven, the same age Picasso had been when he produced the *347* series. That both maintained their creative capacities for a few more years is a poignant point of connection between two great thinkers who were also incessant interpreters of the corporeal.

CONTRA-CLEMENT GREENBERG AND PRO-POSTMODERNISM

Steinberg's writings on Picasso clashed with the dominant views of art critic Clement Greenberg, who argued for the teleological advance of painting from illusionism toward abstraction and flatness.[68] According to this narrative, Picasso made his greatest

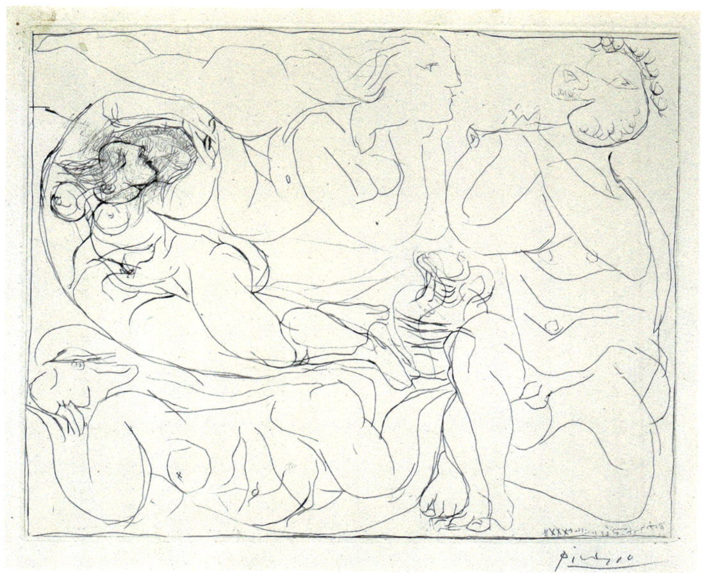

FIG. 44 Pablo Picasso, *Flutist and Three Nude Women*, from the *Vollard Suite*, 1932, published 1939. Drypoint, second state of two, edition of 260, signed in graphite, $11\frac{11}{16} \times 14\frac{7}{16}$ in. (29.7×36.7 cm). Bloch 144, Baer 258 (2002.1989) © 2022 Estate of Pablo Picasso / Artists Rights Society (ARS), New York.

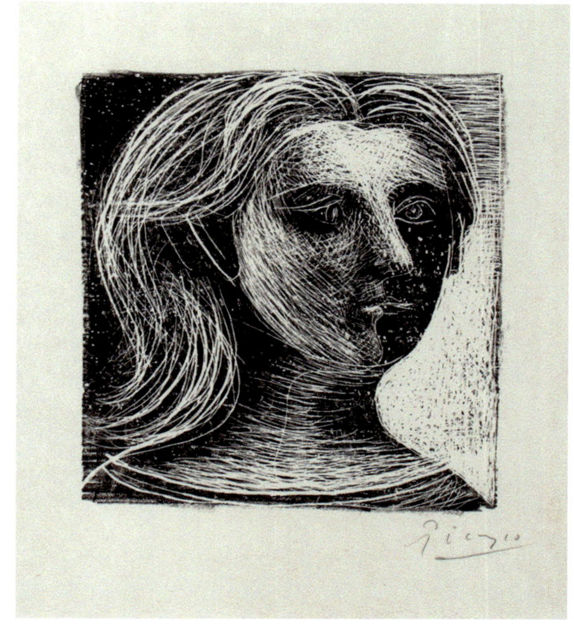

FIG. 45 Pablo Picasso, *Head of a Woman*, 1925, published by Editions des Quatre Chemins in 1926. Lithograph with scraping, edition of 100, signed in graphite, $4\frac{7}{8} \times 4\frac{9}{16}$ in. (12.6×11.6 cm). Bloch 73, Baer 240 (2002.1592) © 2022 Estate of Pablo Picasso / Artists Rights Society (ARS), New York.

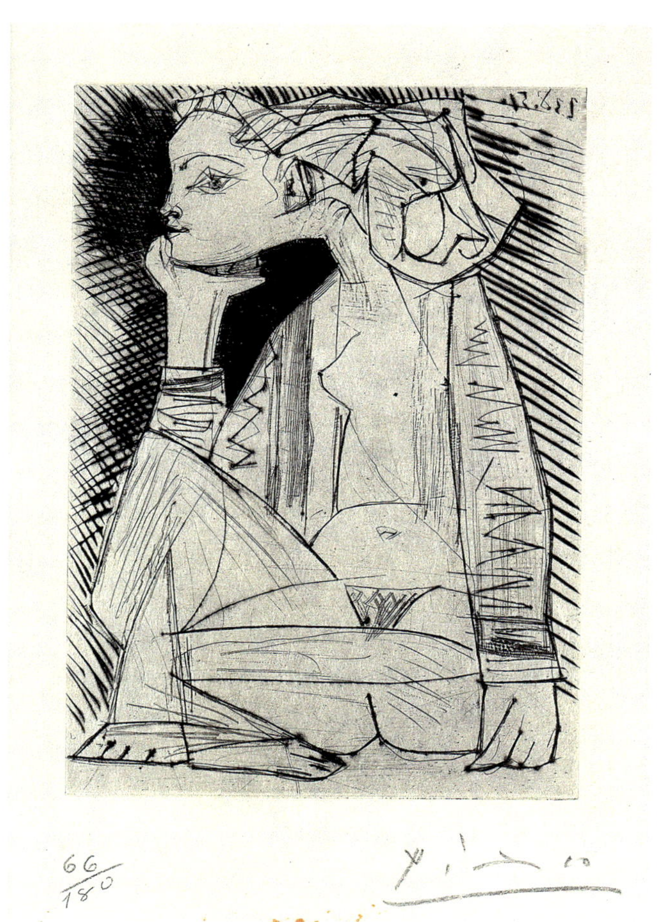

FIG. 46 Pablo Picasso, *Seated Woman in a Suit: Geneviève Laporte*, 1951, published as a frontispiece to *Recordant el Doctor Reventós* (Remembering Doctor Reventós), 1969. Engraving and drypoint, second state of two, edition: 66/180, signed in graphite, $5\frac{11}{16} \times 3\frac{15}{16}$ in. (14.4×9.9 cm). Bloch II 1837, Baer 888 (2002.2595) © 2022 Estate of Pablo Picasso / Artists Rights Society (ARS), New York.

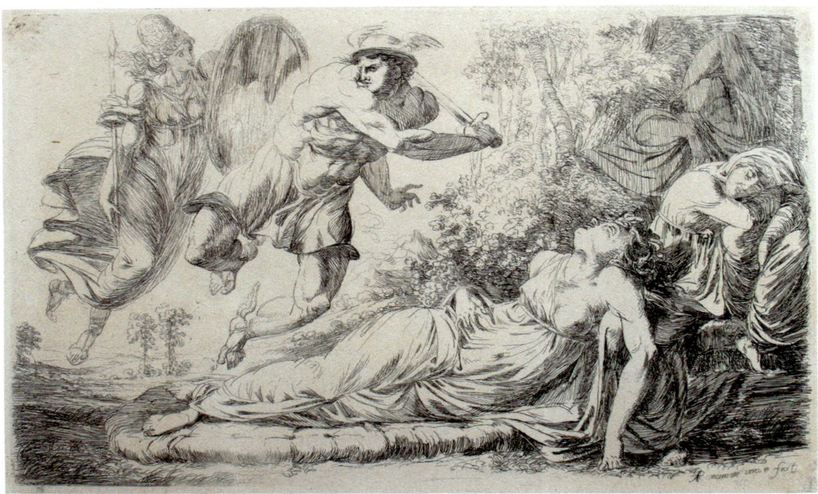

FIG. 47 Alexander Runciman, ***Perseus Slaying Medusa***, 1774. Etching, only state, 6⅛ × 10^{5}⁄$_{16}$ in. (15.6 × 26.2 cm). Le Blanc III.5 (2002.1245)

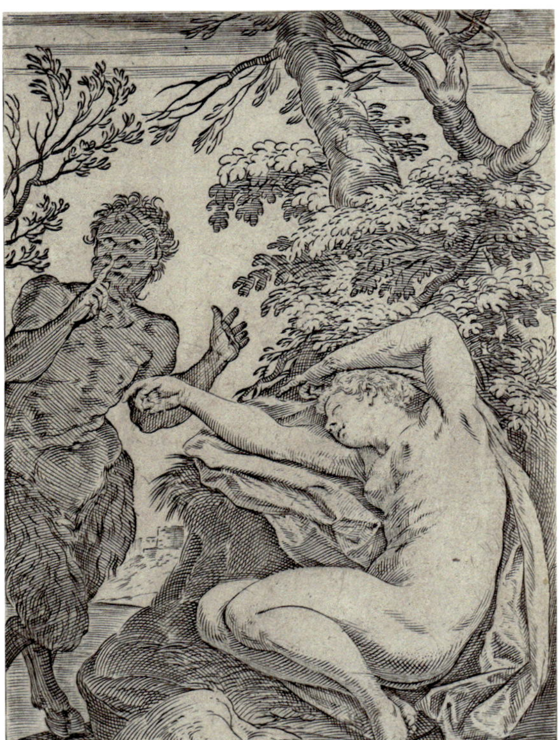

FIG. 48 Agostino Carracci, ***A Satyr Approaching a Sleeping Nymph***, 1590–95. Engraving, only state, 6 × 4^{1}⁄$_{16}$ in. (15.3 × 10.3 cm). DeGrazia Bohlin 184 (2002.162)

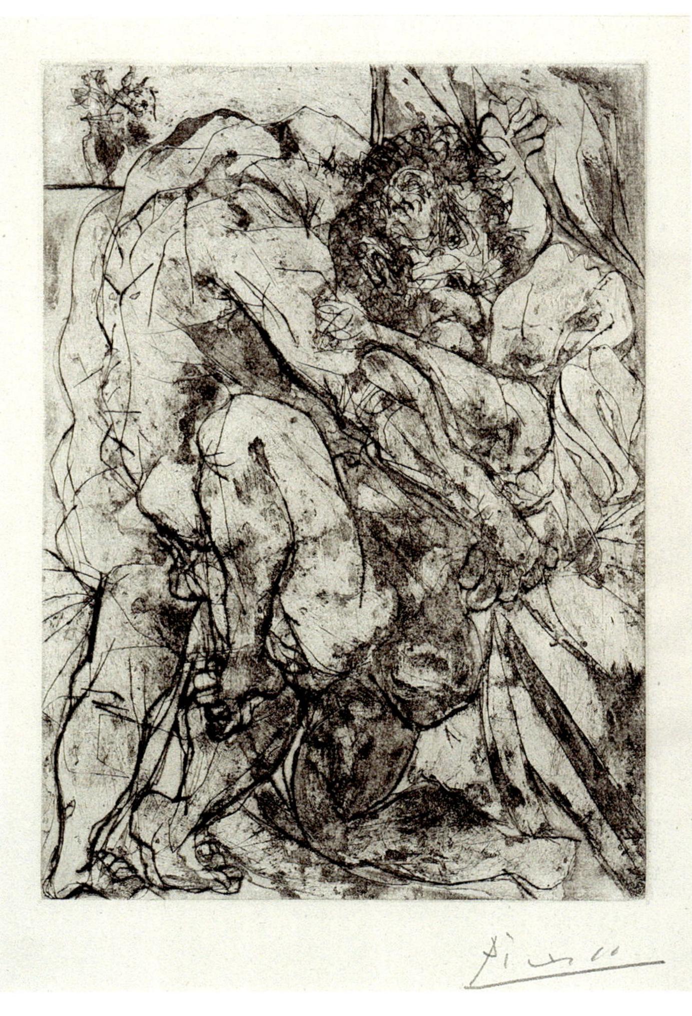

FIG. 49 Pablo Picasso, ***The Rape beneath the Window*** from the ***Vollard Suite***, 1933, published 1939. Etching and aquatint with drypoint, fourteenth state of fourteen, edition of 260, signed in graphite, 10⅞ × 7^{13}⁄$_{16}$ in. (27.7 × 19.7 cm). Bloch 183, Baer 342 (2002.1591)

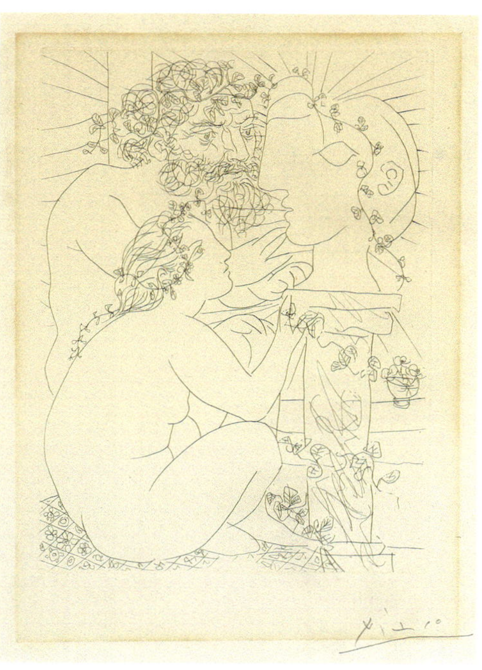

FIG. 50 Pablo Picasso, *Sculptor, Crouching Model, and Sculpted Head*, from the *Vollard Suite*, 1933, published 1939. Etching, second state of two, edition of 260, signed in graphite, 10½ × 7⅝ in. (26.7 × 19.4 cm). Bloch 155, Baer 308 (2002.1988) © 2022 Estate of Pablo Picasso / Artists Rights Society (ARS), New York.

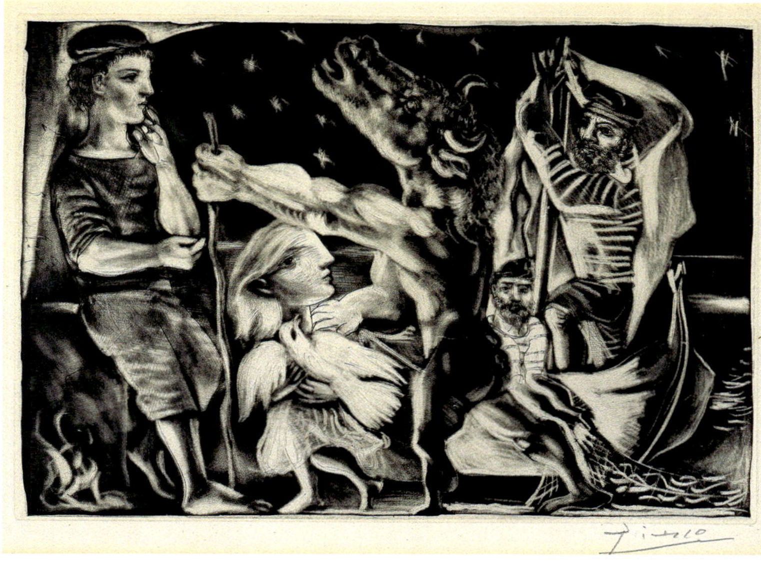

FIG. 51 Pablo Picasso, *Blind Minotaur Guided by a Young Girl in the Night*, from the *Vollard Suite*, 1934, published 1939. Aquatint, etching, and drypoint with scraping and burnishing, fourth state of four, edition of 260, signed in graphite, 9¾ × 13$^{11}/_{16}$ in. (24.7 × 34.7 cm). Bloch 225, Baer 437 (2002.1987) © 2022 Estate of Pablo Picasso / Artists Rights Society (ARS), New York.

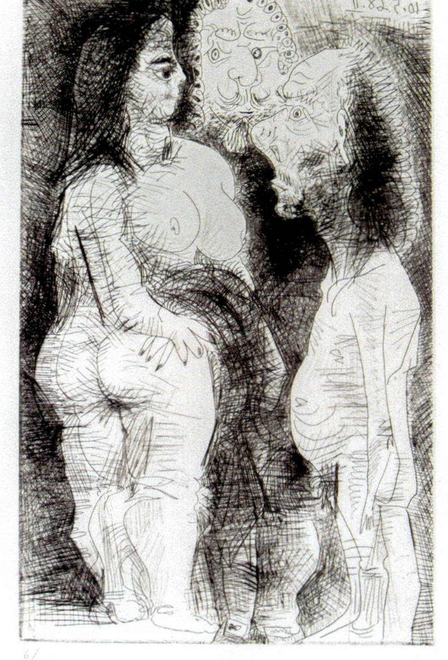

FIG. 52 Pablo Picasso, *Fat Courtesan with an Old Man and a Spectator in Costume*, from *347*, 1968. Etching and drypoint, third state of three, edition: 6/50, signed in graphite, 7⅜ × 4$^{9}/_{16}$ in. (18.7 × 11.6 cm). Bloch II 1552, Baer 1568 (2002.1986) © 2022 Estate of Pablo Picasso / Artists Rights Society (ARS), New York.

contribution to art with his early experiments in Cubism, but regressed when he returned to non-Cubist figuration in the 1930s.[69] Steinberg bristled at Greenberg's judgment that a successful work of art must reference its own material construction, which, for two-dimensional mediums like paintings and prints meant acknowledging the flat planes of the canvas and the paper as such. In his seminal essay, "Other Criteria," developed from a 1968 lecture at the Museum of Modern Art, Steinberg objects to Greenberg's "preventative esthetics" that presumed to tell artists what direction their work must take.[70] Amassing evidence from medieval manuscripts and early modern prints, including, again, those in his own collection, Steinberg further contends that artists have been drawing attention to the flatness of their supports for centuries, purposely juxtaposing them with illusionistic effects. In engravings such as Barthel Beham's *Child with Leaf Ornament* (ca. 1526; fig. 53), for instance, a flat background, a three-dimensional ornamental flourish, and a figure casting a shadow coexist within a constricted space, while the Sistine Ceiling "is a battleground for local illusion, counter-illusion, and emphasized architectural surface—art turning constantly back on itself" (fig. 54).[71]

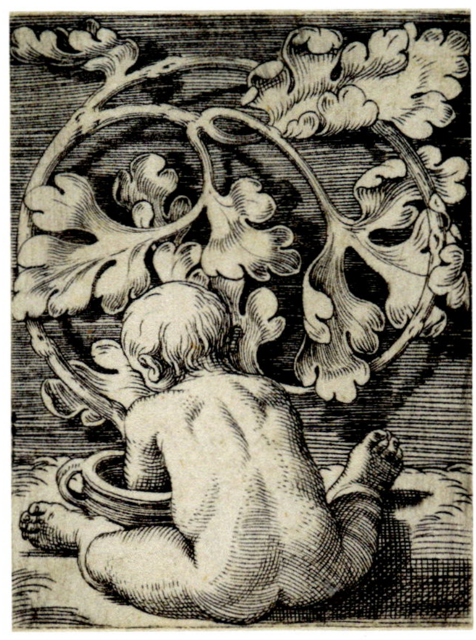

FIG. 53 Barthel Beham, *Child with Leaf Ornament*, ca. 1526. Engraving, only state, 1 15/16 × 1 7/16 in. (4.9 × 3.7 cm). Bartsch VIII.105.51 (2002.768)

Steinberg's print collecting may also underlie his most important contributions to postwar American art—the introduction of the term "postmodern" and the definition of the work of Robert Rauschenberg and others as "flatbed picture planes," conceived horizontally rather than vertically.[72] The term is adapted from the flatbed printing press, a standard press that could print text and images, relief and intaglio. Steinberg connects the bodily posture of manuscript illuminators bent over their parchment to that of printmakers carving into woodblocks or incising copperplates, arguing that postmodern artists revived this "scriptorial tradition" by reorienting the angle of production for their works from the vertical to the horizontal.[73] Rather than an upright body encountering a painting as a mirror or a window on the world, viewers of these new images could, metaphorically, look down on them as onto a horizontal work surface that registers operational processes and records information transmitted by "the brain of the city" (even as most of these works were still displayed on walls).[74] The early modern philosophers René Descartes and John Locke also evoked the printing process to describe the mind, likening it to a copperplate etched with memories or a blank sheet of paper awaiting an impression.[75] They understood the mind as internal and individual; Steinberg's mid-twentieth-century metropolitan brain, however, is bigger than an individual and is captured externally on a work surface that invites not only completed matrices and composed texts, but also fragments, unfinished states, three-dimensional objects, "waste and detritus," both "noise and meaning."[76] An

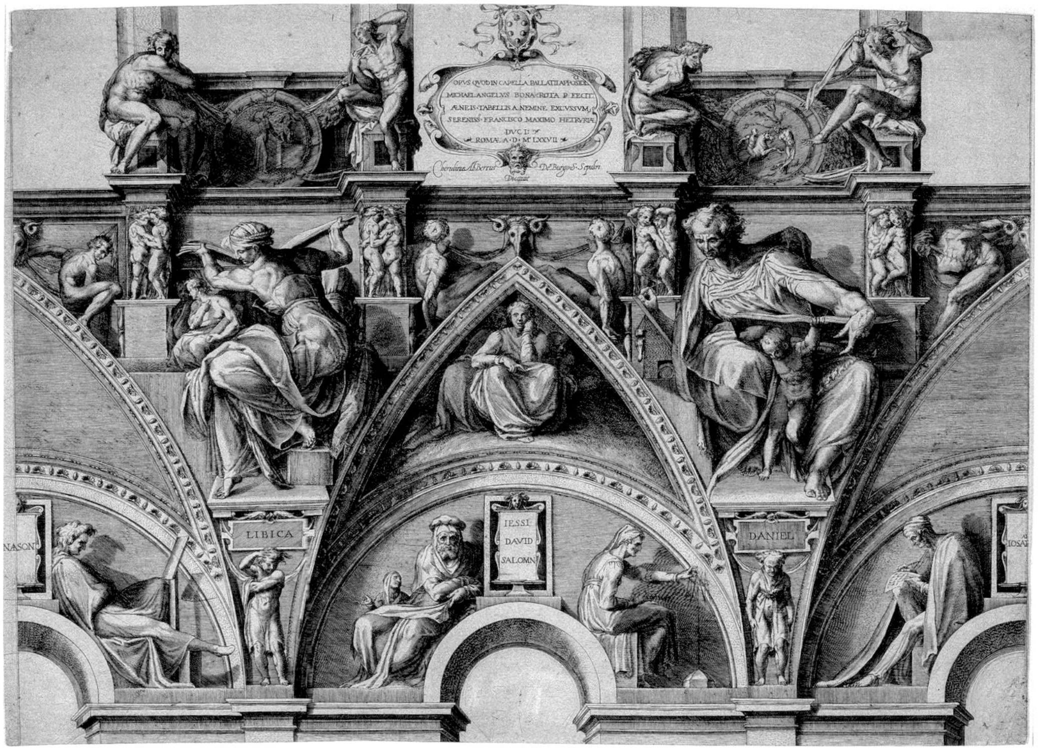

FIG. 54 Cherubino Alberti, *Compartment of the Sistine Ceiling with the Libyan Sibyl and the Prophet Daniel*, after a fresco by Michelangelo, 1577, republished 1628. Engraving, second state of two (?), $16 \times 21\frac{7}{16}$ in. (40.7×54.4 cm, trimmed). Bartsch XVII.76.72 (2002.1722)

awareness of this social, interconnected, and technological brain turns painting into a site of making, as distinct from the vertical picture plane that is primarily a site of seeing.

This new surface bears a relation to the printing press, but also to the centuries-old reproductive prints that Steinberg collected. Just as the flatbed press receives, records, borrows, and appropriates, so, too, have artists received ideas through prints and produced responses to them ranging from the intentionally mimetic to the loosely interpretive or the stealthily stolen. In Rauschenberg, Steinberg recognizes an artist who both makes such borrowings highly visible and foregrounds the processes of appropriation, accumulation, and juxtaposition as the primary content of his work. And as a scholar who expanded his sources to include all manner of printed images, Steinberg was primed to appreciate artists who revel in expanding their sources to include all aspects of material culture. In typical Steinbergian fashion, while he argues that postmodernism's inclusion of what he called "non-art" represents a radical break from modernism's claims of formal purity and its historic sources in art and nature, he also identifies creative impulses that underlie the work of artists across the centuries. It can hardly be coincidental that this ever-perspicacious observer of posture, gesture, and angle of approach fundamentally reconceived the relationship between artwork, artist, and viewer while pondering the facture and uses of the more than four thousand prints he then owned, objects that were produced and stored horizontally and were historically viewed in albums rather than framed on the wall, and that were deeply implicated in networks of cultural communication.

One of the jewels of Steinberg's collection, Jasper Johns's *Ale Cans* (1964; fig. 55), is a fitting coda, extending the definition of prints as the "circulating lifeblood of ideas" into the sixties. On the cover of Steinberg's 1963 book on Johns, a photograph of the artist's *Painted Bronze* (1960) sets the sculpture against a solid-black background. When Johns reinterpreted his two bronzed Ballantine cans in a lithograph the

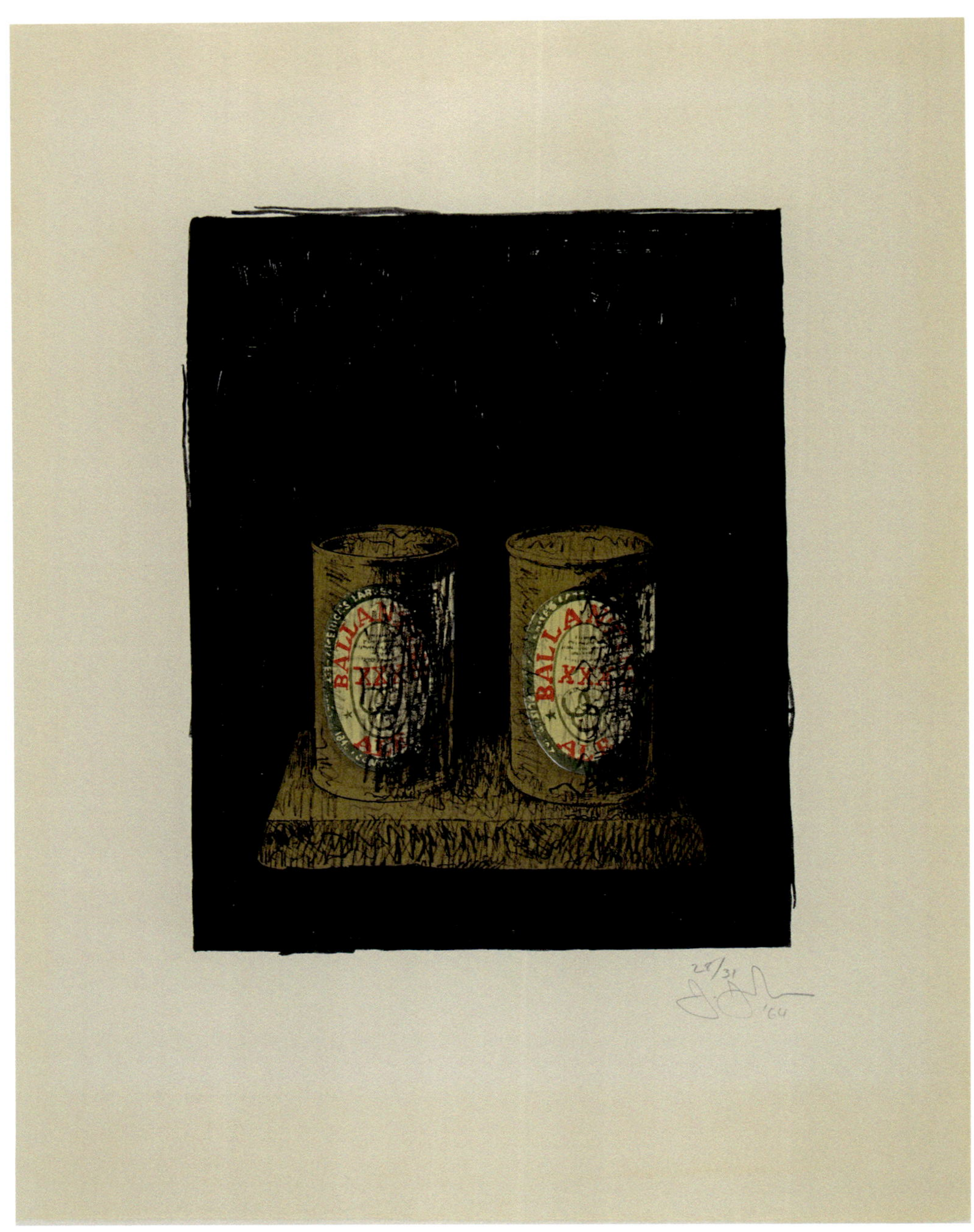

FIG. 55 Jasper Johns, *Ale Cans*, 1964. Color lithograph from seven stones on Japan paper, edition: 28/31, signed in graphite, $14\frac{3}{16} \times 11$ in. (36×27.8 cm). Field 20 (2002.1985) © 2022 Jasper Johns / Licensed by VAGA at Artists Rights Society (ARS), New York.

following year, he adopted the photograph's background color.[77] An apt exemplar of the rich signifying potential of copies, each iteration, from sculpture, to photograph, to lithograph postulates variations on literalness and transcendence, flatness and illusionism, originality and reproduction. And in an ironic reversal of the prints-to-scholarship direction, here Steinberg's scholarship might be said to have occasioned a print.

A LASTING IMPRESSION

As a scholar, Steinberg shared a particular kinship with prints. Though a fully decorated veteran of the art-historical field by the end of his life, he still felt at odds with the mainstream, noting, for example, that the only book of his ever reviewed by *The Art Bulletin* was his final one.[78] Like prints, which were ignored in his graduate program, he, too, was "bursting with information," yet felt marginalized by towering figures like Ernst Gombrich, who pronounced his book on the Pauline Chapel "a dangerous model to follow."[79] Just as Christ's exposed genitals were hiding in plain sight in the art Steinberg chose to investigate, so were prints. Yet it took a maverick scholar unafraid of looking at things tacitly judged as improper or inferior to understand their vital significance. Steinberg's working method reveals a further affinity with prints. He approached his scholarship as a printmaker approaches a matrix. His yellow legal pads were his plates and his lectures were working proofs, which he delivered before returning to the matrix to revise, expand, improve, and tinker. Certain lectures were delivered thirty times over the course of his career. Even final published states were not necessarily definitive. A revision or later edition would sometimes include rebuttals of critical objections. Steinberg was unusual in the extent to which he reworked and republished, paying close attention, like any dedicated craftsman, to a creative engagement with sources, the potential for innovation, and technical proficiency of tone and clarity. And like a prized print, he is to be appreciated for the rarity of his intellectual achievements and the quality of his lasting impression on the field.

NOTES

The five-volume series of Steinberg's *Selected Essays*, edited by Sheila Schwartz and published by the University of Chicago Press (2018–2023), comprises published essays, many revised for the series, as well as previously unpublished lectures and texts. It includes the following titles: *Michelangelo's Sculpture* (2018), *Michelangelo's Painting* (2019), *Renaissance and Baroque Art* (2020), *Picasso* (2022), and *Modern Art* (2023). The first endnote reference in this volume to a published essay by Steinberg cites both the republished volume and the original place(s) of publication. Subsequent references cite only the republished volume.

1 In 2012, the catalogue of the Boston-based antiquarian booksellers Ars Libri listed 4,164 titles from Steinberg's collection. Ars Libri, Ltd, *The Library of Professor Leo Steinberg*, accessed July 21, 2022, https://arslibri.com/collections/LeoSteinbergLibrary.pdf. Sheila Schwartz estimates that Steinberg's library numbered six thousand works in total. The books in the Ars Libri list were purchased by the Fine Arts Academy of Beijing.

2 Steinberg's six Charles Eliot Norton Lectures at Harvard (1995–96) were titled "The Mute Image and the Meddling Text." For a publication history of the series, see Steinberg, *Renaissance and Baroque Art*, 1 and 238n.

3 Panofsky is quoted in Herman Liebaers, *Mostly in the Line of Duty: Thirty Years with Books* (The Hague: Martinus Nijhoff, 1980), 83. The notation "2/2" in Steinberg's ledgers or on the mat of a print indicates that a 2 × 2-inch (35 mm) slide was made of the image for use in a lecture, often the testing ground for subsequent publications.

4 In Steinberg's letter to Faye Hirsch, August 5, 1999, GRI LSRP 930046, T2, he writes that he was "in on the founding of Print Collector's Newsletter [PCN]." Steinberg wrote the following articles for the journal: "A Working Equation or—Picasso in the Homestretch," *PCN* 3, no. 5 (November–December 1972): 102–105; "Ten Irreverent Rimes," *PCN* 5, no. 4 (October–November 1974): 85; "Remarks on Certain Prints Relative to a Leningrad Rubens on the Occasion of the First Visit of the Original to the United States," *PCN* 6, no. 4 (September–October 1975): 97–102; with Diane Karp, "Picasso's Revealer," *PCN* 8, no. 5 (November–December 1977): 140–141; and "A Picture by One Jacob Pynas," *PCN* 11, no. 5 (November–December 1980): 171–174.

5 Marjorie B. Cohn, *A Noble Collection: The Spencer Albums of Old Master Prints* (Cambridge, MA: Fogg Art Museum, Harvard University Art Museums, 1992), 28 (on Mariette); William B. MacGregor, "The Authority of Prints: An Early Modern Perspective," *Art History* 22, no. 3 (September 1999): 390–391 (on De Lairesse); and 395–397 (on De Piles). In the Steinberg collection at the Blanton, the following works show examples of pinpricking: 2002.1648; squaring: 2002.2467; and tracing: 2002.129.

6 These terms are mentioned by Steinberg in "What I Like About Prints," *Art in Print* 7, no. 5 (January–February 2018): 3–28 and in "The Glorious Company," in *Renaissance and Baroque Art*, 209–235. Previously published in Jean Lipman and Richard Marshall, *Art about Art* (New York: Whitney Museum of American Art, 1978), 8–31; Steinberg, "A Picture by One Jacob Pynas"; and Steinberg, "Remarks on Certain Prints Relative to a Leningrad Rubens on the Occasion of the First Visit of the Original to the United States."

7 This illustrated sequence appears in Steinberg, "Words That Prevent Perception," in *Renaissance and Baroque Art*, 24.

8 Steinberg, "Pontormo's Capponi Chapel," in *Renaissance and Baroque Art*, 99–100. Previously published in *The Art Bulletin* 56, no. 3 (September 1974): 385–399; Steinberg, "An El Greco 'Entombment' Eyed Awry," in *Renaissance and Baroque Art*, 125–127. Previously published in *The Burlington Magazine* 116, no. 857 (August 1974): 474–477.

9 Steinberg, "The Glorious Company," 213–216. Previously published in *Art about Art*, 11–12; expanded in a letter to the editor, *The Art Bulletin* 73, no. 3 (September 1991), 505.

10 See also Steinberg, "Rubens' *Ceres* in Leningrad," *ARTnews* 70, no. 8 (December 1971): 42–43.

11 Steinberg, "Deciphering Velázquez's *Old Woman Cooking Eggs*," in *Renaissance and Baroque Art*, 180–185. Previously published in "Review of '*Velázquez:*

A Catalogue Raisonné of His Oeuvre' by José Lopez-Rey," *The Art Bulletin* 47, no. 2 (June 1965): 279–280 and expanded in *Manhattan, Inc.* 6 (October 1989), 156–158 and "The Glorious Company," 228–229. For other artists, see "The Glorious Company," 221–224. In addition to these published examples, Steinberg's ledgers and mat notes indicate other print circulations.

12 For the use of a Matham engraving after Goltzius in Limoges enamel, see Steinberg, "The Glorious Company," 216–217. The other examples cited appear in undated mat notes referencing a piece of majolica based on a Caraglio engraving and a tapestry based on a Salvator Rosa etching, the latter reproduced in *Charles II: Art & Power* (London: Royal Collection Trust, 2018), 227.

13 Steinberg, "The Glorious Company," 278n17.

14 Steinberg, "The Line of Fate in Michelangelo's Painting," in *Michelangelo's Painting*, 213.

15 Steinberg, "Leonardo's *Last Supper*," *The Art Quarterly* 36, no. 4 (Winter 1973): 297–410; Steinberg, *Leonardo's Incessant Last Supper* (New York: Zone Books, 2001). References here are to the book.

16 On Birago's engraving, Steinberg, *Leonardo's Incessant Last Supper*, 19. Steinberg's list of copies in various media is in Appendix E, 227–271 of the book.

17 Steinberg, *Leonardo's Incessant Last Supper*, 22–24, 44.

18 Ibid., 35–38.

19 Ibid., 40–43.

20 Ibid., 115–116.

21 While Leonardo had no direct involvement with the printed reproductions of his fresco, Steinberg makes the intriguing suggestion that he might have incorporated compositional ideas on its painted margins and based Judas's pose on engravings by Andrea Mantegna and Martin Schongauer respectively. *Leonardo's Incessant Last Supper*, 163, 282–283.

22 Steinberg, "Ten Irreverent Rimes," 85.

23 Steinberg, "Who's Who in the *Creation of Adam*: A Chronology of the Picture's Reluctant Self-Revelation," *Michelangelo's Painting*, 79–82, 319n29. Previously published in *The Art Bulletin* 74, no. 4 (December 1992): 552–566. Neither the prints after the *Creation of Adam* nor those after the *Temptation and Expulsion* are in Steinberg's collection at the Blanton.

24 Steinberg, "The Line of Fate in Michelangelo's Painting," 229–231.

25 Steinberg, "The *Last Judgment* as Merciful Heresy," in *Michelangelo's Painting*, 130–159.

26 In "The *Last Judgment* as Merciful Heresy," 143, 153–159, Steinberg discusses copies in this way; see also Steinberg, "A Corner of the *Last Judgment*," in *Michelangelo's Painting*, 184. Previously published in *Daedalus* 109, no. 2 (Spring 1980): 207–273.

27 Steinberg, "The Line of Fate in Michelangelo's Painting," 219–228; Steinberg, "A Corner of the *Last Judgment*," 176–193.

28 Steinberg, "The *Last Judgment* as Merciful Heresy," 134.

29 See Steinberg, "A Corner of the *Last Judgment*," esp. 167–182.

30 Steinberg, "The *Last Judgment* as Merciful Heresy," 147, 186.

31 Steinberg, "A Corner of the *Last Judgment*," 342n96.

32 Steinberg observes other misconstruals in printed versions, including St. Peter returning an intact key to Christ, one that Michelangelo had painted as broken since this symbol of papal authority is now abrogated by Christ's return, and the planting of Simon of Cyrene's cross on clouds rather than on the chapel's embracing cornice, an action meant to resonate around the perimeter of the space, spurring worshippers to take up their cross daily and follow Christ. For the key, see Steinberg, "The *Last Judgment* and Environs," in *Michelangelo's Painting*, 210 and for the clouds, 202.

33 Steinberg, "Michelangelo's Last Paintings," in *Michelangelo's Painting*, 235–304.

34 Steinberg, "The Line of Fate in Michelangelo's Painting," 213–219; for a list of all reproductions, 352–354n47.

35 Steinberg, "Body and Symbol in the *Medici Madonna*," in *Michelangelo's Sculpture*, 103.

36 Steinberg, "A New Michelangelo," in *Michelangelo's Painting*, 94–98. Previously published in *Art & Antiques* (October 1985): 49–55, 92–93; he expands the argument in "Why Michelangelo Huddled Those

Ancestors under That Ceiling," in *Michelangelo's Painting*, 99–129.

37 Bernadine Ann Barnes, *Michelangelo in Print: Reproductions as Response in the Sixteenth Century* (Farnham: Ashgate, 2010) addresses many of the same prints but arrives at different conclusions.

38 Steinberg, "The *Medici Madonna* and Related Works," 90–95; Steinberg, "Body and Symbol in the *Medici Madonna*," 114–126.

39 Steinberg, "The Metaphors of Love and Birth in Michelangelo's *Pietàs*," in *Michelangelo's Sculpture*, 28.

40 Steinberg, "Disconnections: The *Doni Madonna* and Leonardo's *Saint Anne*," in *Michelangelo's Painting*, 11. For the *Bruges Madonna* and the *Epiphany* cartoon, see Steinberg, "The Metaphors of Love and Birth in Michelangelo's *Pietàs*," 33, 37.

41 Ibid., 40–41.

42 Ibid., 1.

43 Steinberg, "The Roman *Pietà*: Michelangelo at Twenty-Three," in *Michelangelo's Sculpture*, 89.

44 Steinberg, "The Metaphors of Love and Birth in Michelangelo's *Pietàs*," 1–2.

45 Ibid., 12–19.

46 Ibid., 23–24.

47 Ibid., 28.

48 Ibid., 22. An alternative explanation is offered by Steinberg's former pupil Jack Wasserman, *Michelangelo's Florence* Pietà (Princeton, NJ: Princeton University Press, 2003), 67–73.

49 Steinberg, *The Sexuality of Christ in Renaissance Art and in Modern Oblivion*, 2nd ed. (Chicago: University of Chicago Press, 1996). Originally published as "The Sexuality of Christ in Renaissance Art and in Modern Oblivion," *October* 25 (Summer 1983): 1–222.

50 Steinberg, *The Sexuality of Christ*, 8.

51 Ibid., 19–20.

52 Steinberg's refutation of his "textist" critics is a major theme in the long "Retrospect" added to the second edition of *The Sexuality of Christ.*

53 Steinberg, "Month in Review," *Arts Magazine* 30, no. 3 (December 1955): 46.

54 Ibid.

55 Further details about these first Picasso purchases can be found in "Leo Steinberg and His Library of Prints" in this volume. Steinberg bought four prints from the *Vollard Suite* between December 1968 and January 1969 (NA.2021.3, inv. J01-J04, 2002.1987, 2002.1988, 2002.1591, 2002.1989) and another one in December 1969 (NA.2021.3, inv. J286), which he traded in 1971 for another Picasso print (NA.2021.3, inv. 1.21, 2002.1970). In December 1969, he also purchased *Head of a Woman* (NA.2021.3, inv. J285, 2002.1592). In 1971, he acquired *Seated Woman in a Suit* (NA.2021.3, inv.1.25, 2002.2595) and *The Spider* (NA.2021.3, inv. 2.49), which he traded toward Matisse's *Josette Gris* (NA.2021.3, inv.2.82, 2002.1576). In 1977, he purchased *Fat Courtesan* (NA.2021.5, inv.7.02, 2002.1986) from the *347* set.

56 Steinberg, "Drawing as If to Possess," in *Picasso*, 41. Previously published in *Artforum* 10, no. 2 (October 1971): 44–53, and expanded in Steinberg, "The Algerian Women and Picasso at Large," in *Other Criteria* (New York: Oxford University Press, 1972), 175.

57 Steinberg, "The Algerian Women and Picasso at Large," 191.

58 Ibid., 143.

59 See Steinberg, "The Philosophical Brothel," in *Picasso*, 71–116. Previously published in *ARTnews* 71, no. 5 (September 1972): 20–29 (part I) and no. 6 (October 1972): 38–47 (part II), revised and expanded in *October* 44 (Spring 1988): 7–74.

60 Leo Steinberg, "Picasso's Sleepwatchers," in *Other Criteria*, 99. Previously published in *LIFE*, December 27, 1968.

61 This Carracci is the lone example in this essay of a print that Steinberg acquired after he had published it.

62 Steinberg, "Picasso's Sleepwatchers," 105.

63 Steinberg, "The Algerian Women and Picasso at Large," 174–175.

64 Steinberg reads Picasso's erotic drawings of this period as consensual consummations, a pictorial rendering of the artist literally in the process of procreation. See Steinberg, "The Algerian Women and Picasso at Large," 411–412n35. However, close looking at Picasso's contorted figures reveals a complex scene. It is not clear that the interaction is mutually desired, and some have reasonably countered that such images depict violence rather than intimacy or inspiration.

Indeed, it was the art historian Hans Bolliger who gave this print the title *The Rape beneath the Window*.

65 Ibid., 130.

66 Steinberg, "A Working Equation or—Picasso in the Homestretch," in *Picasso*, 170–175. Previously published in *PCN* 3, no. 5 (November–December 1972): 102–105.

67 Steinberg, "A Working Equation or—Picasso in the Homestretch," 174. This print is not specifically discussed in the article. For Picasso's final works, see Steinberg, "Picasso's Endgame," in *Picasso*, 176–188. Previously published in *October* 74 (Autumn 1995): 105–122.

68 Michael Hill, "Leo Steinberg vs Clement Greenberg, 1952–72," *Australian and New Zealand Journal of Art* 14, no. 1 (2014): 21–29; Sylvia Harrison, "Leo Steinberg: Pop, 'Post-Modernist' Painting and the Flatbed Picture Plane," in *Pop Art and the Origins of Post-Modernism*, 3rd ed. (Cambridge: Cambridge University Press, 2001), 96–111.

69 Steinberg's summary of Picasso's diminished reputation among art critics is in "The Philosophical Brothel," 110–116.

70 Steinberg, "Other Criteria," in *Other Criteria* (New York: Oxford University Press, 1972), 64; Steinberg, "Mantegna: Did He Paint by the Book?," in *Renaissance and Baroque Art*, 45.

71 Steinberg, "Other Criteria," 71.

72 For further discussion of Steinberg's formulation of the flatbed picture plane, see Peter Parshall's essay in this volume.

73 Steinberg, "What I Like About Prints," 13, 15.

74 Steinberg, "Other Criteria," 90.

75 MacGregor, "The Authority of Prints: An Early Modern Perspective," 404–411.

76 Steinberg, "Other Criteria," 88.

77 Christian Geelhaar, *Jasper Johns Working Proofs* (London: Petersburg Press, 1980), cat. no. 2.

78 Steinberg, "False Starts, Loose Ends," *The Brooklyn Rail*, June 12, 2006, https://brooklynrail.org/2006/06/art/leo. His personal papers at the GRI also attest to his sense of alienation from the field.

79 Ernst Gombrich, "Talking of Michelangelo," *New York Review of Books* 33, no. 18 (January 20, 1977): 19.

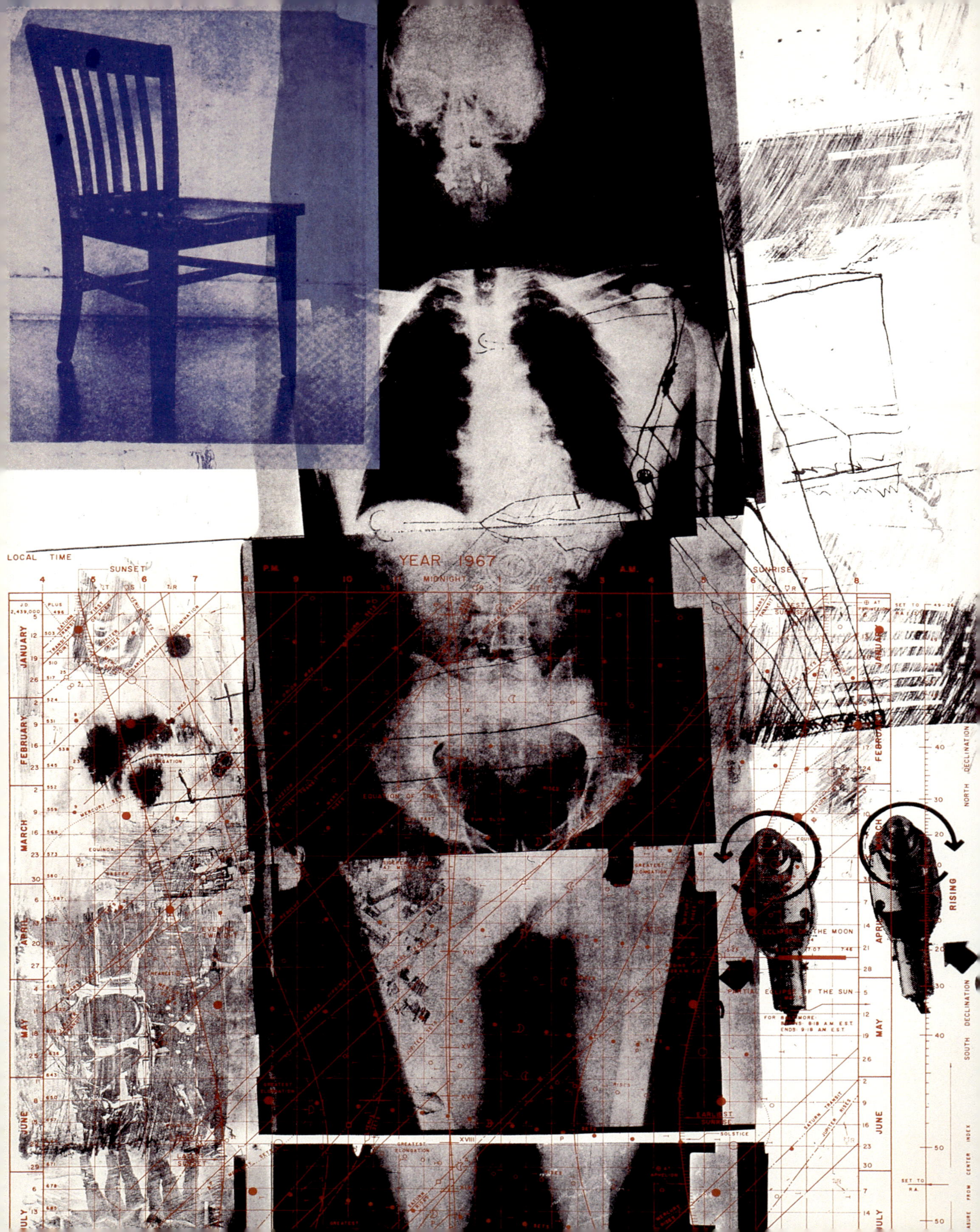
LOCAL TIME
SUNSET
YEAR 1967
MIDNIGHT
P.M.
A.M.
SUNRISE
JANUARY
FEBRUARY
MARCH
APRIL
MAY
JUNE
JULY
EQUATION OF TIME
TOTAL ECLIPSE OF THE MOON
PARTIAL ECLIPSE OF THE SUN
SOLSTICE
RISING
NORTH DECLINATION
SOUTH DECLINATION

Leo Steinberg's Print Affair

PETER PARSHALL

WHY DOES AN ART HISTORIAN COLLECT? MOST OF US do not, at least not in an ambitious and determined way involving the things we study. Some inherited their interest in the field as the result of having grown up with a family collection. This was especially the case in earlier times, particularly among Europeans, and sometimes led to a career in a museum or to becoming a dealer and profiting from the inheritance. In due course, private collecting and curatorial work were recognized to be a conflict of interest, which resulted in the art historian who collects most often being a scholar employed by a university. Steinberg began collecting prints in New York in the early 1960s, when it came to him that one could purchase a work of art by an acknowledged master for a song. He describes his first interest as a kind of rescue operation for a medium that seemed largely disregarded by the discipline. This sense of the print being on a lower echelon among the classic mediums of early modern and later art was indeed reflected in the priorities of academic and curatorial practice. Apart from the widely acknowledged greats (Dürer, Rembrandt, Picasso), in the field of art history prints were considered a service department to the dominant traditions and rarely if ever taught as an independent subject. One consulted them to find out something else: a source for a composition, the record of a lost painting, an unusual iconographical detail. This has all changed, but when Steinberg was a student, and well after that, it was certainly the case.

For at least two centuries, the most prized of old master prints had been expensive, often very expensive. However, in 1962 a delirious translation of a Rubens landscape in an engraving by Schelte Adams Bolswert could be had for only ten dollars.[1] Steinberg came to love the medium of prints for everything it offered him in the works of art themselves and in the evidence of art history in progress. Judging by his own account, he was an impulse buyer, riffling through the boxes and portfolios of print dealers and bookshops in New York and in print stalls on his travels abroad. This manner of acquisition must have been characteristic of image chasers since the Renaissance, when print shopping first became possible. It was a kind of purchasing that printmakers learned early on to exploit in their choices of subject matter and their cultivation of individual styles and techniques, intended in part to catch the eye and open the mind during such fleeting encounters.[2]

As a historian Steinberg recognized the degree to which prints were vital for the circulation of images and ideas, and in this sense alone we can understand his interest in collecting as an endeavor supplementary to—and generative of—his activities as a scholar. Like someone's private library, the tally of nearly seven thousand prints that passed through his collection at various stages is revealing for what it represents as a large facet of his thinking. In this respect, Steinberg's collection stands in a long tradition of prints serving as a pictorial atlas of history and culture, an image bank much like a museum without walls, largely free of written narrative. An important implication of prints as collected items is that with their proliferation one can begin to think about the audience for works of art acquiring something like visual literacy or, as Steinberg puts it, experiencing an elevation in "critical visual awareness."[3] The same principle applies to the digital present, although the term "literacy" would now require a volume to gloss its implications. For a collector, and certainly for a historian, a sizeable collection also constitutes an obligation. For practical purposes alone, the objects need to be put in order, and this ordering will indicate something of how the collection was used and what sort of visual literacy it was meant to support. My point here is to reflect upon the significance of prints in general for Steinberg's thinking as a historian and critic. In short, what does his engagement with the history of prints tell us about his particular approach to interpreting works of art, and in what ways does that interest reflect and embody his unusual visual intelligence?

What Leo Steinberg himself wrote about prints was precious little in proportion to his writings on other subjects. Almost everything specifically to do with them resulted from invitations for occasional pieces from the now defunct *Print Collector's Newsletter.*[4] He put serious effort into these essays, however, and they contain some of his best and most inspiring writing on art. Take, for example, a short piece on a small *Adoration of the Magi* by the little-known seventeenth-century Dutch painter Jacob Pynas. The essay seems to have been prompted by a minor quotation of a figure from a much earlier print that was itself a detail cropped from a lost fresco by Michelangelo.[5] With the ingenuity of a Sherlock Holmes, Steinberg unpacks this well-worn subject in all of its tactical intelligence and subtle humor. He reminds us that minor objects portraying the most familiar subjects sometimes conceal nuances and subtle plays on convention, and that prints are very often a key to uncovering them. Although the implicit comedy of the reference to Michelangelo might have been unintended by the artist, Steinberg would like to see it as part of a *concetto* awaiting discovery. As he put it elsewhere: "I always credit the artist with intention. Whatever may be there unconsciously is not my subject."[6] He presents this incidental moment of intertextuality in defense of artistic intelligence—of the "thinking" painter—a presumption fundamental to his convictions as a critic.

Although Steinberg conferred most of his attention on the established hierarchy of geniuses and canonized masterpieces, here he is doing much more than just logging an entry in a pictorial lexicon of borrowings. He is making an important point about the transmission of a pictorial vocabulary and the generative nature of convention. He was acutely alert to the use of specific poses and gestures adopted and adjusted for their meanings—most notably the crossed legs, the pronated arm, and the slung leg as they were deployed in Michelangelo's sculpture. For Steinberg, these positions were deeply invested with metaphorical significance. There is a distinguished precedent for this idea: Aby Warburg's *Pathosformel* (pathos formula).[7] In Steinberg's case, support for the allegorical interpretation of a pose might include a parade of suspects in many different mediums, extending from antiquity to *New Yorker* cartoons. Unsurprisingly, prints play an important role in these assemblies. In like fashion, he collected obscure literary citations and personal anecdotes to construct a skein of observations, habits, and mores that constitute, like the pictorial lineups themselves, a vernacular record of comparable bodily proclivities. His extended study of Michelangelo's *Medici Madonna* is an excellent demonstration of this cumulative method of explanation, and it teaches us more than we could ever have imagined about the implications of crossing one's legs.[8]

In Steinberg's interview for the Getty's Art History Oral Documentation Project, he recalls the several lecture courses on ancient art that he took with Karl Lehmann while a graduate student at the Institute of Fine Arts in the 1950s. Lehmann's slide exams would entail identification questions drawn from a corpus of some

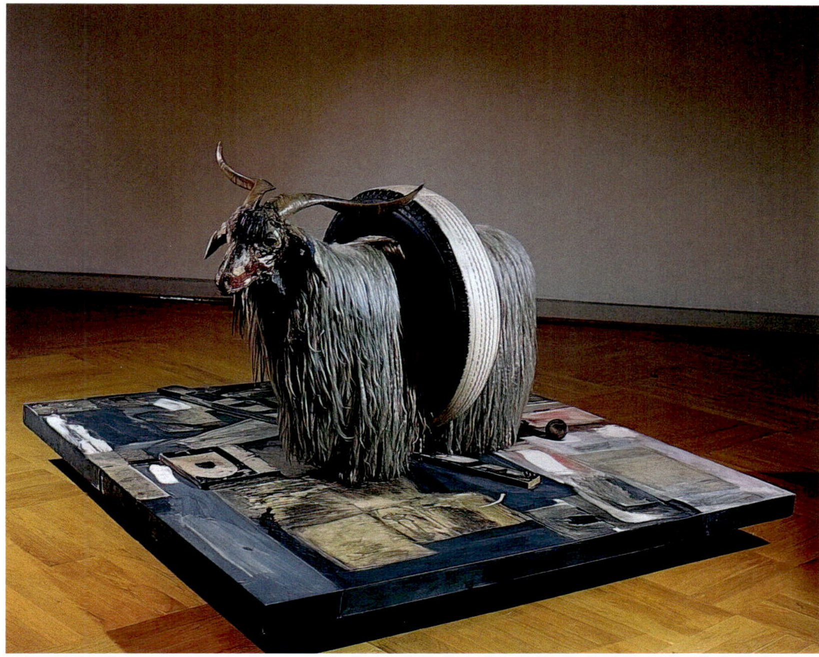

FIG. 56 Robert Rauschenberg, *Monogram* (Combine), 1955–59. Oil on canvas, printed paper, textile, paper, metal sign, wood, rubber shoe heel, tennis ball, taxidermy angora goat with paint and painted rubber tire, 42 × 63¼ × 64½ in. (106.8 × 160.655 × 163.83 cm). Moderna Museet, Stockholm, Purchase 1965 with contribution from Moderna Museets Vänner/The Friends of Moderna Museet © Robert Rauschenberg Foundation.

five thousand objects "including potsherds" for which the students were responsible. Steinberg credits this experience with his ability many years later to review in his mind the whole recorded history of Greek art with sufficient precision to confirm the first appearance of the crossed-leg pose.[9] Add to this the reports of his ability to recite long passages from John Milton's *Paradise Lost* and whole pages of James Joyce's *Ulysses*, and there seems little doubt that we are engaged with a thinker possessed of a prodigious memory—not just of images but also of texts.[10] Hence, the first and most obvious benefit of a print collection to Steinberg's history of art is its value as a pictorial encyclopedia. Yet it makes more sense to understand his infatuation with acquiring prints not as something principally motivated by his investigative method, but as a reflection of it. He liked having large numbers of pictures around because he was natively comfortable with their language and greatly enjoyed speaking it.

By methodologically privileging the visual panorama in the practice of art history, Steinberg was anticipating the emergence of what came to be termed "visual culture" and "*Bildwissenschaft*," related concepts that became central to the "New Art History" of the 1980s. Both laid stress on opening the boundaries of the field and encouraging art historians to consider all manner of visual evidence as part of their brief, and although it was perhaps not quite his intention, Steinberg's contribution to this emancipation was foundational. By intellectual disposition not a joiner, and constitutionally resistant to movements, Steinberg would not have associated himself with either of these rubrics. For him, the postmodern experience of image saturation did not in any meaningful sense constitute a coherent "culture" in its own right. By increasing the latitudes of what qualified as visual evidence, Steinberg was extending a language, and it set him on the flank, but not apart from iconography in its former period of dominance.

Steinberg's readings of body language in particular stand among his most celebrated and contested contributions to the field. His image bank, of which the print collection was a small part, proved to be as extensive as his linguistic lexicon, and together they produced some of the most eloquent passages of ekphrastic prose to be found in the literature of art history. This, too, has proven controversial. Ironically, a discipline rooted in expressing visual experience through words could also be made uneasy by too intimate a relationship between the two.[11] Steinberg's method of argument aimed to bring the reader to agreement by making an interpretation appear self-evident upon encounter with the work of art. Or, as he put it, once the interpretation has been enunciated, "the picture seems to confess itself."[12] Hearing him lecture was, in this respect, watching the formation of a consensus. This was also partly what that he was seeking in the language of images and texts. The more examples he could provide in support of the meaning of a motif, the more credible it became.

In one conspicuous case, Steinberg's proclivity for visual thinking and the example of printmaking resulted in a metaphor that invites being transformed into a model of doing art history. Here I refer to his frequently cited concept of the "flatbed picture plane," a construct he first formulated in explanation of Robert Rauschenberg's *Combines* of the mid-1950s and after, typically framed objects, but sometimes also structures that included all manner of accretions, from fabrics and manufactured items to imported images and curious appendages (fig. 56). Steinberg presented this positional shift as a decisive turning point in the relation of viewer to pictorial object. He first put forward the concept of the flatbed picture plane in a lecture at the Museum of Modern Art in 1968, which was later revised as the landmark title essay in his anthology *Other Criteria*.[13] The term itself he borrowed from the flatbed printing press, adopting as his prototype matrix the horizontal table with its framed block of type where the sheet to be printed is placed in order to receive the downward pressure of the press. Here is what Benjamin Franklin's press looked like, a structure probably not much different from the one Johannes Gutenberg used to print his Bible (figs. 57, 58). When we consider this to be our orientation to the picture plane (rather than the orthodox encounter with an image placed vertically before us on a wall), the full nature of the experience, Steinberg argues, is completely reconceived.

With the appearance of this new conception of the pictorial field, the Renaissance idea of the picture plane as a fictive window onto space (or as a mirror of the visible world) was now converted into a kind of tabletop surveyed from various angles on which that world can be rearranged without regard to any notion of transparency or imagined illusion beyond the surface. The flatbed, Steinberg asserts, was "the characteristic picture plane of the 1960s" and signified no less than "the most radical shift in the subject matter of art, the shift from nature to culture."[14]

> Rauschenberg's picture plane had to become a surface to which anything reachable-thinkable would adhere. It had to be whatever a billboard or dashboard is, and everything a projection screen is, with further affinities for anything that is flat and worked over—palimpsest, canceled plate, printer's proof, trial blank, chart, map, aerial view . . . And it seemed at times that Rauschenberg's work surface stood for the mind itself.[15]

This pictorial surface "let the world in again."[16] It reconfigured the way painting had been traditionally understood in a manner that dissolved the conventional boundary between painting and sculpture. It became a constructed multidimensional domain of its own. Steinberg's thesis is rich in implication for a new understanding of artistic process and the redefinition, if not obsolescence, of the Renaissance picture plane as we knew it. This idea proved to be powerful in the extreme, providing as it did a marking point for the shakeup that, largely through Steinberg's critical writings, came to be termed "postmodernism."[17]

Of interest to us here, however, is a more limited aspect of Steinberg's observation: the fact that this dramatic inversion of a pictorial tradition extending over half a millennium is explicated through the model of a printing press. Should we take this as mere rhetorical flair, or is there more to it? That is the very question Steinberg himself would ask of such a thesis, and therefore we are obligated to consider it further. The question is this: why should Steinberg have chosen a press bed rather than, for example, a tabletop for his model? [18] One can perform precisely the same actions

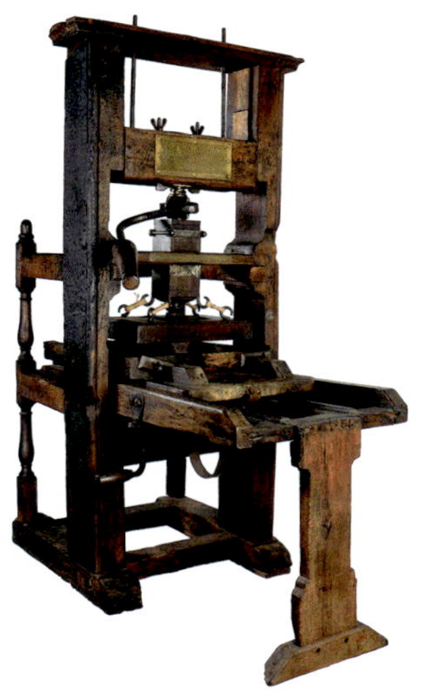

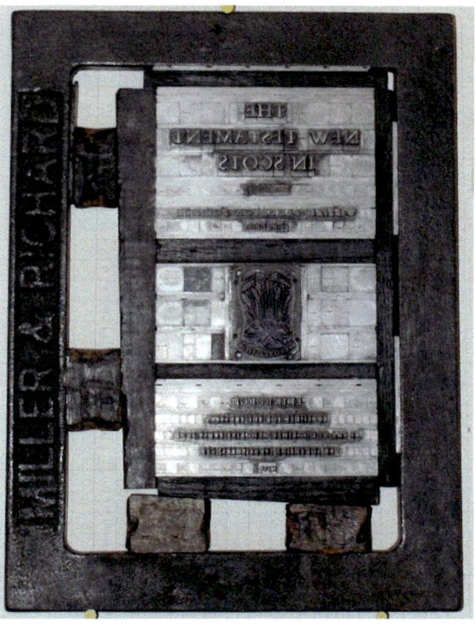

FIG. 57 "Franklin" common press, ca. 1720, said to have been used by Benjamin Franklin in John Watts's printing shop in London in 1726. Division of Work and Industry, National Museum of American History, Smithsonian Institution, Washington, DC.

FIG. 58 Locked-up type form set for inking and printing in a flatbed press. The City of Edinburgh Council Museums and Galleries; People's Story.

there with less encumbrance, and, indeed, Steinberg includes a worktable among his catalogue of analogies to the Rauschenberg plane. The press, with all its requirements for cleanliness and precision, does not accommodate the contrary qualities much valued elsewhere in the aesthetic of flatness and compression, for example "the pressed-leaf effect, the graffito effect, the scratched gravel or fossil impression effect" of a Dubuffet, or in regard to Rauschenberg himself, Steinberg's analogy of a "dump, reservoir, switching station."[19] But it nicely accounts for Rauschenberg's lush and promiscuous use of screenprinted photo-transfers on canvas and his prints made on paper and fabric.

The beauty of the flatbed metaphor is nevertheless its inclusiveness. Books as well as works of art were made using flatbed presses. They were complicated apparatuses that required a variety of skills, including precision typesetting and the ability to proofread in mirror image. The press was a symbol of modernity already from its invention in the fifteenth century and has remained a faithful instrument of reactionary and progressive discourse ever since. One might say that if presses had memories they would carry the record of human accomplishment without peer, retaining all of its mishaps, discarded ideas, and censored affronts along with the full chronicle of constructive accomplishment. Presses likewise took the world in and then returned it in multiple for widespread consumption. The flatbed press invokes structural and procedural properties along with the shift to perpendicular orientation as well: it places a mechanical operation between the maker and the product; it entails the reflective/inversion factor inherent in the print medium; it involves compression and thereby imparts a topography to the printed matter. When we consider the press from these perspectives, the metaphor of the picture plane becomes complicated in ways that do not precisely apply in the sense that Steinberg intends. Possibly he recognized something in the process that captured the essence of Rauschenberg's project. And in its triple assertion of compaction, "flat-bed-press" has a pleasing onomatopoeia and the force of an iterative tautology. But how does it relate to the additive nature of the *Combines*?

One among Steinberg's list of analogies, the palimpsest, seems especially apt to the press metaphor. A palimpsest is typically a written document, either faded or erased, that has been overwritten with another text but remains partly or wholly recoverable beneath the surface. As a material manifestation of printing, it is pregnant with possibility. Perfect examples are Rauschenberg's lithographic photo-transfers that became a signature feature of his work in the period we are considering. These are composed palimpsests layering fragments of newsprint and other previously printed imagery over one another in collage format, but with a planographic surface undifferentiated in its flatness (fig. 59). A mechanically generated repository of memory, partly traceable and partly not, possessed of both orderliness and chaos, logical sequence and free

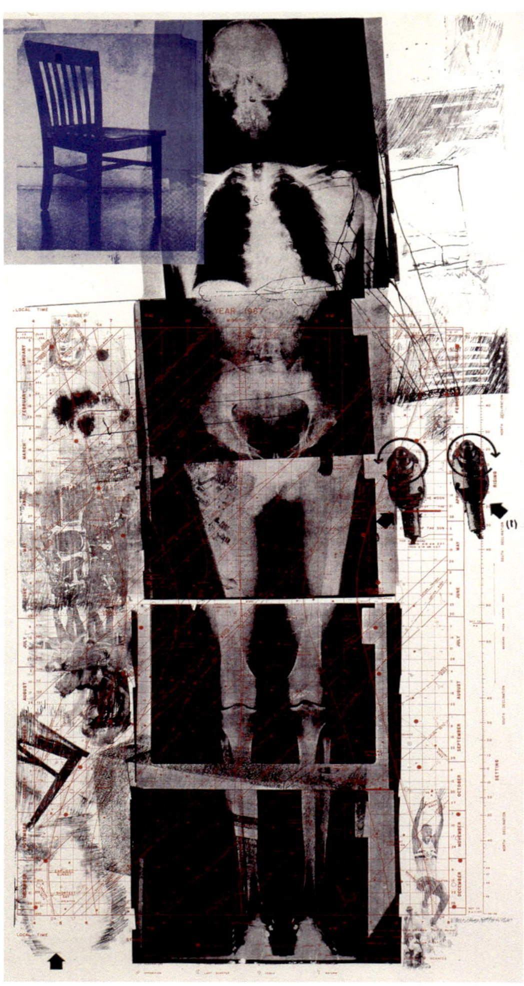

FIG. 59 Robert Rauschenberg, *Booster*, from the series *Booster and the 7 Studies*, lithograph and screenprint, 1967, 71½ × 35⅛ in. (181.7 × 89.3 cm) from an edition of 38, published by Gemini G.E.L., Los Angeles, Museum of Modern Art, New York, John B. Turner Fund © Robert Rauschenberg Foundation.

association, inventive production and media refuse, the palimpsest serves not only as a model of the mind but also of the stratigraphy of the historical record.[20]

The richness of these photo-transfer images is boundless, which is the source of their attraction and also their vulnerability. In a much later reflection, Steinberg provided another angle on his choice of the flatbed metaphor in which he qualified the radicalness of his initial claim. He noted that the so-called flatbed picture plane had, in fact, been around for a very long time. By way of illustration he cites an illuminated manuscript of 1515 as one among a legion of examples in which artists played upon the pretense of spatial illusion, demonstrating their awareness of perspective as a mere contrivance, the parchment effectively just another "workspace" rather than a transparent veil over the world.[21] He was reminding us again that painters were always thinkers, and that their skill set always included the potential for irony. Like his choice of the printing press as a metaphor, it seems not accidental that Steinberg chose a book to make his point, indeed a handmade book produced two generations after Gutenberg's introduction of printing with moveable type.

Rauschenberg's photographic transfers are, among much else, a recapitulation of (recently or distantly) past events. Not only are they suggestively a model of the mind, they are a template for historical retrospection. Like the process of reconstructing history, they are examples of the palimpsest as a stratigraphic record of time and events, dense with detail and often barely discernible through overprintings and added markings. Steinberg describes the experience of a *Combine* as follows:

> [T]he images—each in itself illusionistic—kept interfering with one another; intimations of spatial meaning forever canceling out to subside in a kind of optical noise. The waste and detritus of communication, like radio transmission with

> interference; noise and meaning on the same wavelength, visually on the same flatbed plane.[22]

Although this phenomenon is more frequently demonstrated in Rauschenberg's prints, Steinberg chooses to concentrate on the materially more complex *Combines* to make his point, including those that employ screenprinted photo-transfers. The prints themselves, however, are different. Their extension of the flatbed principle evokes topography only in an illusionistic way. Should we therefore tacitly exclude them from the flatbed class? Do they present a problem of conceptual border control? In any case, their status as palimpsests obtains. Here the value of the palimpsest and the image bank overlap, each representing a dimension of the memory in a different register: diachronic and synchronic. The process of screenprinting itself suggests literally "the horizontal flow of culture in the age of media."[23] In short, it evokes, in both senses of the term, the leveling effect of the press as the initial agent of mass communication.

As a historian, Steinberg took for granted that his engagement with works of art must begin with the sensibility and intelligence of his own time. For him, it was this that held out the possibility of finding something previously neglected in the historical record, and although anachronism had to be guarded against, it should not pose an unbreachable barrier to imaginative interpretation. The palimpsest not only confuses our retrospective understanding of the overwritten past, it also evolves hermeneutically over time, variously obscuring and revealing what lies behind, depending on the questions we bring to it.[24] James Joyce was one of Steinberg's most favored vehicles for penetrating that stratification, which recalls the fact that Steinberg's approach to the past was premised on a discrete but intimate relationship between artistic and literary production, one that is partly exemplified by the history of prints both as objects in their own right and as avenues of transmission.

There is no simple answer to the question of why this particular art historian collected as he did. An intellect of this stature, having engaged the most challenging figures in the Western canon and devoted decades to the investigation of single works of art, also maintained wide latitudes of interest and seems to have enjoyed it all. We will continue to read him for the sheer intelligence he brought to the discipline and for his elegant and evocative prose. Ready access to many works of art at home brings sundry pleasures, and for Steinberg one of these was certainly having close at hand an available version of the historical record catalogued and boxed for efficient recovery. In this respect, his collection was very different from the view of history presented by the flatbed plane—a landscape dense with hummocks of impasto, plywood trapdoors, forests of clutter, and at least one goat.

NOTES

1 Steinberg, "What I Like About Prints," *Art in Print* 7, no. 5 (January–February 2018): 7–10, adapted from a lecture given at the Blanton Museum in 2003 to celebrate its acquisition of Steinberg's print collection.

2 Peter Parshall, "Prints as Objects of Consumption in Early Modern Europe," *Journal of Medieval and Early Modern Studies* 28, no. 1 (1998): 19–36.

3 Steinberg, "What I Like about Prints," 18. "The most important contribution of prints is to have raised—for an entire civilization—the level of critical visual awareness. Prints made it possible, as never before, to compare images at something like the molecular level."

4 Published between 1970 and 1996.

5 Steinberg, "A Picture by One Jacob Pynas," *Print Collector's Newsletter* 11, no. 5 (November–December 1980): 171–174.

6 "The Gestural Trace: Leo Steinberg," transcript of an interview with Steinberg conducted by Richard Cándida Smith in 1998 for the Art History Oral Documentation Project at the Getty Research Institute, https://primo.getty.edu/primo-explore/fulldisplay?vid=GRI&docid=GETTY_ALMA21126736220001551&context=L.

7 Aby Warburg, *The Renewal of Pagan Antiquity* (Los Angeles: Getty Research Institute, 1999). The concept of Pathos formula was first fully articulated in Warburg's lecture on Albrecht Dürer in 1905; the idea later found a place in his *Mnemosyne Atlas*. Warburg proposes that certain motifs or topoi (most famously the drapery flourishes on ancient Greek maenad reliefs) bore emotional content and that this was recognized by the Renaissance artists (Sandro Botticelli, for example) who redeployed them.

8 Steinberg, "Body and Symbol in the *Medici Madonna*," in *Michelangelo's Sculpture: Selected Essays*, ed. Sheila Schwartz (Chicago: University of Chicago Press, 2018), 96–128.

9 "The Gestural Trace," 79–81.

10 Schwartz, "Preface and Acknowledgments" to *Michelangelo's Sculpture*, viii.

11 See, for example, Ernst Gombrich, "Talking of Michelangelo," *New York Review of Books* 33, no. 18 (January 20, 1977). Supposedly Walter Friedlaender, one of his teachers, used to say: "I don't trust Leo Steinberg, he writes too well." "The Gestural Trace," 20. This was presumably said tongue-in-cheek, but one wonders if it contained a degree of seriousness. Steinberg himself recounts it with evident pride.

12 Steinberg, "Michelangelo's Last Paintings" in *Michelangelo's Painting: Selected Essays*, ed. Sheila Schwartz (Chicago: University of Chicago Press, 2019), 238. Previously published as *Michelangelo's Last Paintings* (New York: Oxford University Press, 1975).

13 See Steinberg, "Other Criteria," in *Other Criteria* (New York: Oxford University Press, 1972), 82–91; the essay was partly reframed and republished in *Encounters with Rauschenberg* (Chicago: University of Chicago Press, 2000), a lecture delivered at the Menil Collection, Houston, in 1998 (see especially 21–45).

14 Steinberg, "Other Criteria," 82, 84.

15 Ibid., 88.

16 Ibid., 90.

17 Steinberg effectively introduced the term "postmodernism" into critical discourse in the 1960s. For an indication of how widely the concept of the flatbed plane was applied as an index of postmodern culture see Douglas Crimp, "On the Museum's Ruins," first published in *October* 13 (Summer 1980) and revised for *The Anti-Aesthetic: Essays on Postmodern Culture*, ed. Hal Foster (Port Townsend, WA: Bay Press, 1983), 43–56.

18 Painting an actual tabletop with illusionistic motifs, stories, and comical figures was already a common practice in the Renaissance (see, for example, Hans Herbst, *Painted Tabletop*, oil on wood, 1515, Landesmuseum, Zurich). Steinberg surely knew of this practice but its relevance to the issue at hand is marginal.

19 Steinberg, "Other Criteria," 81–82, 88.

20 For a detailed and provocative consideration of the silkscreen/lithographic method and Rauschenberg's innovative use of it in his breakthrough print *Booster*, see Jennifer L. Roberts, "Sifted: Screenprinting and the Art of the 1960s," in *Three Centuries of American Prints from the National Gallery of Art*, ed., Judith

Brodie (Washington, DC: National Gallery of Art, 2016), 240–244.

21 Steinberg, "What I Like About Prints," 13–15.

22 Steinberg, "Other Criteria," 87–88.

23 Andrianna Campbell, "'Souvenirs without Nostalgia,' Gluts in Present Time," in *Robert Rauschenberg*, ed. Leah Dickerman and Achim Borchardt-Hume (New York: Museum of Modern Art, 2016), 33n11.

24 This was the gist of his disagreement with Gombrich and others who charged Steinberg with overinterpretation; "The Gestural Trace," 33, 121, 146.

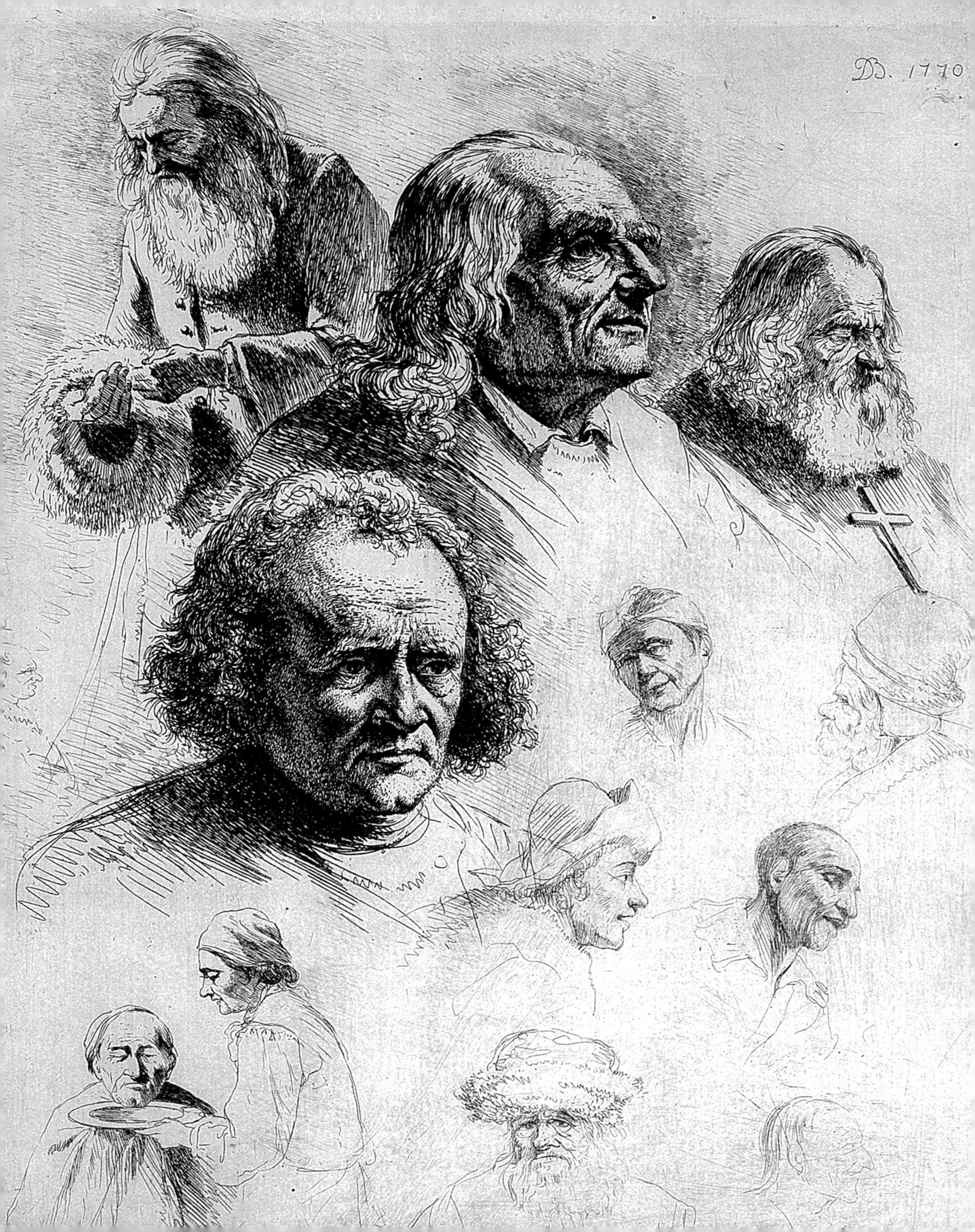
DB. 1770

The Leo Steinberg Collection: Highlights of Western Printmaking

HOLLY BORHAM

THE LEO STEINBERG COLLECTION SPANS SIX CENTURIES, with a strong emphasis on the years between 1500 and 1800. It includes work by artists of nineteen different nationalities, demonstrating the transnational reach of printmaking techniques that developed in association with both book production and metalwork in Italy and Germany in the fifteenth century. **Woodcut** was the first printmaking technique employed in Europe, where it was in practice by at least the 1420s and used primarily for book illustration. By the mid-fifteenth century, printing establishments used the same kind of screw press developed for moveable type in the late 1440s by Johannes Gutenberg in Mainz to integrate the printing of texts with woodblocks and **metalcuts**.[1] Along with the expansion of paper production in the early fifteenth century, these innovations allowed images to be combined easily with text and widely distributed. Just as woodcut developed alongside book production, so the **intaglio** processes of **engraving** and **etching** had their genesis in the metalsmith's workshop. The same skills and tools required to incise decorative designs into arms and armor, as well as ornamental plaques (nielli), transferred easily to copper and iron plates, which could then be inked, wiped, and printed on paper. The earliest engravings appeared in the 1430s; the type of press capable of applying the requisite pressure to force paper down into a plate's incised lines was invented in the 1460s.[2] By the mid-1490s, Augsburg armorer Daniel Hopfer (1471–1536) had pioneered the less-demanding etching technique, in which acid, rather than the engraver's skilled handling of the **burin**, "bites" the lines into a printing plate.[3]

The relative economy, reproducibility, and transportability of prints expanded the potential for the circulation and ownership of images across social classes and beyond territorial boundaries; this, in turn, encouraged artists to represent such practical and popular subjects as designs for ornament and decorative objects, social and political satires, and scenes from nature and daily life, in addition to traditional religious and mythological ones. Due to Steinberg's voracious curiosity, his collection includes examples of the wide range of subject matter depicted in prints over the centuries and records significant technical developments in the medium. This selection of highlights features prints produced in all of the major European printmaking centers, by both renowned and obscure or lesser-known artists using an array of printmaking techniques. Together, they chart the evolution of printmaking as well as providing a window onto Steinberg's scholarly interests and his broad and often idiosyncratic tastes. Not least, when viewed in the context of his writings, such works from the collection convey a sense of the richness of a life shaped by a passion for prints. As Steinberg himself described his early forays into the field: "If at first I imagined myself stepping into a vast unmapped terrain, I soon discovered that I had, in fact, entered a club composed of a small band of dedicated enthusiasts, spread out over continents and centuries; people who had been fascinated by the world of prints and had spent decades cataloguing collections for the benefit of like-minded amateurs in generations to come. I would look at a print picked from a junk heap on Portobello Road, find it catalogued and described by a librarian working in Vienna during the Napoleonic Wars, and end up enjoying a sense of fellowship with kindred spirits across ages and oceans."[4]

THE SIXTEENTH CENTURY

> UNKNOWN FRENCH ARTIST
> PUBLISHED BY THIELMAN KERVER
> Leaf from *Hore intemerate virginis marie* (Book of Hours)
> PLATE 1

Among the early highlights of Steinberg's collection is a leaf from a Book of Hours (1501–02), designed to prompt prayer throughout the day, and one of the most commonly owned types of books during the Middle Ages.[5] Printed by Thielman Kerver in Paris at the turn of the sixteenth century, with moveable type and illustrations in metalcut, the book nevertheless retains features typical of illuminated manuscripts produced by hand, like the vellum (animal skin) support, rubrication (red lines to guide handwriting), and the red, blue, and gold initials.[6] These vestiges of scribal culture attest to the enduring appeal of the earliest Western techniques of book production, as well as the opportunities they afforded printers to customize such features as support type and the degree of hand coloring, depending on the intended client.

> MICHAEL OSTENDORFER
> *The Pilgrimage to the Beautiful Virgin at Regensburg*
> PLATE 2

During the sixteenth century, entrepreneurial printers, hoping to appeal to a broader market, commissioned single-leaf woodcuts, either with or without accompanying text, on both religious and secular themes. These prints, some rudimentary in design and execution and others highly refined, depict such contemporary events as political and religious disputes, military campaigns, and astrological anomalies, as well as portraits, and "moralities" intended to communicate proverbial wisdom and provide social commentary.[7] A two-block woodcut by Michael Ostendorfer (ca. 1490–ca. 1559) showing *The Pilgrimage to the Beautiful Virgin at Regensburg* (1519–23), a reference to a thirteenth-century painting known as the *Schöne Maria* housed in a temporary wooden church there, represents a popular religious subject with aesthetic sophistication.[8] The ruins of the town's Jewish quarter, razed in 1519 when the Jews were expelled from the town after more than a century of persecution, surround the church. When a stonemason involved in the destruction of the synagogue unexpectedly survived a fall from the vaults, the miracle was credited to the Beautiful Virgin. City authorities quickly erected a church on the site and introduced a papal indulgence for those who made the pilgrimage.

Ostendorfer's print includes three representations of the Virgin: Regensburg artist Albrecht Altdorfer's painted banner on the central tower, emblazoned with the Virgin and Child and the city's symbol of crossed keys, beckons pilgrims from afar; in the forecourt, worshippers prostrate themselves before a stone statue of the Beautiful Virgin carved in 1516 by Erhard Heydenrich; and men and women from various walks of life circle the chapel and press toward the painted icon visible through the church door. Although wildly popular, the Regensburg pilgrimage was not without its detractors. Martin Luther's critique in his 1520 *An den Christlichen Adel deutscher Nation von des Christlichen standes besserung* (Address to the Christian Nobility of the German Nation) was echoed by Albrecht Dürer, whose annotated impression of this print condemns the phenomenon as counter to biblical teaching and motivated by material gain.[9] Commissioned by the city council of Regensburg, Ostendorfer's

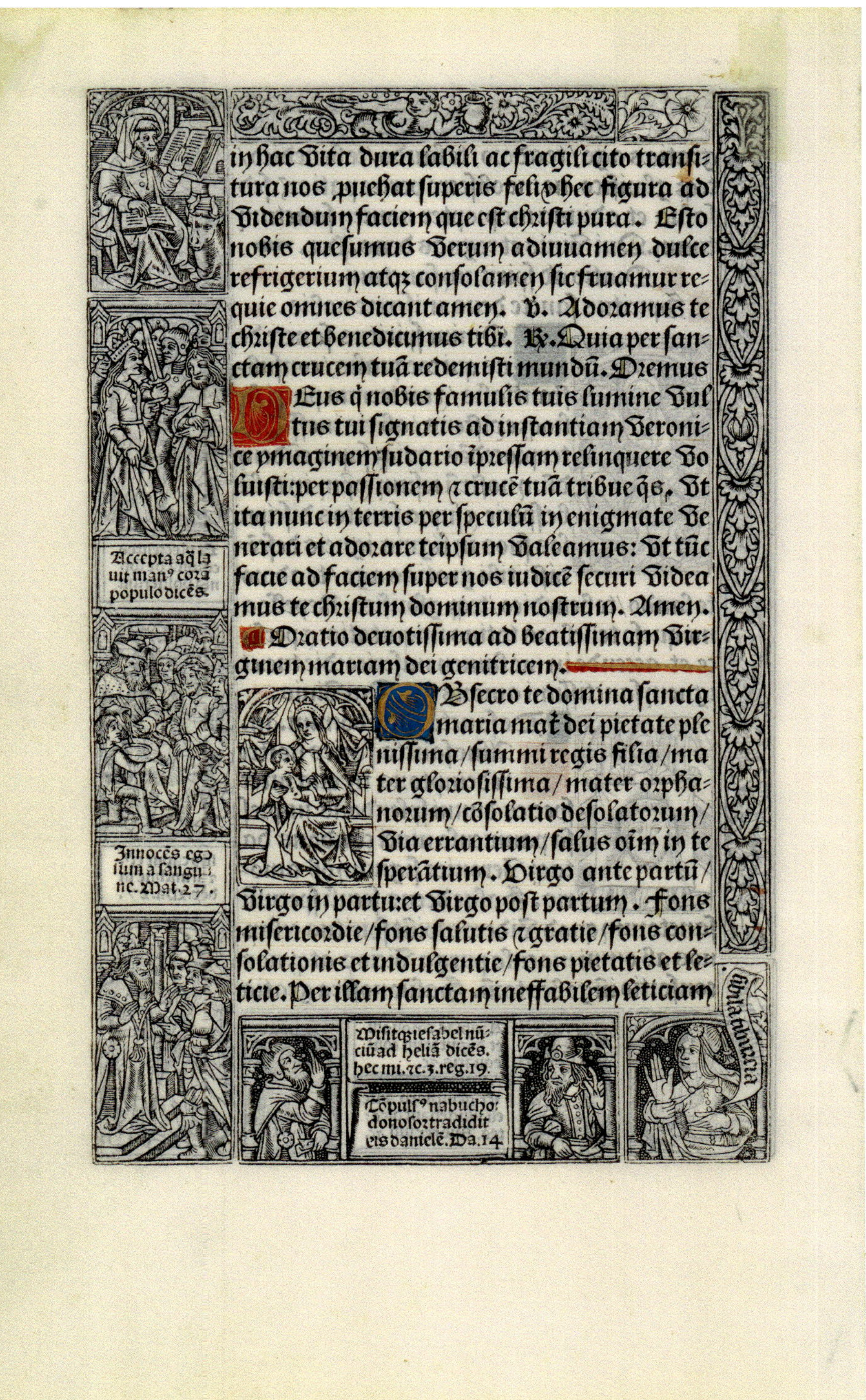

1 UNKNOWN FRENCH ARTIST
PUBLISHED BY THIELMAN KERVER

Leaf from *Hore intemerate virginis marie* (Book of Hours) 1501–02

Letterpress and metalcut with hand coloring on vellum, 6 11/16 × 4 1/8 in. (17 × 10.5 cm). (2002.289)

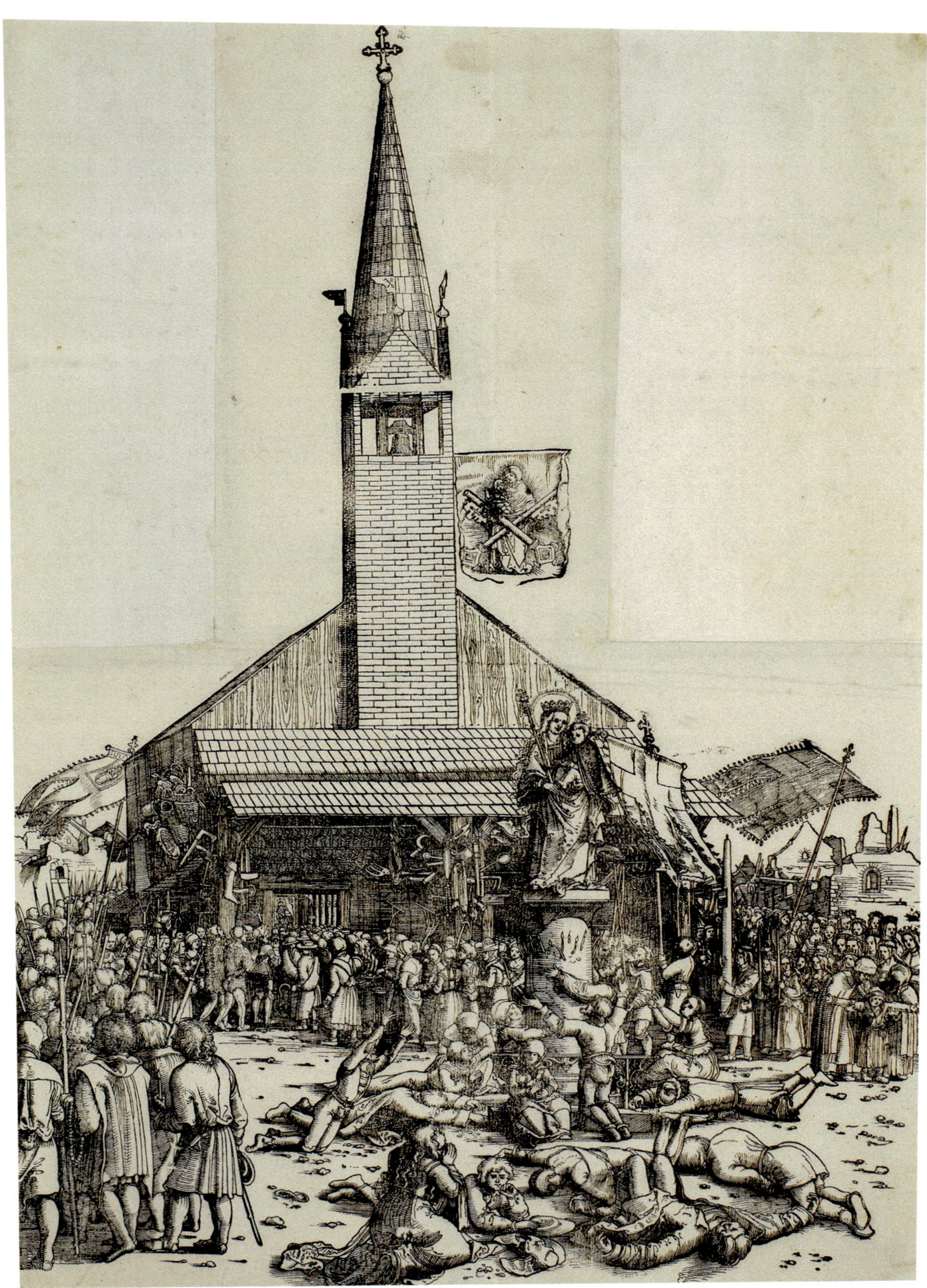

2 MICHAEL OSTENDORFER

The Pilgrimage to the Beautiful Virgin at Regensburg 1519–23

Woodcut, 21¾ × 15 in. (55.4 × 38.2 cm), trimmed at right and left of the tower, with later additions. Hollstein 6 (2002.2333) woodcut functioned variously as a devotional print, a record of indulgences granted, an advertisement for a tourist attraction, a fundraising tool for a new church edifice, and an "eyewitness" account of a current event.[10] The print was widely circulated, assisted by the more than one hundred thousand pilgrims who visited during the site's initial heyday and carried the original edition of fifteen hundred impressions far beyond the borders of Regensburg.[11] Although by 1525 the pilgrimage site had lost its popularity, the woodblock was reprinted until the early seventeenth century, with German text replacing the original Latin in later editions. Steinberg's impression, trimmed at the lower and side margins, is from the sixteenth century.

MARTIN WEIGEL
Women Snaring Men
PLATE 3

The theme of feminine wiles is tied to the image of a bird trap in a woodcut by Augsburg artist Martin Weigel (ca. 1553–ca. 1580) known as *Women Snaring Men* (1550–80), based on a woodcut made in about 1534 by Erhard Schön, originally paired in a broadsheet format with a text by Nuremberg poet Hans Sachs.[12] But Weigel's print does not need an accompanying poem—its humorous admonition is clear. Crouching behind a bird blind fashioned out of foxtails and crowned with a fool's cap—symbols of the trickery of women and the foolishness of men—a young woman pulls a lever, ensnaring two victims in her net. She is guided by an accomplice who peers through a wild-man mask incorporated into the blind. A third victim appears to be perched precariously, or perhaps impaled, on the branches of an ominous black tree. The equal number of stylishly attired men and women on either side of the trap suggests they will ultimately pair off under the watchful eye of a male figure who surveys the scene from an upper window and who has been variously interpreted (in Schön's woodcut) as the poet offering commentary or as a procurer supervising his business dealings.[13] Not only do such woodcuts provide valuable insights into the social mores of the time, but their extremely low rate of survival also indicates that they were purchased inexpensively and discarded. Unlike prints by Albrecht Dürer, which were avidly collected in his own day and are, therefore, preserved in significant numbers, there is no other known impression of Weigel's crudely carved woodcut.[14]

DANIEL HOPFER
Two Candelabra Designs
PLATE 4

Daniel Hopfer's *Two Candelabra Designs* (ca. 1525) points to the close association between metalwork and printed ornament. Reminiscent of typical Roman candelabra forms, whose rectangular or triangular bases support a series of bulbous shafts separated by flared dishes or vases, surmounted by urn-like forms intended to hold a candle or incense, Hopfer's designs also employ such *all'antica* motifs as sphinxes, rams' heads, putti, acanthus leaves, and rosettes. Situated at the crossroads between Italy and Germany, Augsburg artists had relatively easy access to Italian designs, which Hopfer embellished, recombined, and augmented with such inventive figures as the winged chimeric creature atop the right candelabrum.[15]

As Landau and Parshall suggest, Hopfer's designs would have appealed to "artisans looking to buy figural models or ornamental patterns to enhance the appeal of their own products" as well as to collectors who simply admired their beauty.[16] Although Hopfer presents these two candelabra as three-dimensional models, such ornament prints were rarely intended as fixed prototypes for craftsmen. The candelabra and any number of other designs for decorative objects and ornamental motifs could be scaled and adapted to roles as diverse as border decoration in books, architectural reliefs, or even freestanding columns.[17]

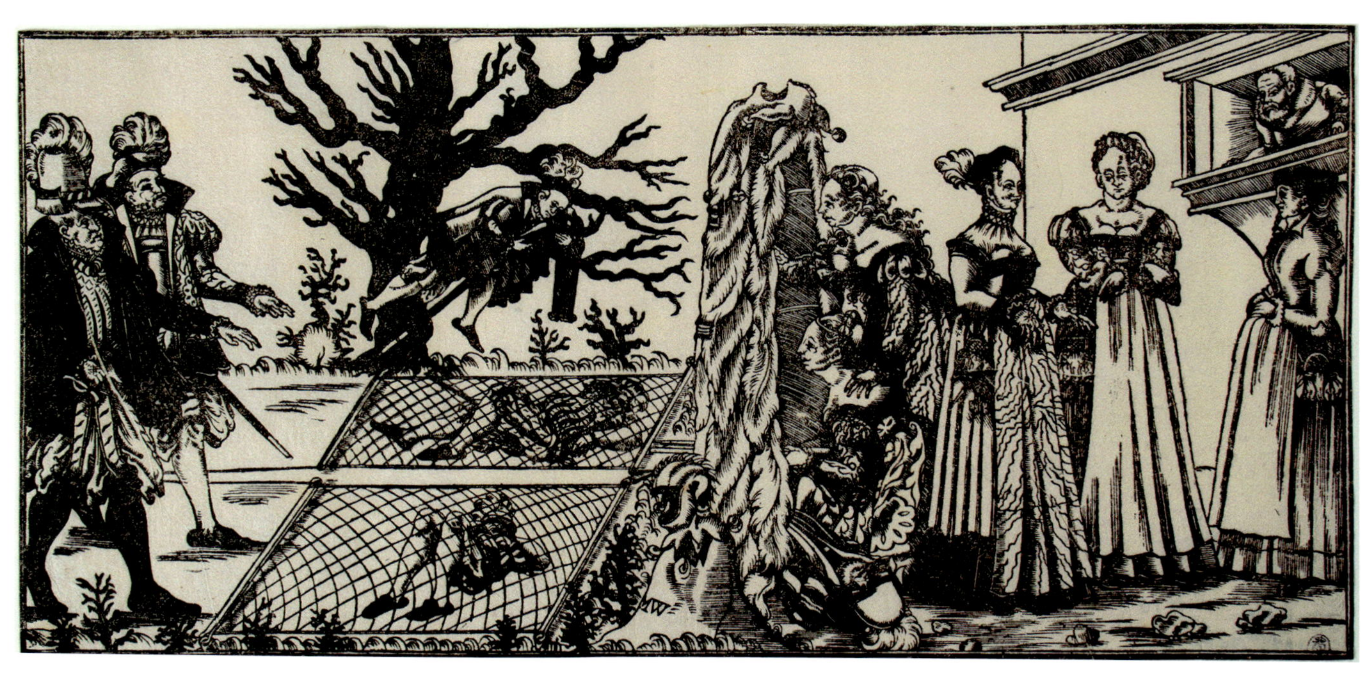

3

MARTIN WEIGEL

Women Snaring Men 1550–80

Woodcut, 6⁹⁄₁₆ × 13⁹⁄₁₆ in. (16.7 × 34.5 cm). Strauss 31 (2002.854)

4

DANIEL HOPFER

Two Candelabra Designs CA. 1525

Etching, second state of two, 8¹¹⁄₁₆ × 6³⁄₁₆ in. (22.1 × 15.8 cm). New Hollstein 142 (2002.840)

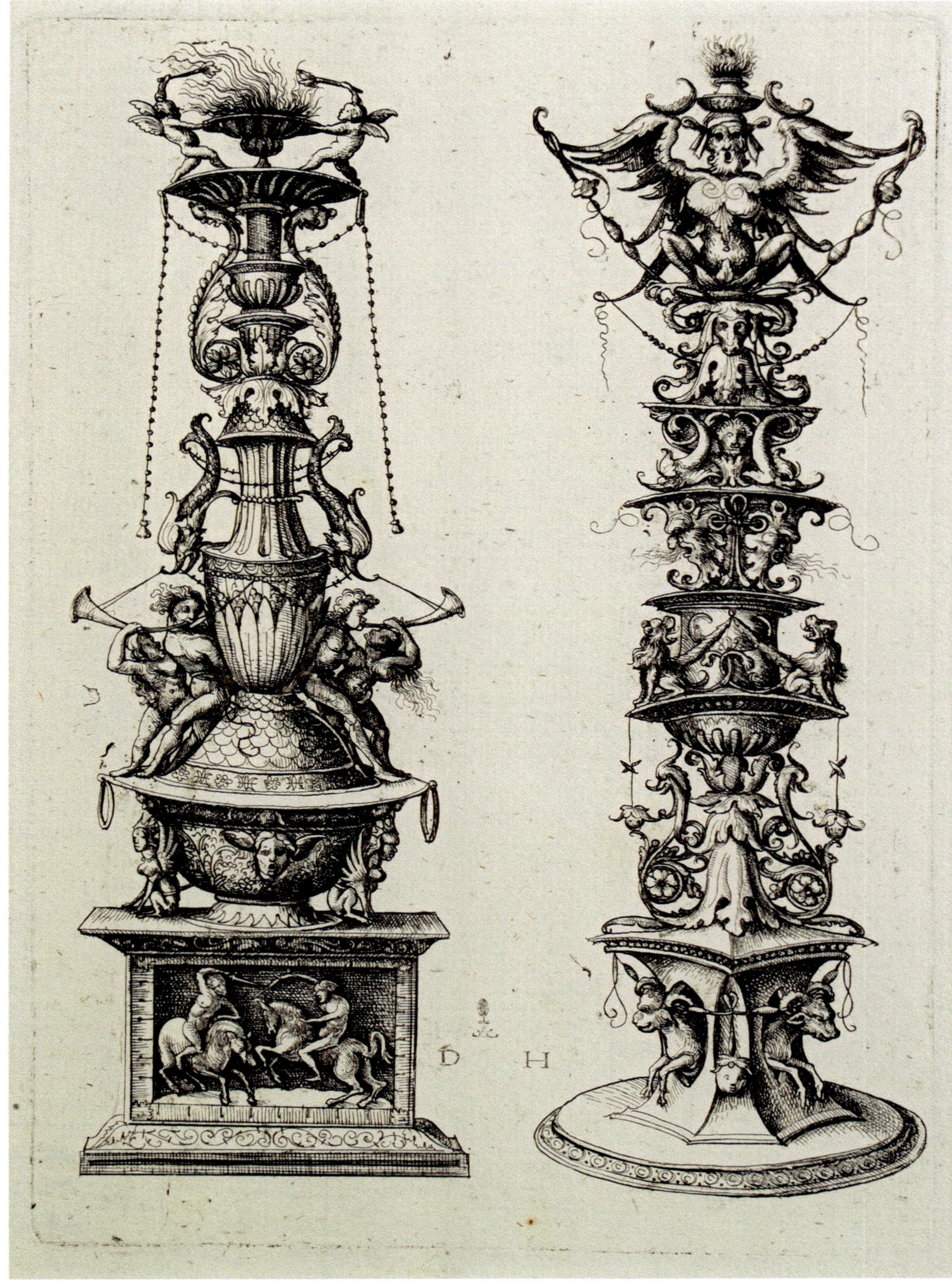
D H

ALBRECHT DÜRER
St. Christopher Facing Right
PLATE 5

Steinberg made his first purchase of prints by Albrecht Dürer (1471–1528) in 1962, with four woodcuts from the *Small Passion* (1509–10), and continued collecting his works until 1990.[18] There are fourteen prints by the German master in the Steinberg Collection at the Blanton. Dürer apprenticed in Nuremberg with his goldsmith father and then with local painter and woodcut artist Michael Wolgemut, ultimately setting a standard of technical excellence in both engraving and woodcut for generations to come.[19] However, he was no less renowned as a draftsman, painter, and art theorist. In his writings, Dürer addresses technical issues of proportion and perspective, as well as moral and epistemological questions about artistic license. His interest in the natural world reflected his belief that empirical observation should be at the root of artistic invention; in addition to landscape, flora, and fauna, often depicted in minute detail, his artworks incorporate devotional, mythological, and allegorical scenes, ornamental and architectural designs, astronomy, and portraits.[20]

St. Christopher Facing Right (1521) is one of Dürer's most intimate religious prints. (It was also Steinberg's single most expensive print purchase.) Light entering from the left strikes the central pair, while rays emanating from the Christ child's halo and the hermit's candle punctuate the nocturnal landscape. The resulting luminosity is appropriate to a scene depicting Christ revealing himself to the giant Christopher who ferries him across a river—though it is notable that Dürer's distinctive "AD" monogram is also illuminated, as if to declare that the artist is similarly touched by heavenly inspiration.[21] Dürer's engraving of the patron saint of travelers, executed shortly after his return from a trip to the Netherlands, was apposite.

ALBRECHT DÜRER
Knot with a Heart-Shaped Shield
PLATE 6

Dürer's *Knot with a Heart-Shaped Shield* (1505–07) is one of six ornamental woodcuts that he copied after a series of engravings thought to have been designed by Leonardo da Vinci (1452–1519) in around 1490–1500, and which the German artist might have encountered during his Italian sojourn in 1505–07. Scholars have speculated variously that these interlaced designs relate to applied mathematics or represent a theological expression of the perfection and completeness of God's creation; they might also be intended to assert the preeminence of classicism through the production of an ever-finer line—or even have been produced as embroidery patterns.[22] The series provides a rare example of Dürer copying the work of another artist, and the absence of his monogram in the first state suggests he was reluctant to sign an image he had not invented. In Steinberg's impression, a posthumous printing, a subsequent owner of the block added the monogram, testifying to the enduring market for works by Dürer after the artist's death and his critical role in elevating the status of printmaking to an art form in itself.

MARCANTONIO RAIMONDI
David and Goliath
PLATE 7

As Dürer's artistic renown spread rapidly through his prints, even Raphael (1483–1520) took notice. According to Giorgio Vasari, in 1515 the pair exchanged artworks; Dürer sent Raphael a now-lost watercolor self-portrait and received in return a red-chalk drawing of three male nudes.[23] Another point of contact between these masters of the Northern and Italian Renaissance was the printmaker Marcantonio Raimondi (1480–1534). Soon after he arrived in Venice in 1506, Marcantonio notoriously began making engravings after Dürer's religious woodcuts, shamelessly applying the famous "AD" monogram to his versions and offering them as original works by the German artist. Dürer lodged a complaint with the Venetian Senate the same year in what was the first recorded dispute over intellectual property.[24] By 1510, Marcantonio had moved on to Rome, where Raphael quickly engaged him to translate his drawings and paintings into print. This collaboration disseminated Raphael's designs and invigorated his reputation, and while the celebrated partnership was not the first of its kind, it set the course for the development of so-called reproductive printmaking.[25] Steinberg amassed an impressive group of Marcantonio's prints, which likely interested him both for their sheer artistic merit and for their significant role in the "circulating lifeblood of ideas." Of Marcantonio's *David and Goliath* (ca. 1520) he writes, "Busy as he was, Raphael found time to invent compositions specifically for his chief engraver [Marcantonio]. One shows David about to behead the giant Goliath, whom he had just felled with a slingshot and pebble, causing the Philistines to take to their heels with the Israelites in pursuit, while a messenger in the left foreground leaves the picture to bring the good news to King Saul. Compositions such as these were studied by artists throughout Western Europe; like a centrifuge, pictorial energy exploded outward from a rotating hub."[26]

GIOVANNI BATTISTA SCULTORI
David and Goliath
PLATE 8

When Giulio Romano (1499?–1546), Raphael's pupil, relocated to the Gonzaga court at Mantua, he carried that energy with him, introducing the city's artists not only to the new Roman style but also to the concept of reproductive engraving. There he employed printmaker Giovanni Battista Scultori (1503–1575), who, in turn, trained the next generation of engravers, including Giorgio Ghisi, and established Mantua as a disproportionately influential center for the medium. Scultori's *David and Goliath* (1540) interprets a fresco lunette in Giulio's decoration of the Palazzo del Te, the ducal villa on the outskirts of the city.[27] Inspired by Raphael's composition, with the muscular shepherd boy bearing Goliath's sword aloft as he straddles the sprawling giant, Scultori's version so dramatically compresses the pictorial space that the scene resembles a classical bas-relief, an effect heightened by the stone walls in the background. The semi-sculptural quality of the somewhat flattened figures contrasts with Goliath's richly articulated helmet, which recalls the origin of the engraver's art in arms and armor.

MARCANTONIO RAIMONDI AND AGOSTINO DE MUSI
Lo Stregozzo (The Witches' Procession)
PLATE 9

Among the most striking works in Steinberg's collection, *Lo Stregozzo* (The Witches' Procession, 1520s) may originate in the circle around Raphael's workshop, although scholars debate the authorship of both the design and the engraving.[28] In the foreground of Steinberg's impression, the blank tablet, which Marcantonio used for his signature after the monogram controversy with Dürer, indicates that it is a first state. The second state includes an "AV" monogram on the horn blown by the boy at the front of the procession, suggesting that Agostino dei Musi, called Agostino Veneziano (ca. 1490–ca. 1540), completed or reprinted Marcantonio's plate.

Both the unusual subject and some of the figures derive from printed books and images. In the fifteenth and sixteenth centuries, concerns about witchcraft infiltrating communities expanded in tandem with print publishing, encouraging an unprecedented proliferation of demonological material. The *Malleus Maleficarum* (The Hammer of Witches, 1486), the standard medieval treatise on witchcraft, was written by Heinrich Kramer and first published in Speyer. It initiated a spate of printed matter on witchcraft, ranging from treatises by inquisitors and legal scholars to humanist dialogues and popular pamphlets.[29] Dürer's engraving of *The Witch* (ca. 1500; fig. 60), showing a wild, muscular figure with windswept hair riding backward on a goat, provided a direct model

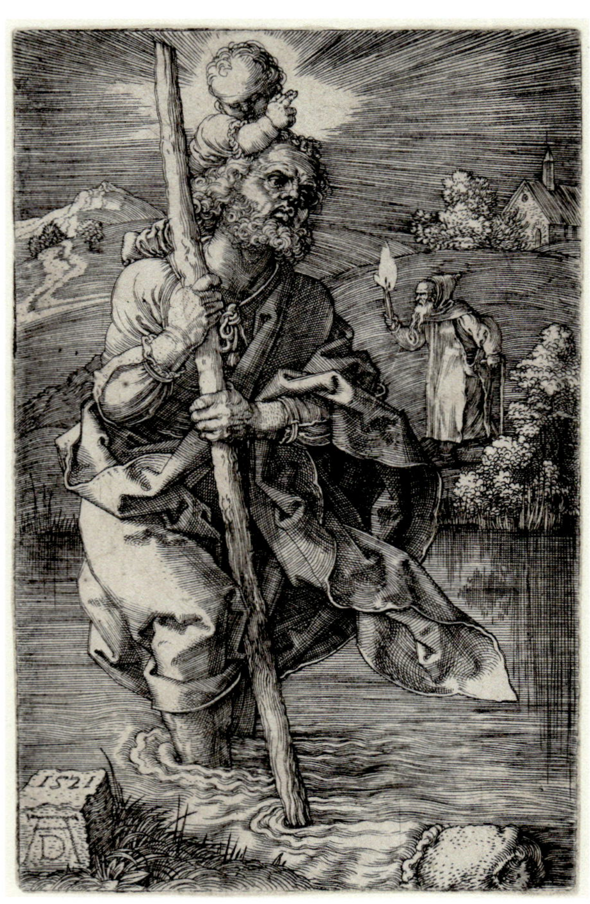

5

ALBRECHT DÜRER

St. Christopher Facing Right 1521

Engraving, only state, 4⅝ × 2¹⁵⁄₁₆ in. (11.8 × 7.4 cm). Meder 52 b/d, Schoch I.94 (2002.830)

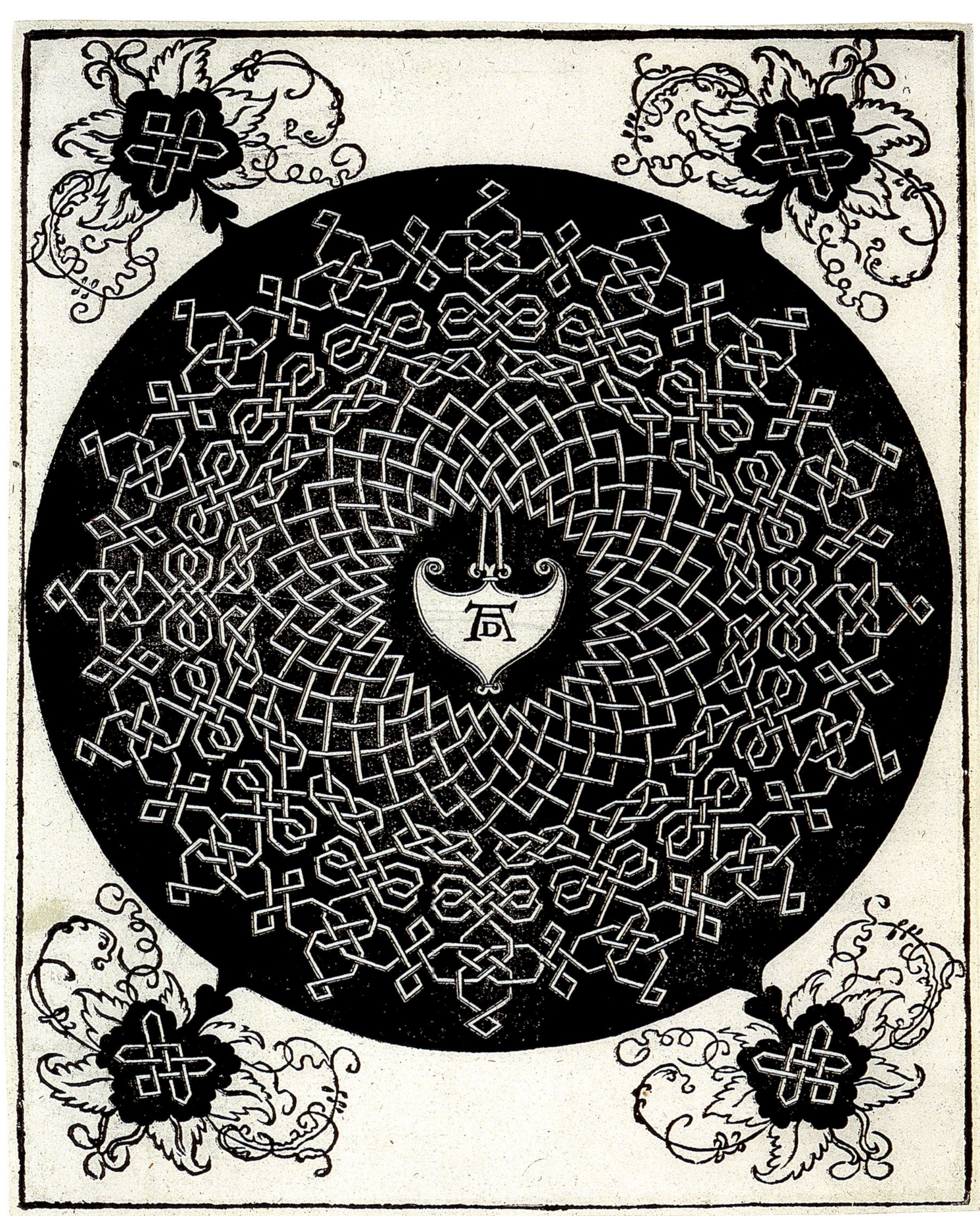

6 ALBRECHT DÜRER

Knot with a Heart-Shaped Shield from *The Six Knots* 1505–07

(FROM THE SECOND EDITION PRINTED AFTER 1528)

Woodcut, second state of two, 10 11/16 × 8 5/16 in. (27.2 × 21.1 cm). Meder 274 2c/c, Schoch II.142 (2002.834)

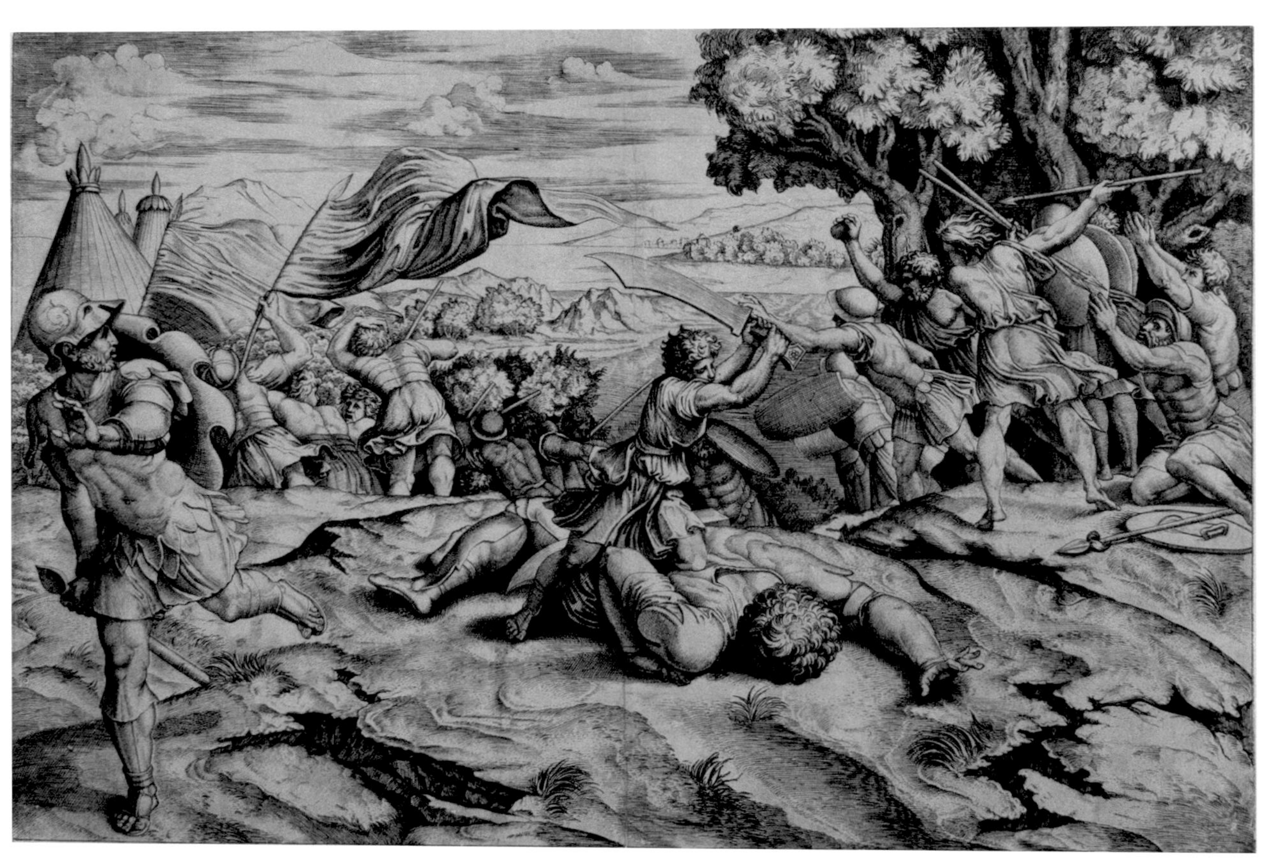

7 MARCANTONIO RAIMONDI

David and Goliath, after a design by Raphael CA. 1520

Engraving, first state of two, 10½ × 15⅜ in. (26.6 × 39 cm). Bartsch XIV.12.10, Shoemaker 53 (2002.1708)

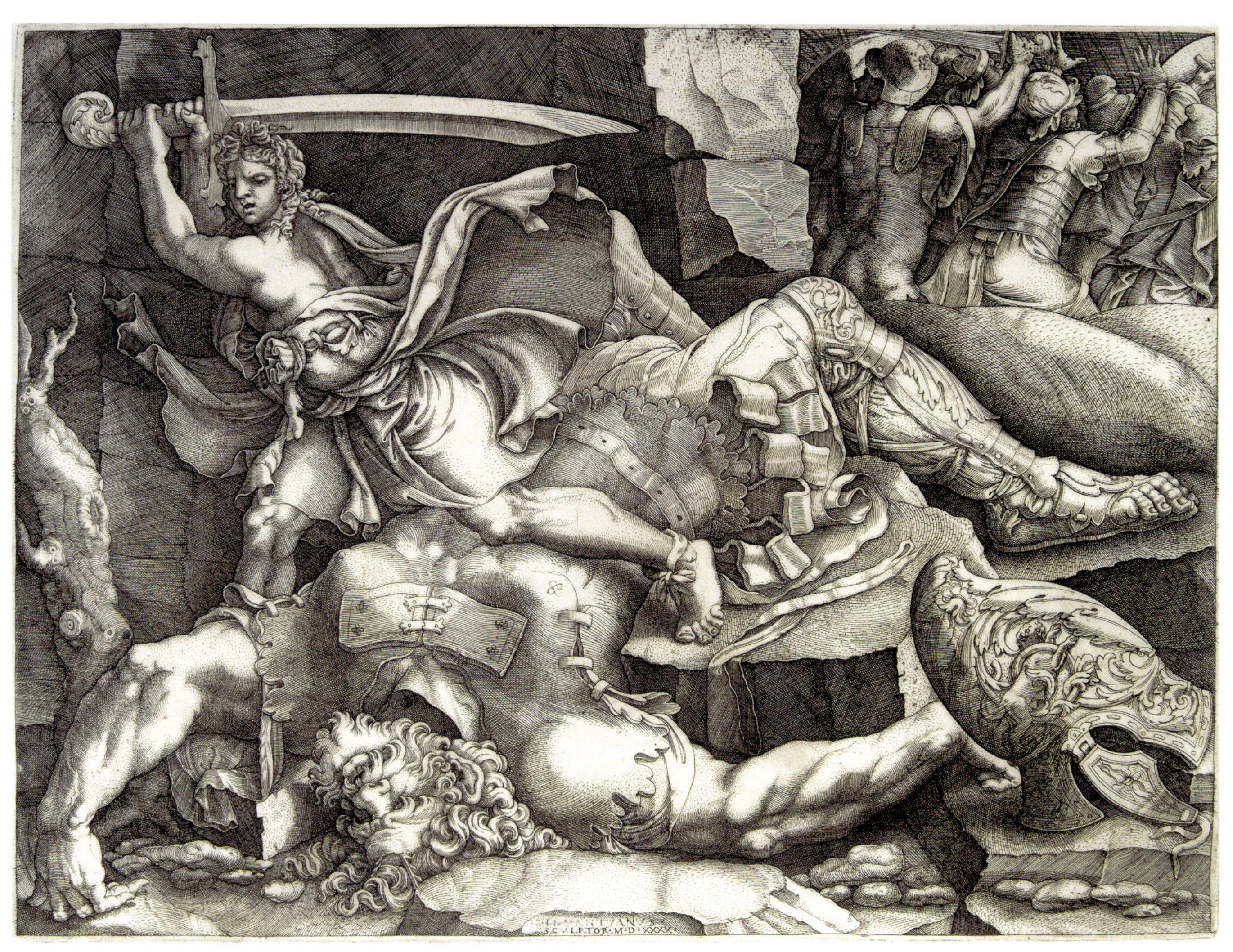

8 GIOVANNI BATTISTA SCULTORI

David and Goliath, after a drawing for a fresco by Giulio Romano 1540

Engraving, second state of two, 14 × 17 13/16 in. (35.6 × 45.2 cm). Massari (1980) 7 (2002.1677)

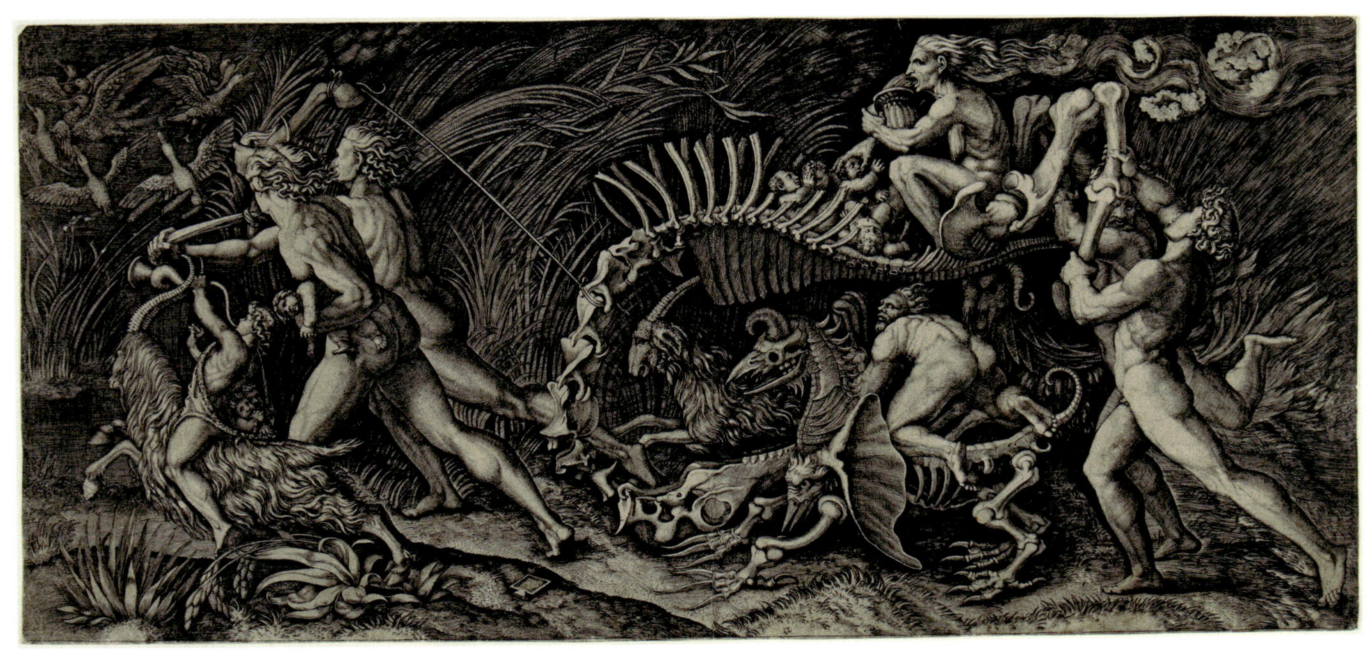

9 MARCANTONIO RAIMONDI AND AGOSTINO DE MUSI, CALLED AGOSTINO VENEZIANO
Lo Stregozzo (The Witches' Procession), after a drawing by Raphael or Giulio Romano 1520s
Engraving, first state of two, 11 13/16 × 24 13/16 in. (30 × 63 cm). Bartsch XIV.321.426.I (2002.1676)

for *Lo Stregozzo*'s nude woman steering a skeletal monster through a marshy netherworld. On her way to a witches' Sabbath, she stuffs wriggling babies—key ingredients in a potion to facilitate flight—into her cauldron, from which rising vapors mingle with her streaming hair. Symbols of evil and death such as goats, skeletal hybrids, and a crouching nude who presents his backside, comprise part of her retinue. The witch's apparent age and rippling musculature diverge from contemporaneous depictions of ideal femininity, while the male nudes conveying her osseous chariot embody a classical perfection. This fusion of a subject of current fascination with an archeological interest in both natural history and classical antiquity, filtered through the burin of a highly skilled engraver to convey a range of tonalities and textures, results in a strikingly original and visually arresting print. Nonetheless, it also demonstrates how artists north and south of the Alps borrowed motifs from one another. In addition to the quotations from Dürer, who had himself been inspired by the figure of Envy in Andrea Mantegna's *Battle of the Sea Gods* (before 1471), the crouching demon and the lead runner in *Lo Stregozzo* reference figures from Michelangelo's Sistine Ceiling and his *Battle of Cascina*.[30] The circulation of this imagery continued in the following century, and is evident, for example in Jusepe de Ribera's *Hecate: Procession to a Witches' Sabbath* (before 1620), a painting in oil on copper.[31]

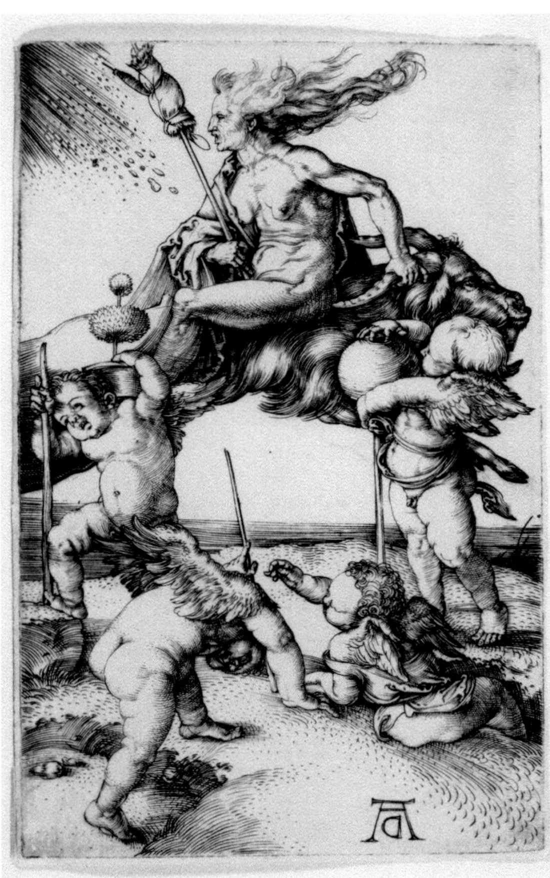

FIG. 60 Albrecht Dürer, *The Witch*, ca. 1500. Engraving, first state of two, 4⅝ × 2¹³⁄₁₆ in. (11.7 × 7.2 cm). Meder 68 1a/b, Schoch I.28. The Metropolitan Museum of Art, Fletcher Fund, 1919.

> ATTRIBUTED TO JUSTE DE JUSTE
> *Nude Figure Leaning on a Socle*
> PLATE 10

Steinberg's collection includes three equally enigmatic prints from a group of seventeen etchings attributed to an artist known as Juste de Juste, or perhaps, Jean Viset, although recent scholarship disputes both these attributions.[32] The works depict muscular yet emaciated male nudes in marionette-like poses: twelve of the prints show singular figures, as in *Nude Figure Leaning on a Socle* (ca. 1543), while the other five depict acrobatic groups of five or six men in pyramid

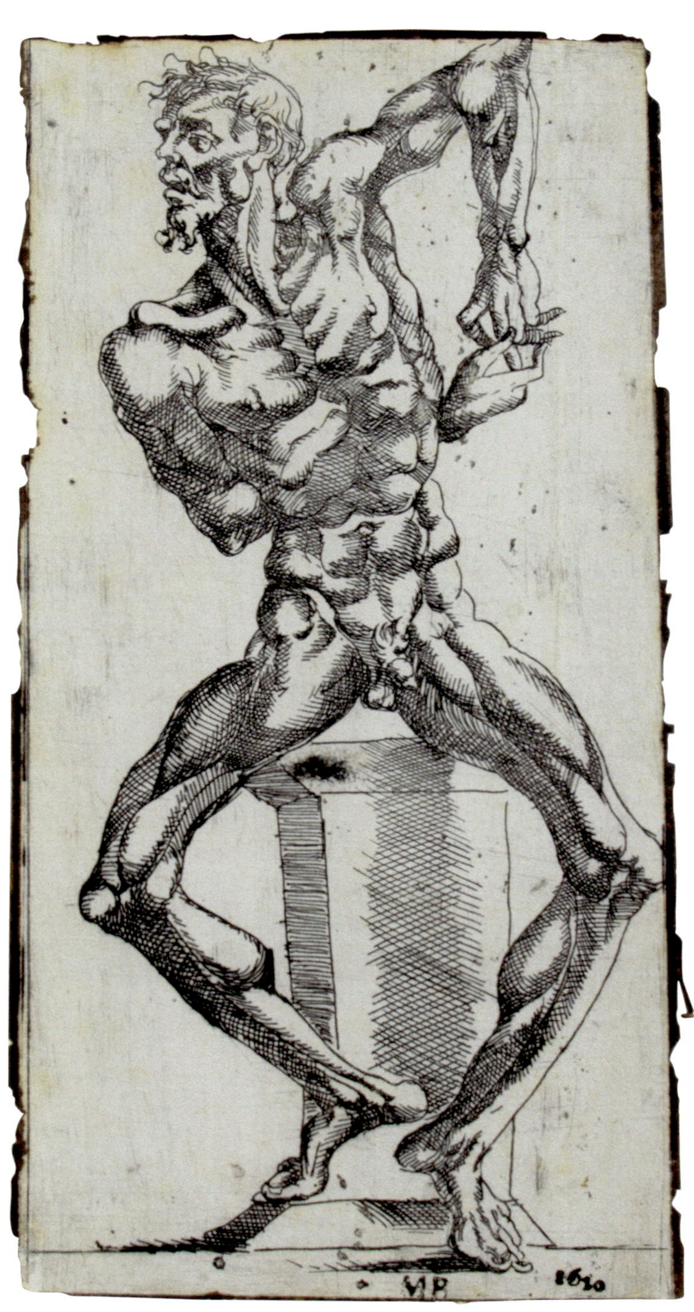

10

ATTRIBUTED TO JUSTE DE JUSTE

Nude Figure Leaning on a Socle CA. 1543

Etching, only state, 6 15/16 × 3 9/16 in. (17.6 × 9.1 cm).
Zerner J17 (2002.1845)

formations. Attempts to decipher the artist's monogram inscribed on some of the pyramid prints have led scholars to posit Juste or Viset, both of whom were active at Fontainebleau. Based on watermark analysis and stylistic divergence from other contemporaneous artists at the French court, however, Catherine Jenkins rejects the Fontainebleau designation. Her comparison of these figures to those in Italian anatomical studies of the period, including écorchés (flayed figures), as well as to the muscular body types of Maarten van Heemskerck, a Haarlem-based artist who spent time in Italy, suggests that the etcher of this series may not be French at all.[33]

These jaunty, almost manic, figures have long intrigued artists, scholars, and collectors alike. German artist Georg Baselitz (b. 1938), for example, has also collected prints from this series, which inform his figural style of small heads and forceful bodies,[34] and he often competed in bidding wars against the print historian and collector Jan van der Waals (1947–2009) when such works came up at auction.[35] In Steinberg's collection, the three impressions join many other prints of single figures by artists like Jacques de Gheyn II (fig. 7), Abraham Bosse (pl. 27), Käthe Kollwitz (pl. 48), and George Grosz (pl. 49), a reflection, as much as anything, of his abiding interest in human form and posture.

ANTONIO FANTUZZI
Jupiter and Antiope
PLATE 11

Steinberg's collection includes works by several artists firmly associated with the School of Fontainebleau, one of the most influential centers of early etching. In about 1530, François I lured French, Italian, and Netherlandish artists to redecorate his royal chateau at Fontainebleau after he had begun rebuilding the original medieval structure.[36] Led by Rosso Fiorentino (1494–1540) and Francesco Primaticcio (1504–1570), this international group of artists contrived a new style characterized by an abundance of sensual ornamental detail and realized in painting, architecture, sculpture, printmaking, and the decorative arts. The etchings of the School of Fontainebleau, produced in an incredible burst of creative energy between 1542 and 1547, were to prove integral to the widespread proclamation of French political and cultural authority.[37]

Antonio Fantuzzi (active 1537–1545), who alone made more than a quarter of the etchings produced at Fontainebleau, was critical to the printmaking project there.[38] In *Jupiter and Antiope* (ca. 1544), an episode from Ovid's *Metamorphoses*, he presents an erotic scene in which the parted drapery echoes Antiope's parted legs, and the fruit and vegetables allude to her fertility. Although not all of his etchings relate directly to designs for Fontainebleau, Jenkins suggests that this composition was intended for a room with a beamed ceiling, indicated by the rectangular block at the upper center.[39] Since the chateau has been so radically altered over the years, etchings like these represent important records of its original splendor.

RENÉ BOYVIN
Echevellée et nue par nuit brune
(Disheveled and naked by dark night)
PLATE 12

The Galerie François 1er at Fontainebleau is one of the few rooms that retains much of its original decoration; it is a brilliant example of the elaborately combined painted and stucco decoration that once embellished much of the chateau's interior. The Flemish painter and designer, Léonard Thiry (ca. 1500–ca. 1550), one of Fiorentino Rosso's principal assistants at Fontainebleau from 1536, worked on the gallery and helped to transform its stucco frames into printed ones in his designs for the twenty-eight-plate series *Livre de la conquête de la Toison d'or* (Jason and the Golden Fleece, 1563).[40] In plate eighteen, *Echevellée et nue par nuit brune* (Disheveled and naked by dark night), engraved by René Boyvin (ca. 1525–1598/1625) in Paris, the decorative motifs of masks, satyrs, nymphs, grotesques, cartouches, and swags epitomize the Fontainebleau style, an amalgam of artifice, eroticism, classicism,

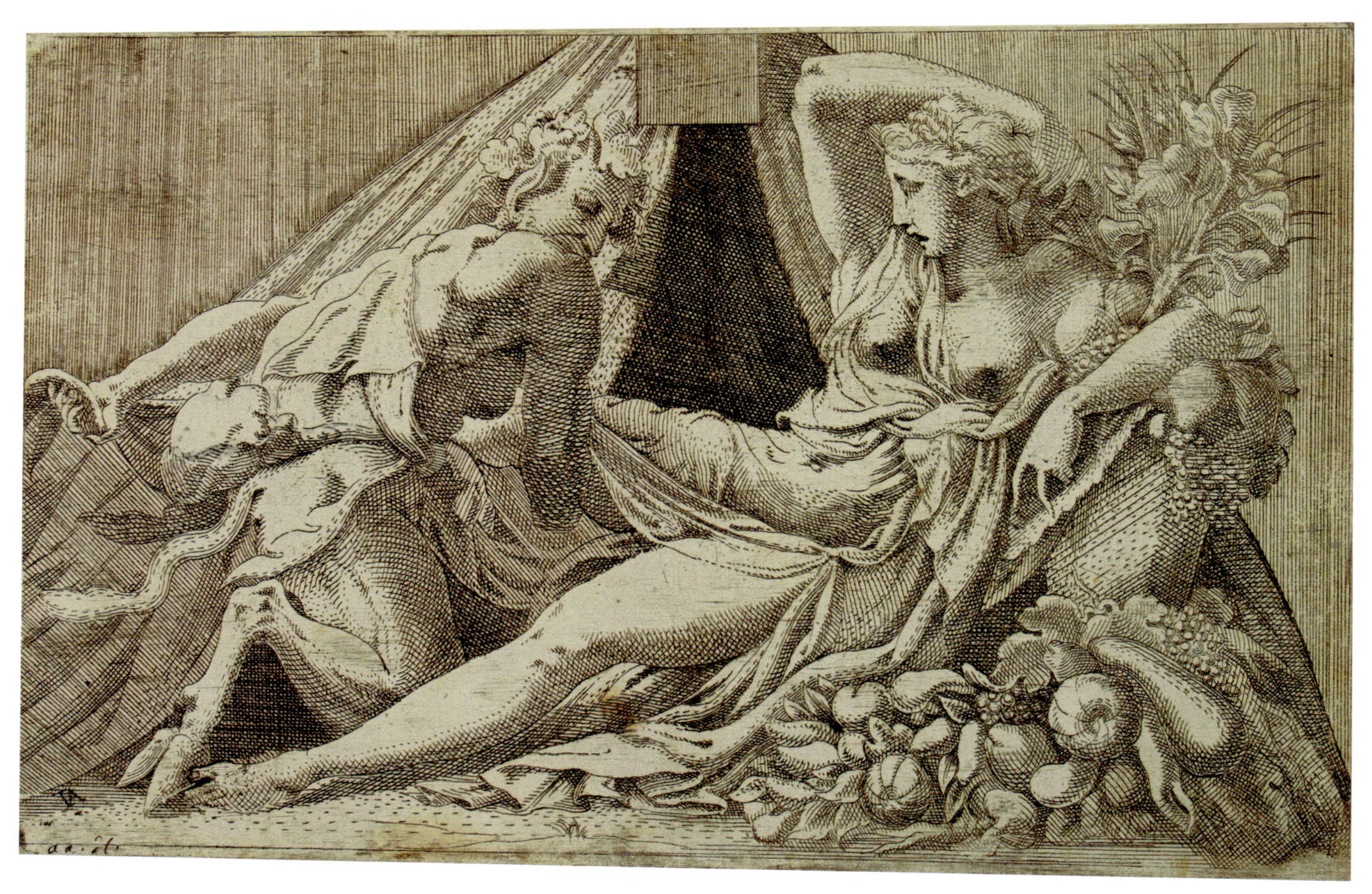

11 ANTONIO FANTUZZI

Jupiter and Antiope, after a design by Francesco Primaticcio CA. 1544

Etching, only state, 6 15/16 × 10 9/16 in. (17.6 × 26.9 cm). Jenkins AF71 (2002.1838)

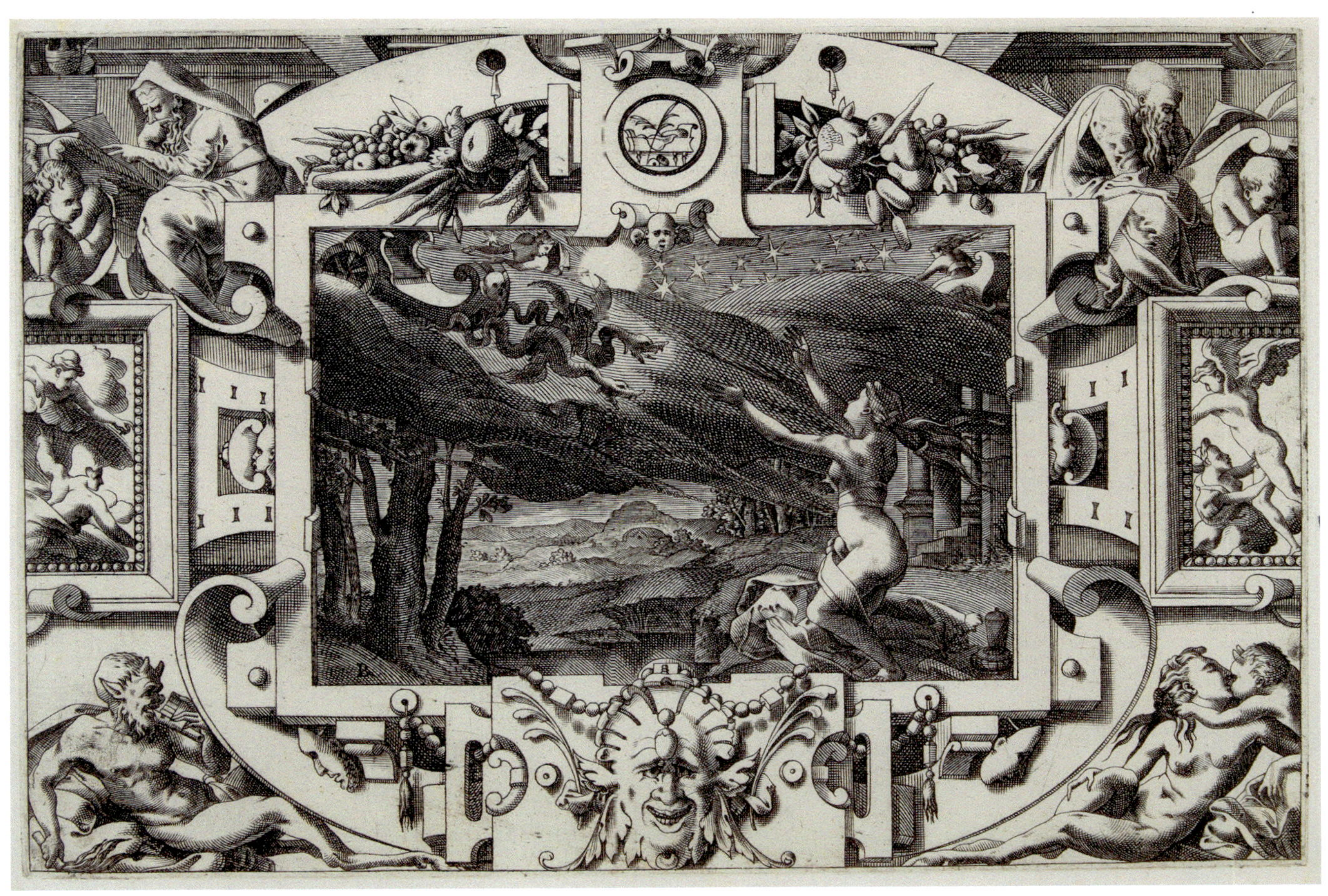

12 RENÉ BOYVIN

Echevellée et nue par nuit brune (Disheveled and naked by dark night), plate 18 from *La Toison d'Or* (The Golden Fleece), after a drawing by Léonard Thiry 1563

Engraving, second state of three, 6¼ × 9$\frac{1}{16}$ in. (15.9 × 23 cm). Robert-Dumesnil 8.56 (2002.310)

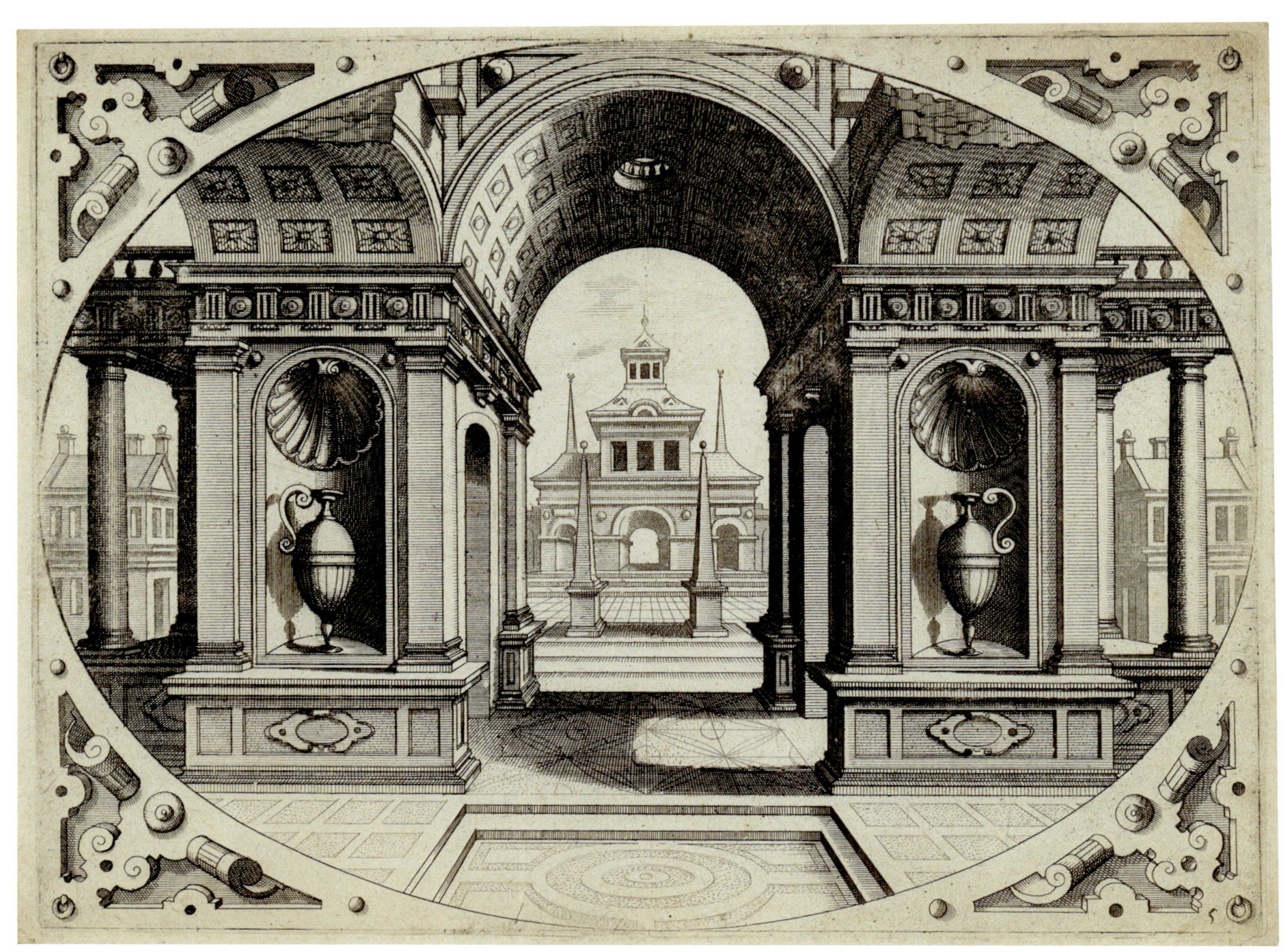

13 JAN VAN DOETECUM AND LUCAS VAN DOETECUM

Plate 5 from *Oval Architectural Perspective Views for Intarsia Work*, after a design by Hans Vredeman de Vries CA. 1560–62 (FROM THE SECOND EDITION PRINTED IN 1601)

Etching, second state of two, 6 5/16 × 8 5/16 in. (16 × 21.1 cm). New Hollstein 188 (2002.2082) abundance, and Michelangelism.[41] Rosso is believed to have developed the ribbon-like scrolls of late-Gothic and Moresque ornament into three-dimensional bands resembling strips of rolled leather, known as strapwork; he combined them with these other motifs to frame and articulate the painted murals in the Galerie François 1er.[42] A vast number of prints made after these decorative designs served to disseminate the style across Europe into the seventeenth century.

JAN VAN DOETECUM AND LUCAS VAN DOETECUM
Plate 5 from *Oval Architectural Perspective Views for Intarsia Work*
PLATE 13

Prints by Netherlandish artists, many of them unfashionable at the time (with the exception of Rembrandt), entered Steinberg's collection during its formative years. As he wrote: "[B]eginning around 1961, I started to look at prints and buy them in bookshops and flea markets and from dealers, finding the unsalable stock they wanted to get rid of, like Goltzius engravings or prints after Rubens . . ."[43] While it might not have been particularly popular with collectors of the 1960s, by the mid-sixteenth century, Netherlandish book and print publishing, centered in Antwerp, was on par with that in such other major cities as Rome, Venice, Nuremberg, and Paris.[44] As in Italy, the owners of the local publishing houses took charge of all aspects of print production. They commissioned designs from artists, contracted with engravers and etchers, employed printers to operate presses, and organized distribution through various networks. Antwerp's most prominent print-publishing house, Aux Quatre Vents (At the Sign of the Four Winds), was run by married proprietors Hieronymus Cock and Volcxken Diericx from 1548 to 1600 (with Diericx as the sole owner after Cock's death in 1570).[45] Shortly after founding the venture, Cock invited Giorgio Ghisi from Mantua to Antwerp, where he engraved five large plates for Aux Quatres Vents.[46] Ghisi's presence encouraged young engravers like Cornelis Cort (1533–1578), who would later engrave the virtuosic *Martyrdom of St. Lawrence* (1571; pl. 16), and his work also provided specific models for Netherlandish printmakers. In plate five (of twenty) from *Oval Architectural Perspective Views for Intarsia Work* (ca. 1560–62) by Jan and Lucas van Doetecum after Hans Vredeman de Vries, for example, barrel vaults and pilaster-framed niches echo the architecture in Ghisi's engraving after Raphael's *School of Athens*.[47]

The van Doetecums' print also exhibits two features that were to prove essential to the success of the genre.[48] Firstly, Cock and Diericx introduced the concept of the print series to the market, encouraging buyers to collect complete sets of images rather than single sheets. This inevitably increased sales. In addition, the van Doetecums, who worked for Aux Quatre Vents for more than a decade, created the varied widths characteristic of engraved lines by using the more expedient process of etching, biting their plates multiple times, and sometimes even going over the etched lines with a burin to produce a pointed end.[49] In this composition, Vredeman de Vries blends classical architecture—coffered barrel vaults, niches, and a colonnaded courtyard—with such local vernacular elements as gabled roofs and chimneys as well as strapwork ornament to create a style that could be applied across the visual and decorative arts. This series was intended for woodworkers, who used the etchings as models for inlaid designs in paneling and cabinetry, but like other ornamental and architectural prints, they also have aesthetic value in their own right.[50]

GIORGIO GHISI
The Prophet Joel
PLATE 14

After his stint in Antwerp and an extended period in France, Giorgio Ghisi (1520–1582) returned to Italy in the late 1560s, where he continued to reproduce the work of prominent painters, including Michelangelo. Unlike his contemporary Raphael, however, Michelangelo did not hire a talented engraver to reproduce his designs. Nevertheless, both during his lifetime

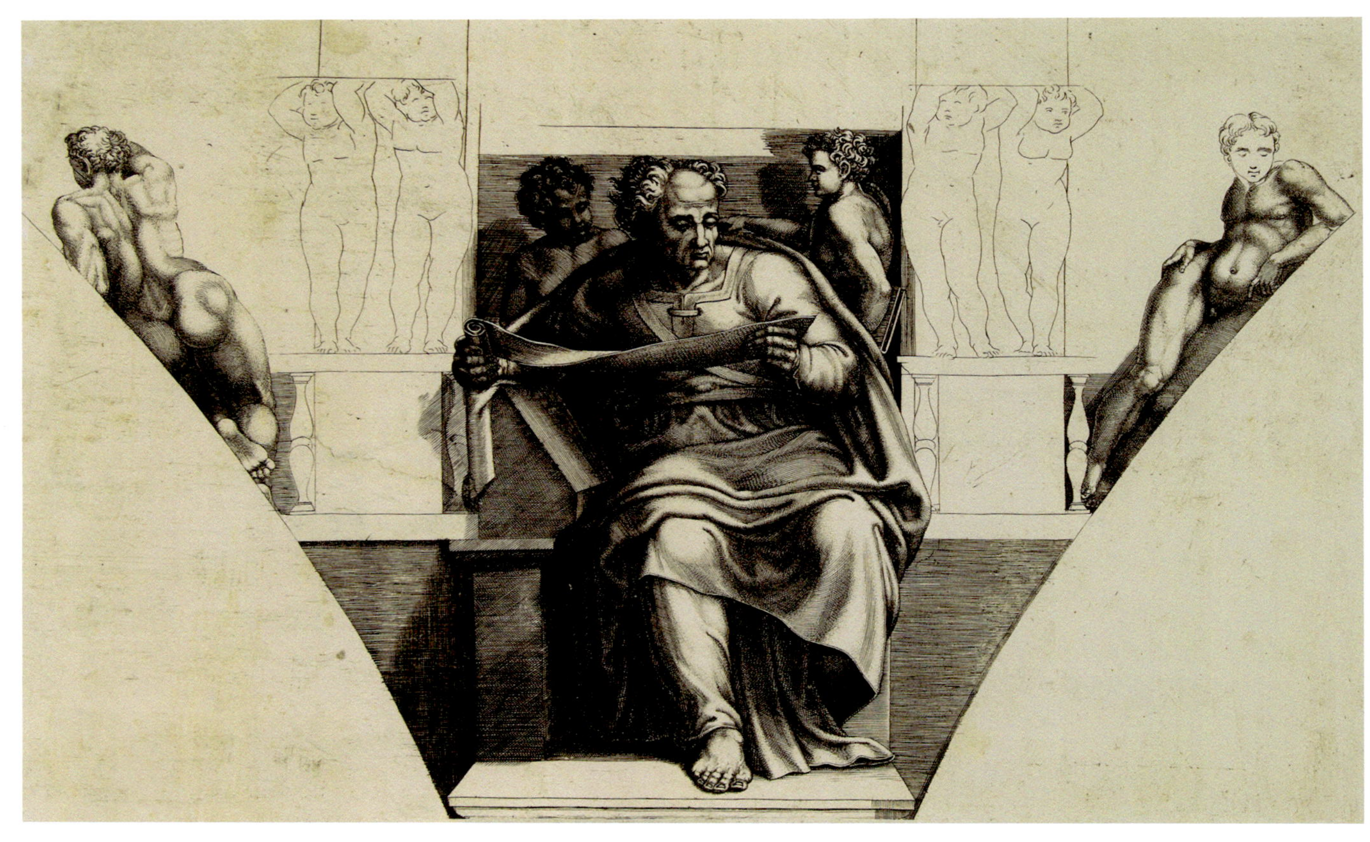

14 GIORGIO GHISI

The Prophet Joel, after a fresco by Michelangelo EARLY 1570s

Engraving, first state of five, $9^{13/16} \times 15^{3/4}$ in. (25 × 40 cm). Boorsch and Lewis 44 (2002.1743)

and for centuries afterward, printmakers drawn to Michelangelo's paintings, drawings, sculpture, and architecture disseminated knowledge of his works far beyond the confines of their original locations.[51] While the central Creation frescoes of the Sistine Ceiling are among the most instantly recognized works of art in the world today, in the decades after their completion in 1512, the prophets, seers, *ignudi* (nudes), and ancestors of Christ in the transitional space between the ceiling and the walls were the most commonly reproduced motifs. Ghisi's engravings are the most accurate of these published through the end of the eighteenth century.[52] What Michelangelo rendered in paint on a curved surface high above the viewer's head—invented architecture, brightly cloaked figures, supple flesh tones, and marble and bronze statues—Ghisi translated into six large-scale, black-and-white images on a flat page. He adjusted the figures' proportions to account for the different vantage point and intensified the shading, emphasizing their musculature to compensate for the absence of coloristic effects.

Among Steinberg's many prints of the Sistine Chapel frescoes is an extremely rare proof state of *The Prophet Joel* (early 1570s), which elucidates Ghisi's method of working section by section, incising outlines and then creating shading with hatching and crosshatching. He inked and printed this sheet before returning to the plate to complete the composition, which, in the final version, includes a lower half printed from a second plate. Since Ghisi's engravings were not published as a set until 1570, the 1540 date printed on several of them was perhaps intended to give an additional air of authenticity, allowing him to claim in a flooded market that his work was the "original."[53]

ATTRIBUTED TO NICOLÒ BOLDRINI
Six Saints
PLATE 15

Like Raphael, the renowned Venetian painter Titian (1485/90–1576) used prints to broadcast his fame. And there were many skilled woodcutters with whom he could work in Venice, a major center of book and map production. Early in his career, Titian created designs expressly for woodcut, some of which were large, multiblock prints. By the 1530s, he began designing prints that reinterpreted his paintings.[54] According to Giorgio Vasari, the artist drew directly on the block for *Six Saints* (1525–35), a composition that reprises in reverse the lower half of his altarpiece for the Venetian church of San Nicolò dei Frari.[55] Excluding the upper, heavenly scene of the Virgin and Child crowned by putti, Niccolò Boldrini's bold carving sets the lower figures of Sebastian, Francis, Anthony of Padua, Peter, Nicholas, and Catherine of Siena against a purely linear background that removes them from a pictorial context and serves, like a gold-ground painting, to make the figures more iconic and yet more immediate. A faint square behind Sebastian's head indicates that a recarved plug was inserted to make a correction or repair to the woodblock. Compared to the painting, in which Sebastian gazes downward, the woodcut version increases the pathos of Sebastian's anguished visage, recalling one of Laocoön's sons from the famed Hellenistic sculpture that was a favorite of Renaissance artists. While lack of textual sources has engendered scholarly debates over how many of Titian's woodcuts were actually carved by Boldrini,[56] the artist's collaboration with Cornelis Cort, his chief engraver, is well documented.

CORNELIS CORT
The Martyrdom of St. Lawrence
PLATE 16

In 1565, after establishing himself as a highly proficient reproductive engraver at Aux Quatre Vents in Antwerp, Cornelis Cort (1533–1578) traveled to Italy, where Titian commissioned him to engrave eight compositions under his direct supervision in the painter's own home.[57] During the second of Cort's two lengthy stays in Venice (in 1565–66 and 1571–72), Titian likely supplied the printmaker with a drawing that combined elements from his two painted versions of *The*

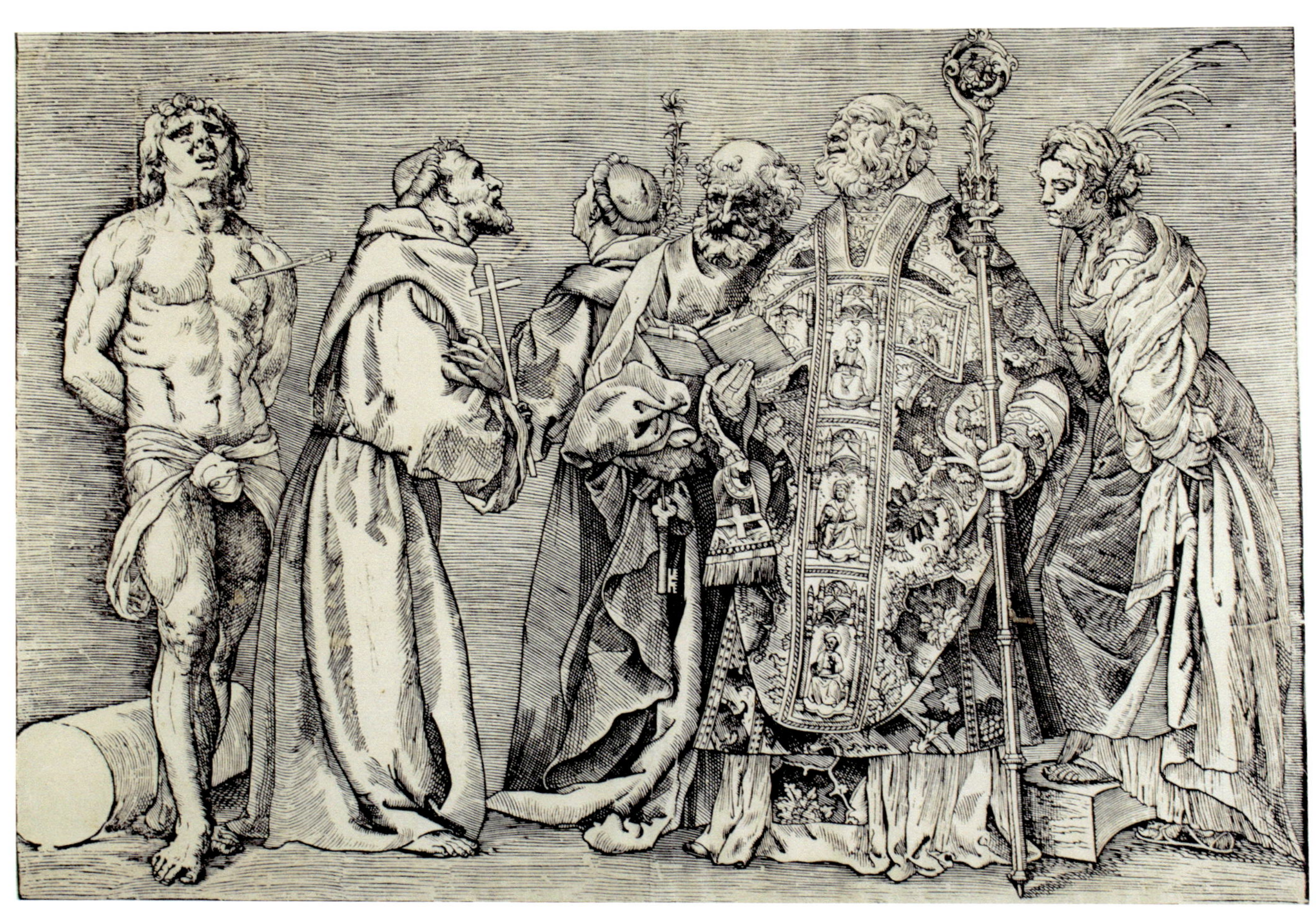

15

ATTRIBUTED TO NICOLÒ BOLDRINI

Six Saints, after a drawing and painting by Titian 1525–35

Woodcut, 14¾ × 21⅛ in. (37.4 × 53.7 cm). Rosand and Muraro 35 (2002.1653)

16

CORNELIS CORT

The Martyrdom of St. Lawrence, after paintings by Titian 1571

Engraving, only state, 19⁷⁄₁₆ × 13¾ in. (49.4 × 35 cm). New Hollstein 126 (2002.2097)

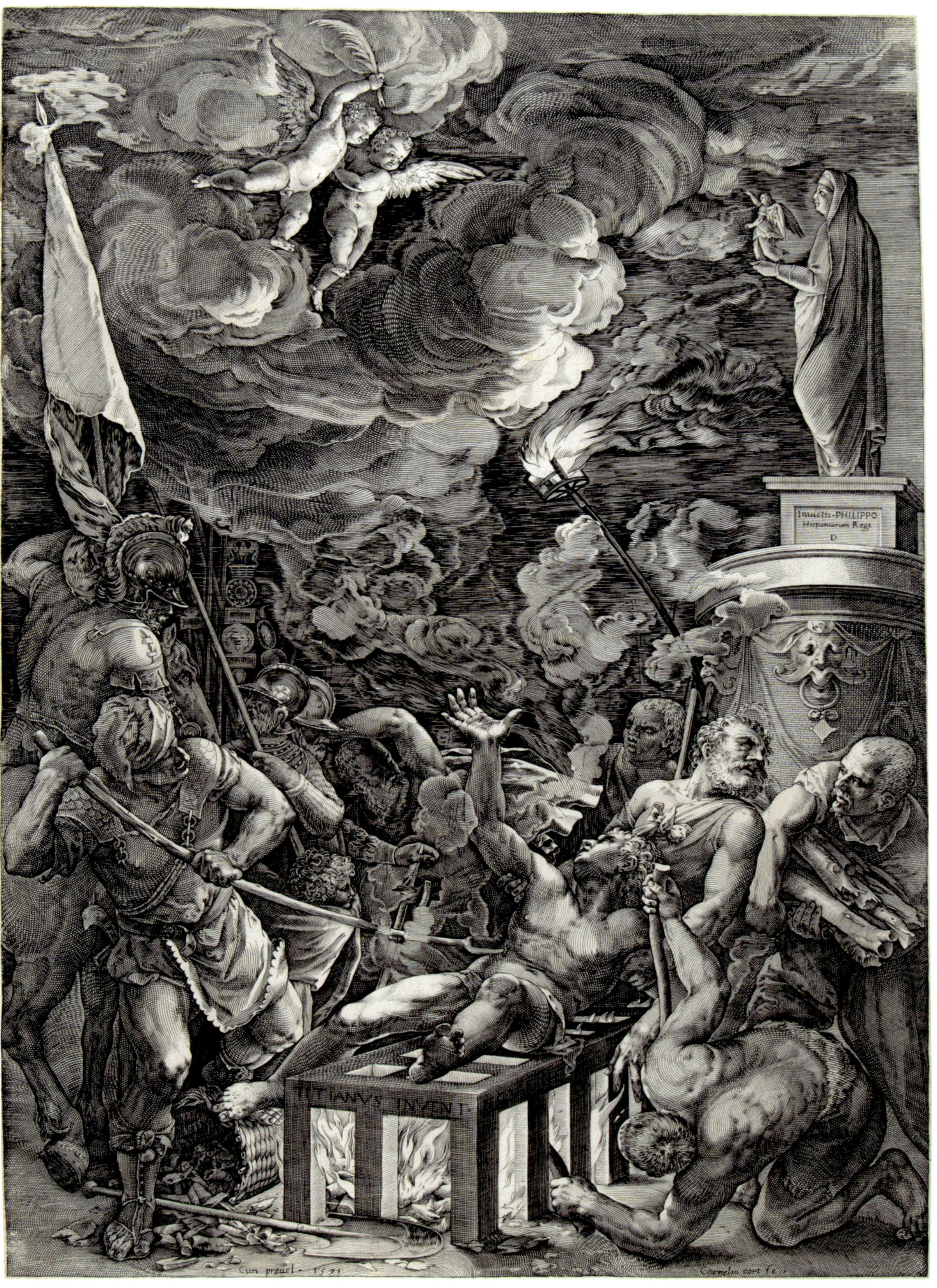
Inuictis · PHILIPPO
Hispaniarum Regi
D
TITIANVS INVENT.
Cum preuel · 1571
Cornelio cort fe ·

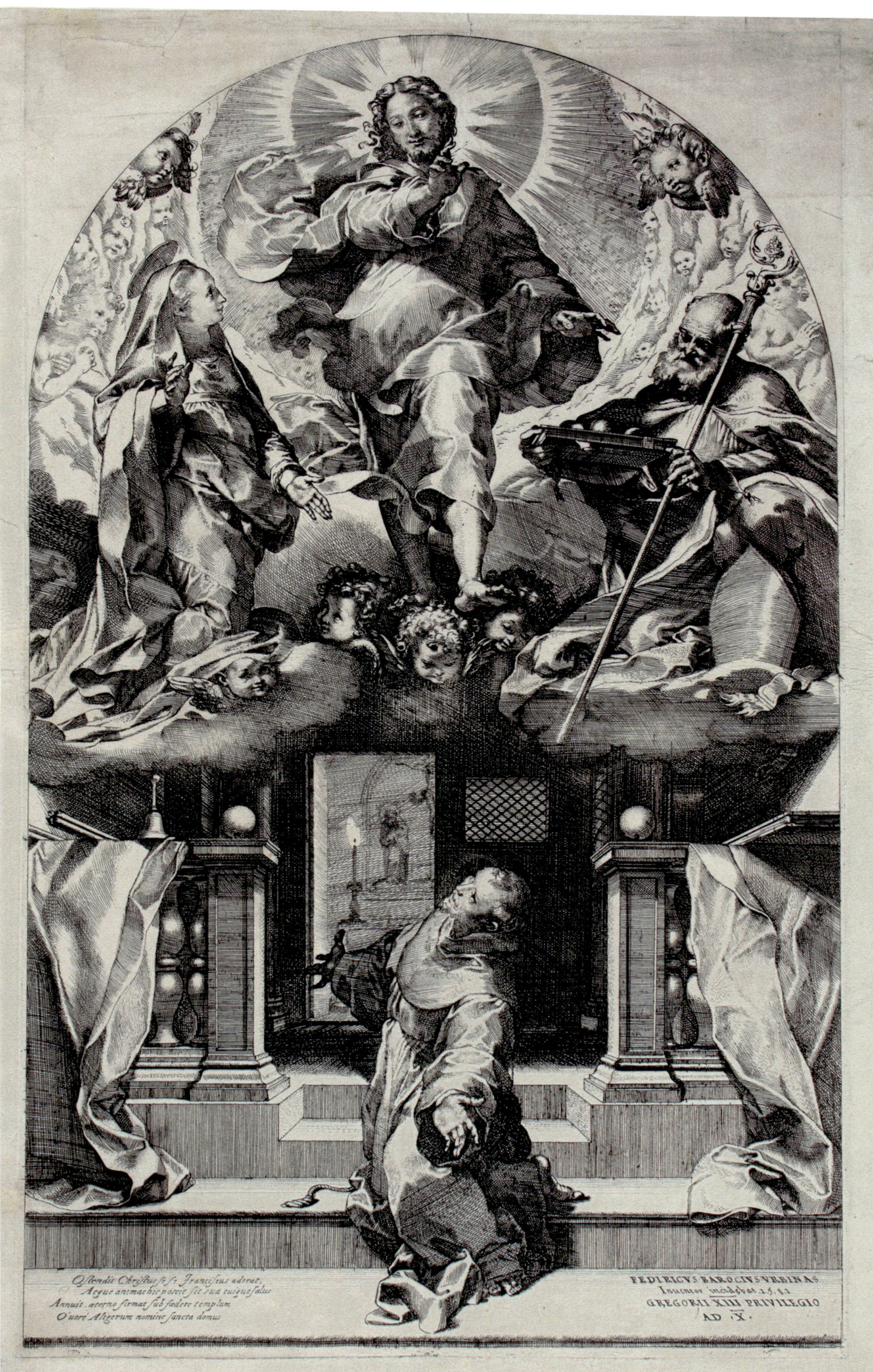
Ostendit Christus se, s. Franciscus adorat,
Aeque animae hic poscit sit sua cuique salus
Annuit. aeterno firmat sub foedere templum
O uere Aligerum nomine sancta domus
FEDERICVS BAROCIVS VRBINAS
Inuentor incidebat. 1581
GREGORII XIII PRIVILEGIO
AD X.

Martyrdom of St. Lawrence, one of which he had recently completed for King Philip II of Spain. (The resulting print evidently captivated Steinberg; his collection at the Blanton includes two versions by Cort, in addition to an anonymous copy in reverse.) Inscriptions on Cort's engraving (1571) reveal the specific roles of the artists in its production: on the martyr's grill, "TITIANUS INVENT" credits Titian as the designer; at the lower right, "Cornelio cort fe" is Cort's signature; "Cu[m] prevel. 1571" at lower center indicates the copyright protection granted to Titian by the Venetian authorities, a practice that artists increasingly employed to prevent unauthorized copying of their designs and to maintain control of their markets.[58] Cort translates the nocturnal scene into a mesmerizing interplay of lines comprising the billowing smoke and clouds, which nearly distract from the gruesome scene below of St. Lawrence's roasting on the grill. The expressive quality of the artist's distinctive swelling and tapering burin work—known as the "*schwellende Taille*" (swelling line)—made him a sought-after engraver who produced prints after Netherlandish and Italian artists of his own day and earlier, including Federico Barocci, Frans Floris, and Raphael.[59] Cort's engraving style would be fully developed by the next generation of Netherlandish engravers, most notably by artists in the circle of Hendrick Goltzius.

FEDERICO BAROCCI
Il Perdono di San Francesco (The Pardon of St. Francis)
PLATE 17

A painter best known for the brilliant coloring, graceful poses, and profound spiritual tenor of his work, Federico Barocci (1535–1612) had two of his designs engraved by Cort. After the printmaker's death in 1578, Barocci produced four prints of his own, including one after his altarpiece of 1576 for the church of San Francesco at Urbino.[60] *Il Perdono di San Francesco* (The Pardon of St. Francis, 1581) depicts the kneeling saint receiving a heavenly vision of the Virgin, St. Nicholas, and Christ, who promises indulgences (reduced time in purgatory) for pilgrims who visit the saint's chapel near Assisi, pictured in the background. Although Barocci was not the first printmaker to etch and engrave on a single plate, this print represents the successful combination of the techniques.[61] After coating the copperplate with an acid-resistant ground, drawing his design with an etching needle, and applying acid to the plate, Barocci protected areas he wished to remain lightly etched by covering them with more ground. He then added further lines and reapplied acid to more deeply etch any exposed lines, resulting in a plate that would print in a spectrum of lights to darks.[62] Barocci returned to the plate with an engraving burin to strengthen dark areas, add fine stippling, and introduce more middle tones.[63] He thus constructed complex pictorial effects appropriate to a scene that juxtaposes heaven and earth. While pilgrims to San Francesco's chapel probably purchased this print as a guarantee of spiritual reward, much like Ostendorfer's Regensburg woodcut earlier in the century, Barocci's earthly rewards included an exclusive monopoly on the subject of *Il Perdono* for ten years, as well as direct payments from individual worshippers who purchased the print during his lifetime.[64]

HENDRICK GOLTZIUS
Holy Family with the Young St. John the Baptist from *Meisterstiche* (Masterpieces)
PLATE 18

The work of Hendrick Goltzius (1558–1617) reflects the crosscurrents between Italian and Netherlandish artists at the end of the sixteenth century that gave rise to an international Mannerist style in print, one that remained influential in the next generation through the work of his pupils. In his early years, Goltzius engraved for Aux Quatre Vents in Antwerp, but by 1582, his ability as a designer and engraver of his own compositions allowed him to become an independent print publisher in Haarlem.[65] In works like the *Farnese Hercules* (1592; fig. 3), he combined his knowledge of Italian art—acquired through the study of Italian prints, engraving

17 FEDERICO BAROCCI
Il Perdono di San Francesco (The Pardon of St. Francis) 1581
Etching and engraving, only state, 21⅛ × 12¾ in. (53.7 × 32.4 cm). Pillsbury and Richards 73 (2002.1775)

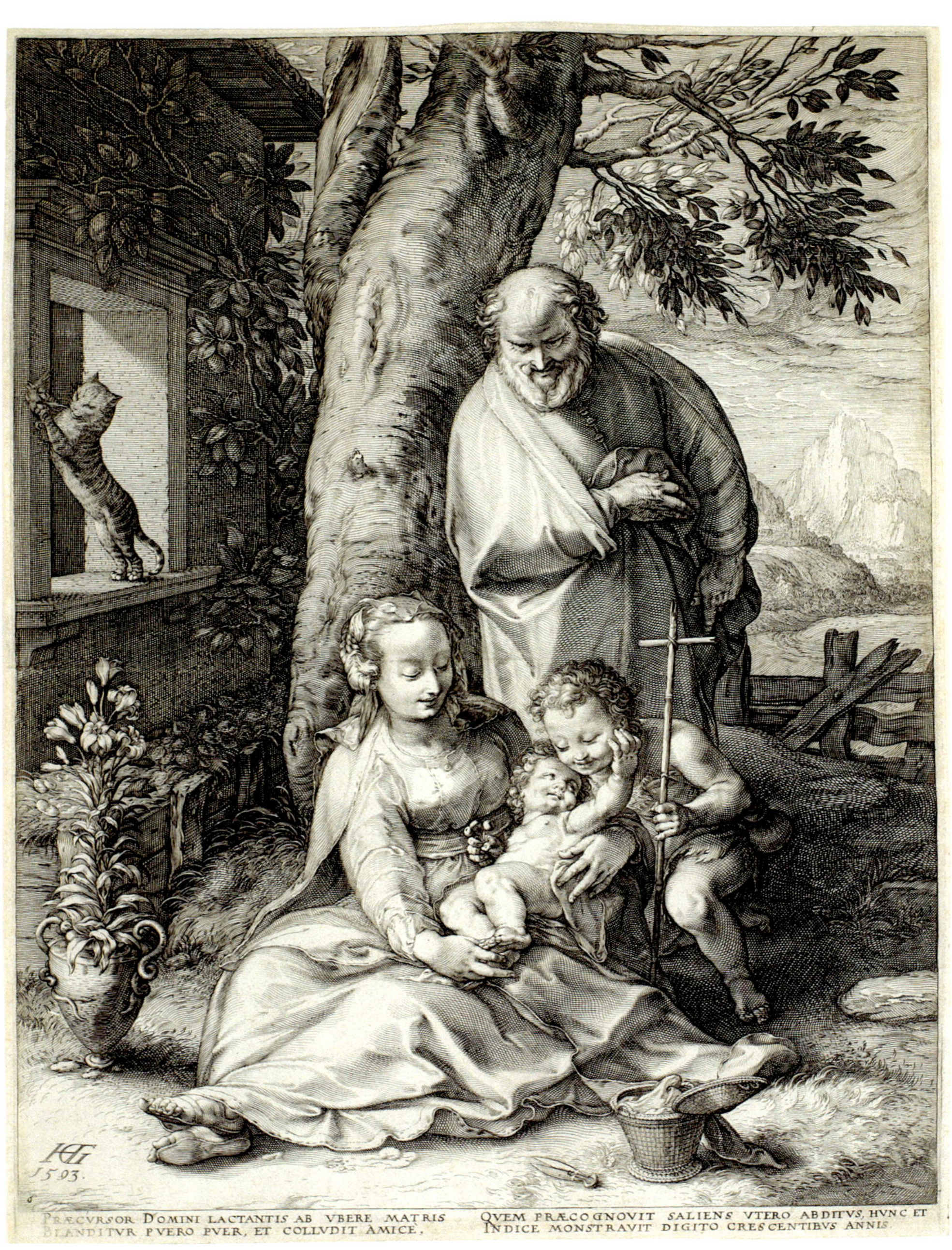

18 HENDRICK GOLTZIUS

Holy Family with the Young St. John the Baptist from *Meisterstiche* (Masterpieces) 1593

Engraving, third state of three, 18¾ × 14 in. (47.7 × 35.5 cm). New Hollstein 13 (2002.2180) after other Netherlandish artists who had traveled to Italy, and visiting Italy himself—with innovative burin work that introduced an even greater variety to Cort's swelling and tapering lines. Here, the muscles of the ancient marble statue seem to strain against Goltzius's distinctive graphic system of mesh-like webs. At the same time, he was also deeply engaged with the work of virtuoso printmakers of the past. In his series of six large-format engravings known as the *Meisterstiche* (Masterpieces, 1593–94), analogous to the three famous *Meisterstiche* of Albrecht Dürer, Goltzius ingeniously inverts the concept of reproductive engraving. Each of the six plates depicting the birth and early life of Christ is rendered in the style of a distinguished predecessor. Demonstrating a "chameleon-like ability"[66] to invent new compositions and emulate the hand of such masters of engraving as Federico Barocci and Lucas van Leyden as well as the great Dürer, Goltzius claims artistic preeminence over them all.[67] In *Holy Family with St. John the Baptist* (1593), Goltzius combines compositional elements from two paintings by Barocci, which he probably encountered in reproductive engravings by Cornelis Cort, to create a tender scene with sweetly sentimental figure types characteristic of the Italian painter.[68] To convey Barocci's graceful style, Goltzius restricts his singularly bold crosshatching to such rounded forms as John the Baptist's shin and left arm, and employs a range of subtler, yet still energetic lines in the rest of the composition.

THE SEVENTEENTH CENTURY

JAN SAENREDAM
Vanitas
PLATE 19

Trained by Hendrick Goltzius, Jan Saenredam (1565–1607) was among a talented group of artists, including Jacques de Gheyn II, Jacob Matham, and Jan Muller, whose engravings after Goltzius's designs extended the idiom of Mannerist print, with swelling and tapering burin lines that seem to caress the sensuously graceful human figures they shape.[69] In this engraving, *Vanitas* (1600), after a drawing by Abraham Bloemaert (1566–1651),[70] a female personification of Vanity cradles a vase in one hand and, with the other, gestures toward precious objects arrayed on a table; an equally beautiful calligraphic inscription that translates as "vanity of vanities, all is vanity," a quotation from Ecclesiastes 1:2, cautions the viewer against prizing transitory things. Saenredam transforms the inscription, usually confined to a caption in the lower margin, into both a literal and figurative frame that ironically reinforces not only the seductive pull but also the admonitory message of the image. The sinuously intertwined letters echo the shape of the rising smoke, an oft-used symbol of *vanitas*. Through the proliferation of handwriting manuals and penmanship competitions in the Netherlands, calligraphy achieved a high status among the learned elite.[71] Like other engravers who relied on scholars to supply Latin captions for their images, Saenredam likely turned to a local humanist for the design of the textual elements, which he then engraved to mimic the strokes of a quill pen.[72]

JAN VAN DE VELDE II
Ignis (Fire) from *The Four Elements*
PLATE 20

Jan van de Velde II (1593–1641) was the son of a famed calligrapher who had written the manual *Spieghel der Schryfkonste* (Mirror of the Art of Writing, 1605). He represents a link between two exemplary styles of Netherlandish printmaking.[73] Apprenticed to Jacob Matham, stepson of Hendrick Goltzius, Van de Velde was trained as an engraver in the Mannerist idiom. The strong tonal contrasts of his enchanting "night pieces" as well as his fluidly executed etched landscapes, influenced those of Rembrandt himself. *Ignis* (Fire, 1622), is one from a series depicting the four elements by Van de Velde after designs by Willem Buytewech. The Latin captions, composed by a humanist contemporary of Van de Velde's, describe both the dangerous

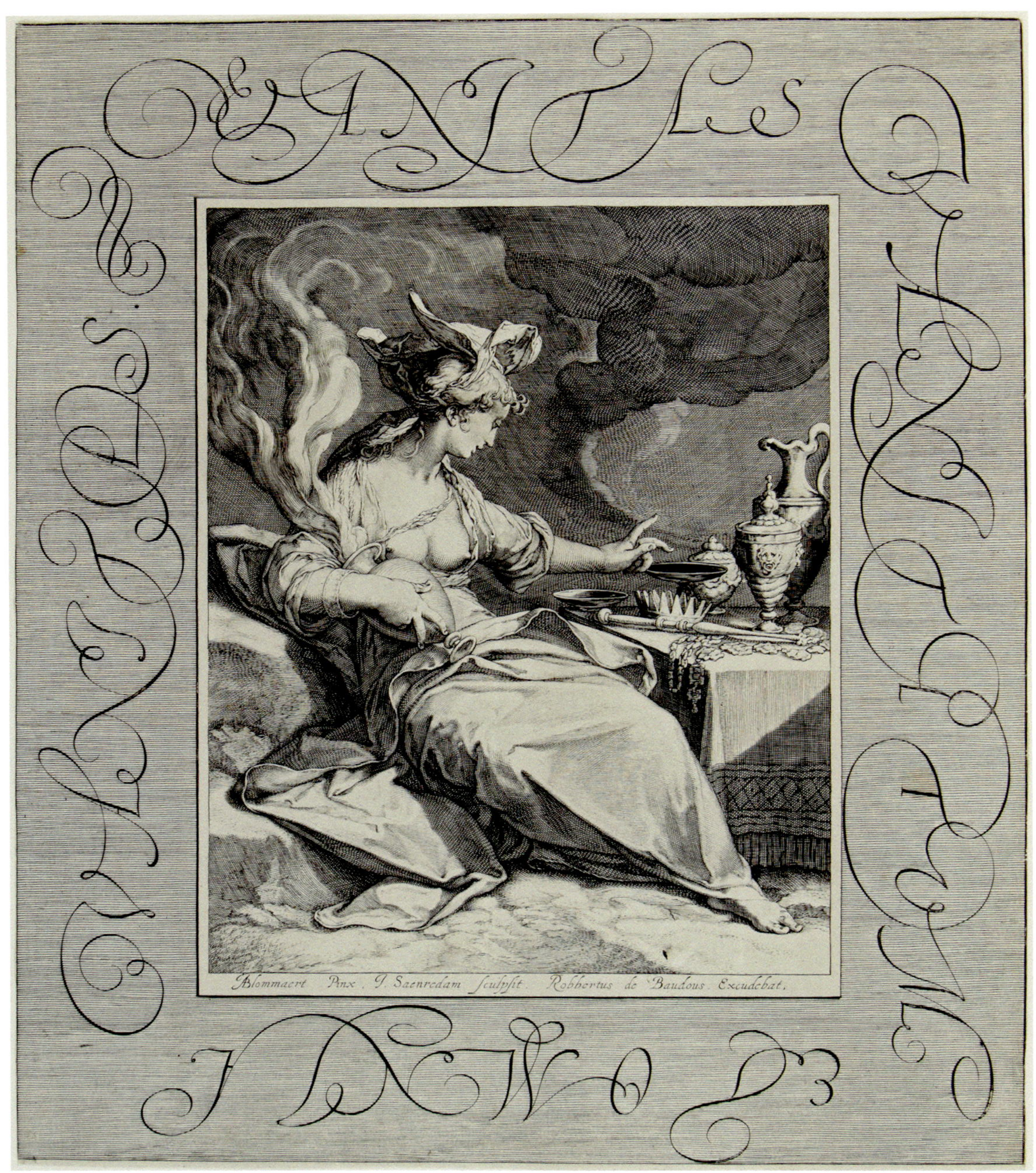

19 JAN SAENREDAM

Vanitas, after a drawing by Abraham Bloemaert 1600

Engraving, second state of two, 14¾ × 12⅝ in. (37.5 × 32 cm). Hollstein 112 (2002.2268)

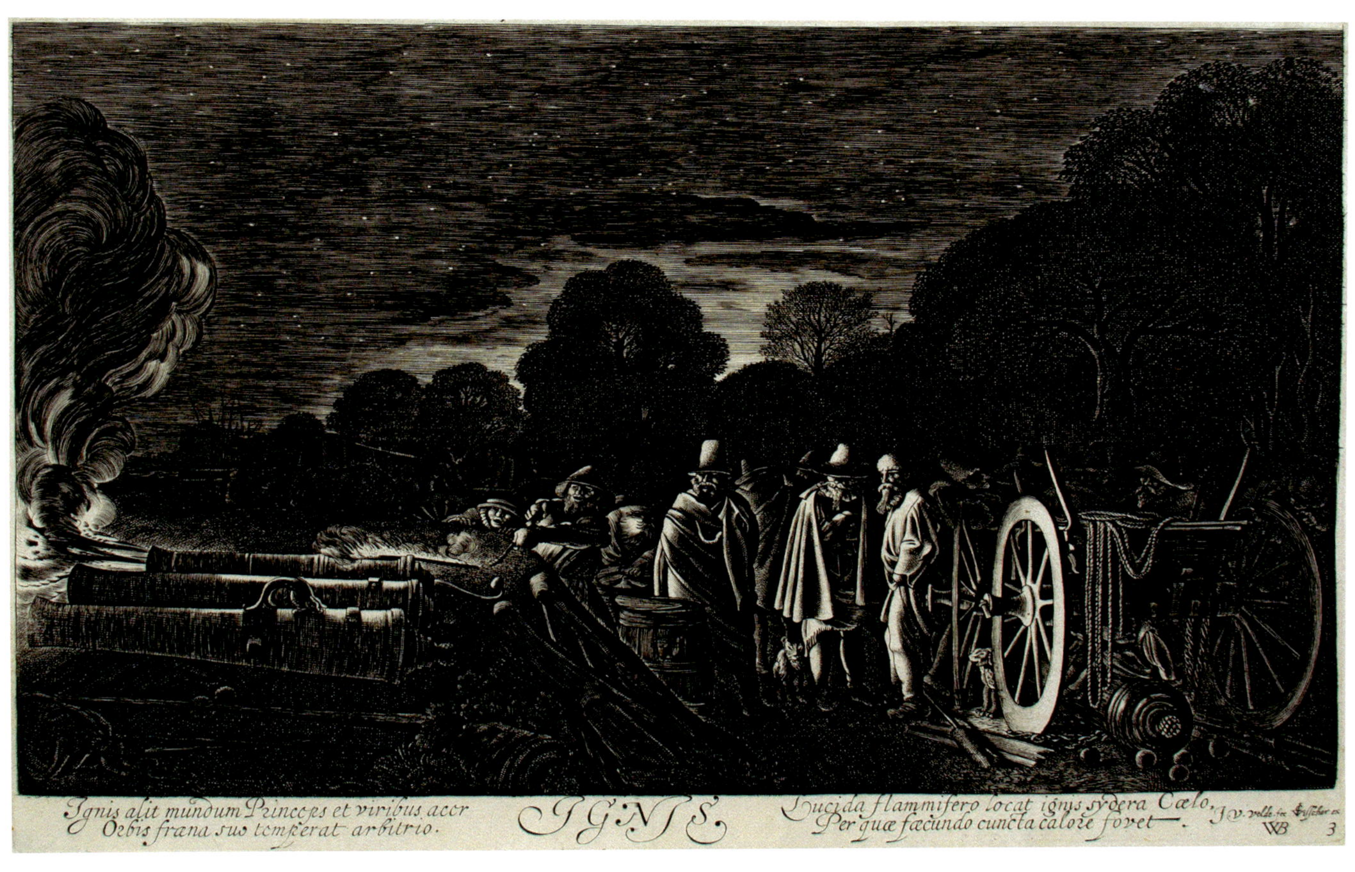

20 JAN VAN DE VELDE II

Ignis (Fire) from *The Four Elements*, after a design by Willem Buytewech 1622

Etching and engraving, second state of five, $7\frac{5}{16} \times 11\frac{7}{16}$ in. (18.5 × 29 cm). Hollstein 20 (2002.2313)

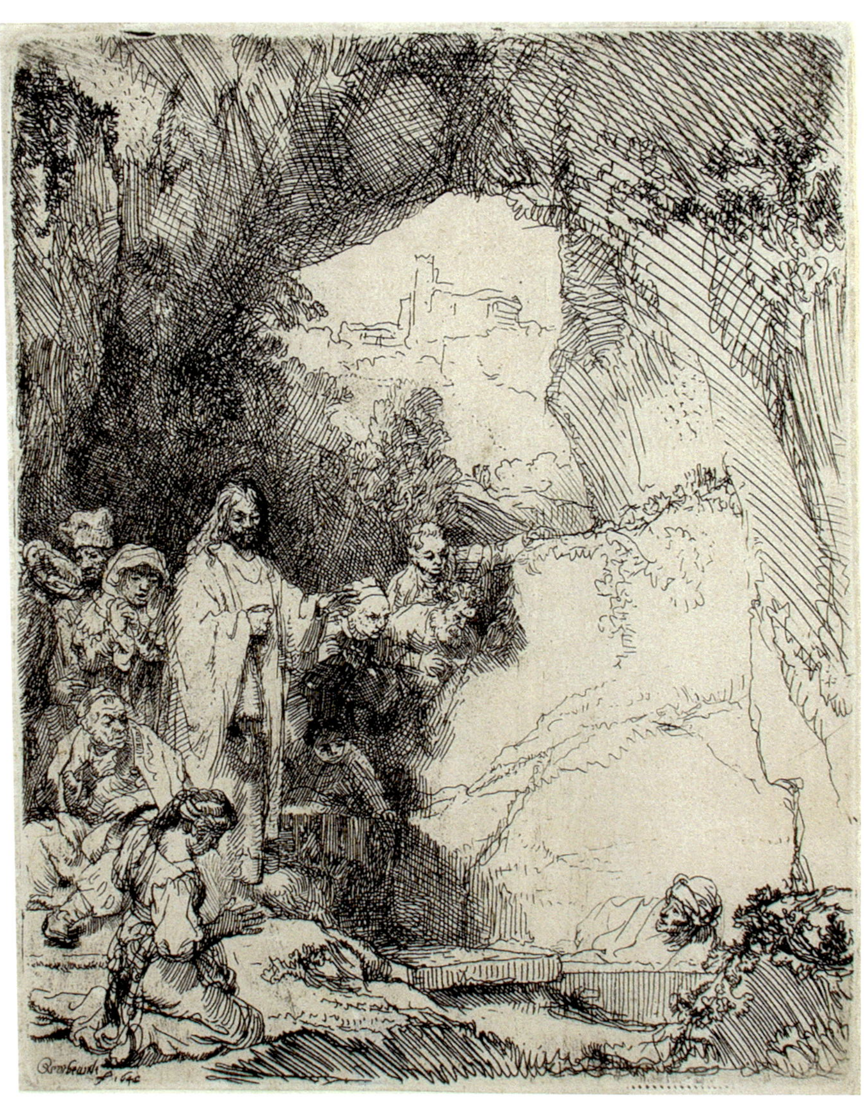

21 REMBRANDT HARMENSZ. VAN RIJN

The Raising of Lazarus 1642

Etching, first state of two, 5⅞ × 4 7/16 in. (14.9 × 11.2 cm). White and Boon B72 (2002.2353) power of fire (suggested by the firing cannon) and its importance to human life, as the source of the stars and all warmth.[74] Here Van de Velde combines the deep lines of the engraver's burin with the lighter touch of the etching needle to describe a star-speckled sky and shows cloaked captains looking on as militiamen fire a cannon, which goes off in a burst of swirling smoke. The centrality of the cannon, a manmade contraption, to this depiction of fire reflects the tensions between religious factions in the Netherlands in the 1610s and the resumption of the Eighty Years' War with Spain in 1621. Rather than personifying the elements as single figures as many of his predecessors had done,[75] Van de Velde bases his image on the outdoor genre scenes that formed the background to many earlier images of this kind,[76] indicating the growing interest in depictions of landscape and everyday life in seventeenth-century Dutch art.[77]

REMBRANDT HARMENSZ. VAN RIJN
The Raising of Lazarus
PLATE 21

Although Rembrandt's prints were relatively expensive for Steinberg, his collection at the Blanton includes six, and he evidently treasured them. Rembrandt van Rijn (1606–1669) was the quintessential *peintre-graveur*, a term invented by print collector and scholar Adam von Bartsch in the nineteenth century to distinguish those artists who made prints after their own designs from those who reproduced the work of others. Although this designation retroactively introduces problematic concepts about originality and value to periods in which these distinctions were irrelevant, the concept of the *peintre-graveur* is entirely appropriate to Rembrandt, who was equally skilled as a painter and printmaker, producing more than three hundred prints in his lifetime.[78] Renowned in both fields for his creation of extraordinary tonal effects and his sensitivity to the nuances of human expression, he addressed a wide range of subjects in his prints, including portraits, self-portraits, biblical and mythological scenes, landscapes, genre, and ***tronies*** (figures with exaggerated facial expressions, often in historical or exotic costume), imbuing them with an individuality that belies their replicative nature. Rembrandt's fluid etchings have the immediacy of drawings and are far removed in this respect from the systematic linear patterns typically employed by engravers of the period. He also designed, etched, and printed his own plates rather than submitting his designs to a printmaker, reveling in the variations he could achieve by adding **drypoint**, selectively wiping the ink, printing on various papers, and dramatically reworking his compositions.[79] These innovations were driven not only by his interest in artistic experimentation but also by a shrewd awareness of the nature of the print market. Rembrandt printed proof impressions (intermediate versions before the final state) on expensive paper imported from Asia, for example, attesting to his strategy of creating demand for multiple states by introducing monetizable variations into what is otherwise a replicative medium. Since the market for Rembrandt's prints has never waned, his plates have been sold and reprinted repeatedly, and numerous impressions of his prints (as well as copies and fakes) survive.[80] The first modern catalogue raisonné, now a fundamental armature of art history, was published to distinguish original Rembrandt prints from such imitations, further confirming the artist's centrality to the development of art-historical scholarship.[81]

Steinberg described one of his prints by the Dutch master in almost sacramental terms: "Whenever I commune with Rembrandt's little etching of *The Raising of Lazarus* (1642)—watching the corpse heave its weight out of its coffin at the bidding of Christ—I'm joining eight witnesses to a miracle."[82] This resurrection seems to occur head first, with the corpse's sketchily indicated body following. As he regains his senses, Lazarus and his kneeling sister exchange an astonished gaze. Figures of all kinds surround Christ—young and old, female and male, absorbed and uncomprehending. A mass of densely crosshatched lines indicating the tomb's depths contrasts with largely blank areas of the paper where thin squiggles connote vegetation and cracks in the back wall of the cave, while vigorous zigzags define the foreground. The freedom of Rembrandt's etched lines, at times painterly and at others more sketch-like, his wide range of subject matter, and his experimental approach to the printmaking process, are aspects of the medium that his Dutch contemporaries, as well as Italian and French etchers such as Giovanni Benedetto Castiglione (pl. 31), Stefano Della Bella (pl. 32), Giovanni Battista and Giovanni Domenico Tiepolo (pl. 34), Jean-Jacques de Boissieu (pl. 35), Jean-Honoré Fragonard (pl. 36), and Félix Buhot (pl. 46) would continue to explore through the nineteenth century and beyond.

> ADRIAEN VAN OSTADE
> *The Breakfast*
> PLATE 22

Second only to Rembrandt as the major Dutch etcher of his day, Haarlem-based Adriaen van Ostade (1610–1685) specialized in scenes of village life.[83] *The Breakfast* (ca. 1664) is a sympathetic portrayal of a scruffy-yet-cozy farmhouse, populated by a jovial group engaged in lively conversation (although the seated woman's less-animated posture suggests that she may be enduring, rather than enjoying, the company). Playing cards scattered on the floor and an upturned jug provide evidence of previous revelry. The Latin inscription by the Roman poet Tibullus below the image translates as "We spend time for an untroubled table—After a lengthy wait, a fair day comes" and celebrates the simple pleasures of food and friendship. However, the text would have been unintelligible to the home's inhabitants, suggesting that, like so many scenes of peasant life in Netherlandish art, this one was intended for educated collectors.[84] At the same time, a painting hangs high on the back wall of the cluttered interior, and what appears to be a broadsheet is affixed to the side of a cabinet. These two objects bridge the divide between the depicted figures and the likely viewer, as all are collectors of art and printed matter.

> MARCUS DE BYE
> Plate 6 from *Goats*
> PLATE 23

As the taste for scenes of contemporary life expanded during the seventeenth century, Dutch artists became increasingly specialized in their subject matter. Painter, draftsman, and etcher Paulus Potter (1625–1654) dedicated himself to pastoral scenes, receiving particular acclaim for his portrait-like images of animals. After his untimely death, Marcus de Bye (1639–ca. 1688), a painter and printmaker from The Hague, made multiple series of animal prints after drawings by Potter, most likely given to him by the painter's widow.[85] Some of these, such as the eight plates of etchings showing *Goats* (1654–88), focus on familiar livestock, while others feature more exotic beasts like leopards and lions.[86] These prints appealed to Dutch collectors for the same reasons that landscape prints exploded in popularity during this period—public pride in the newly independent Dutch Republic and its hard-won foreign territories, interest in Italian art theory that encouraged scientific approaches to the study and imitation of nature, and Christian notions articulated by both Reformed and Counter-Reformation thinkers advocating careful attention to the natural world as an act of piety to the Creator.[87] Although goats were traditionally associated with Satanism and witchcraft as in *Lo Stregozzo* (pl. 9), De Bye's series, showing nannies,

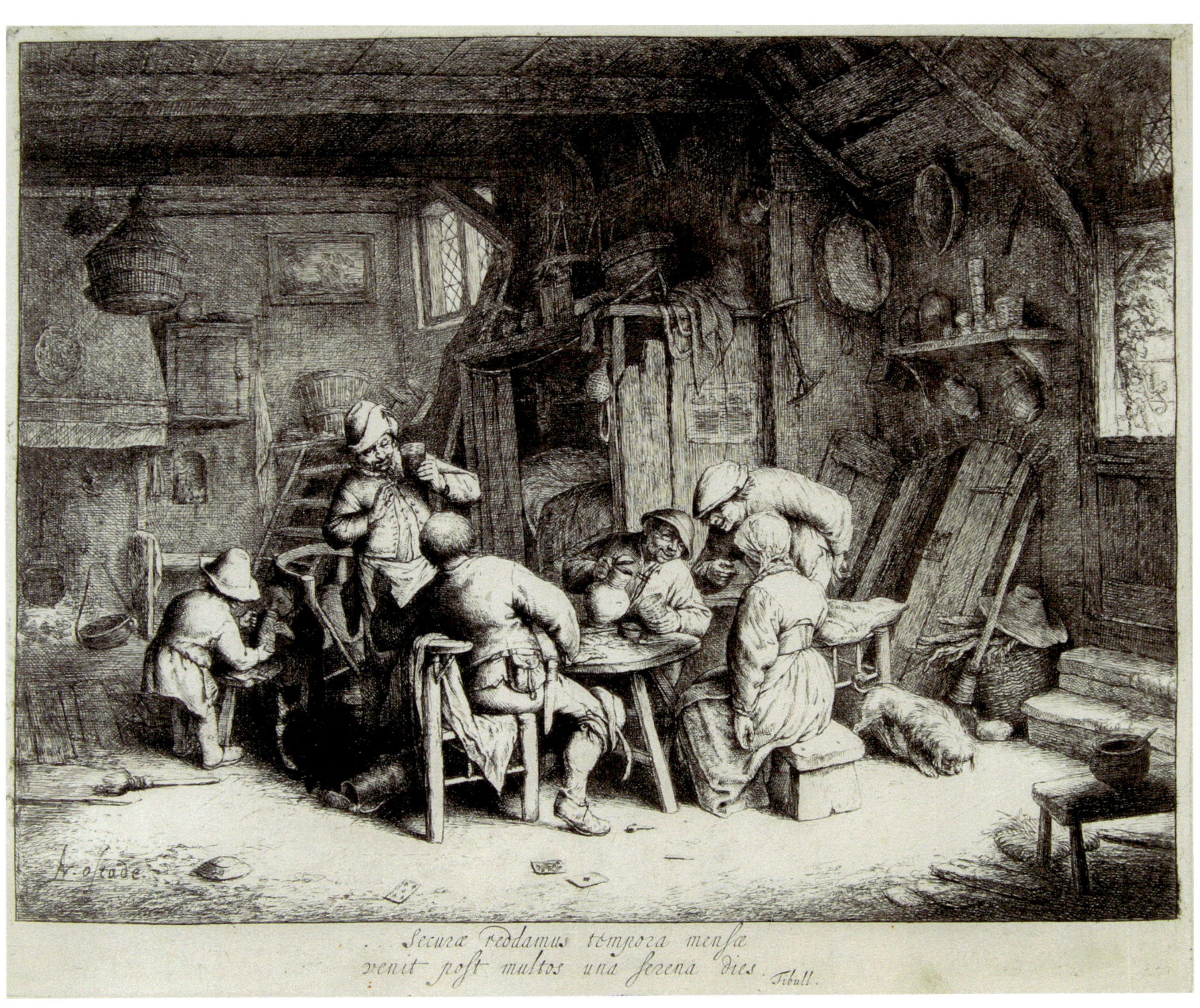

22 ADRIAEN VAN OSTADE

The Breakfast CA. 1664

Etching, eighth state of twelve, 8⁹⁄₁₆ × 10¼ in. (21.8 × 26 cm). Hollstein 50 (2002.2422)

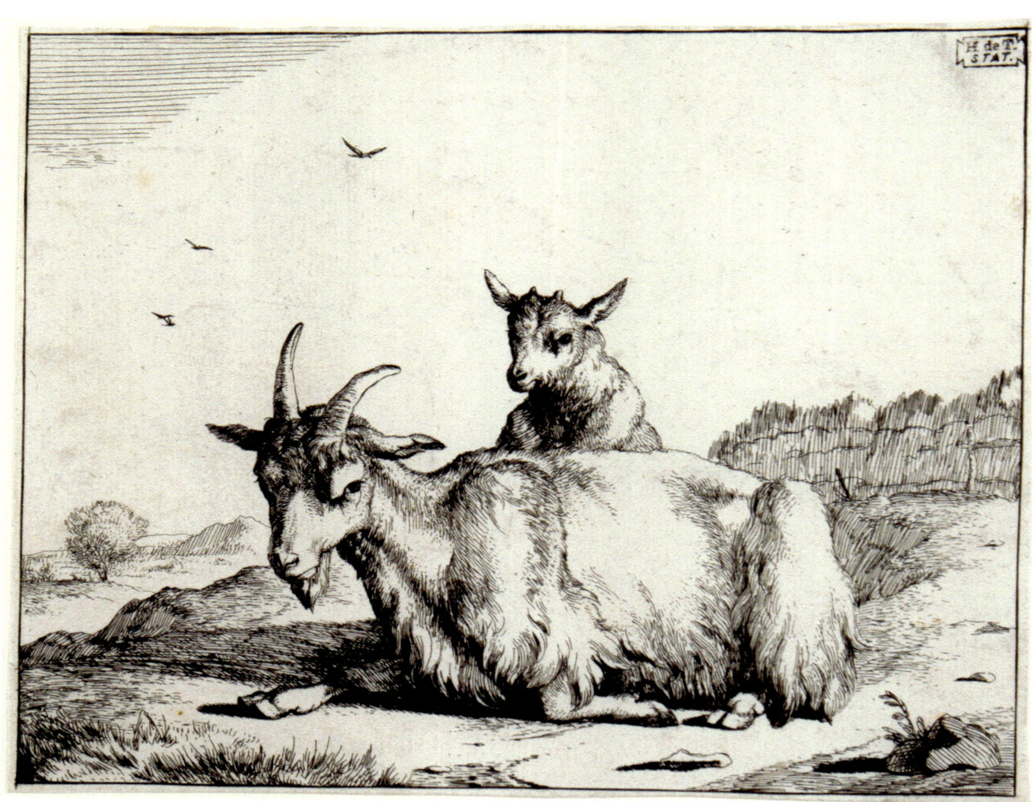

23 MARCUS DE BYE

Plate 6 from *Goats*, after a design by Paulus Potter 1654–88

Etching, third (?) state of four (trimmed), 4 5/16 × 5 7/16 in. (10.9 × 13.8 cm). Hollstein 6 (2002.2615.6/8)

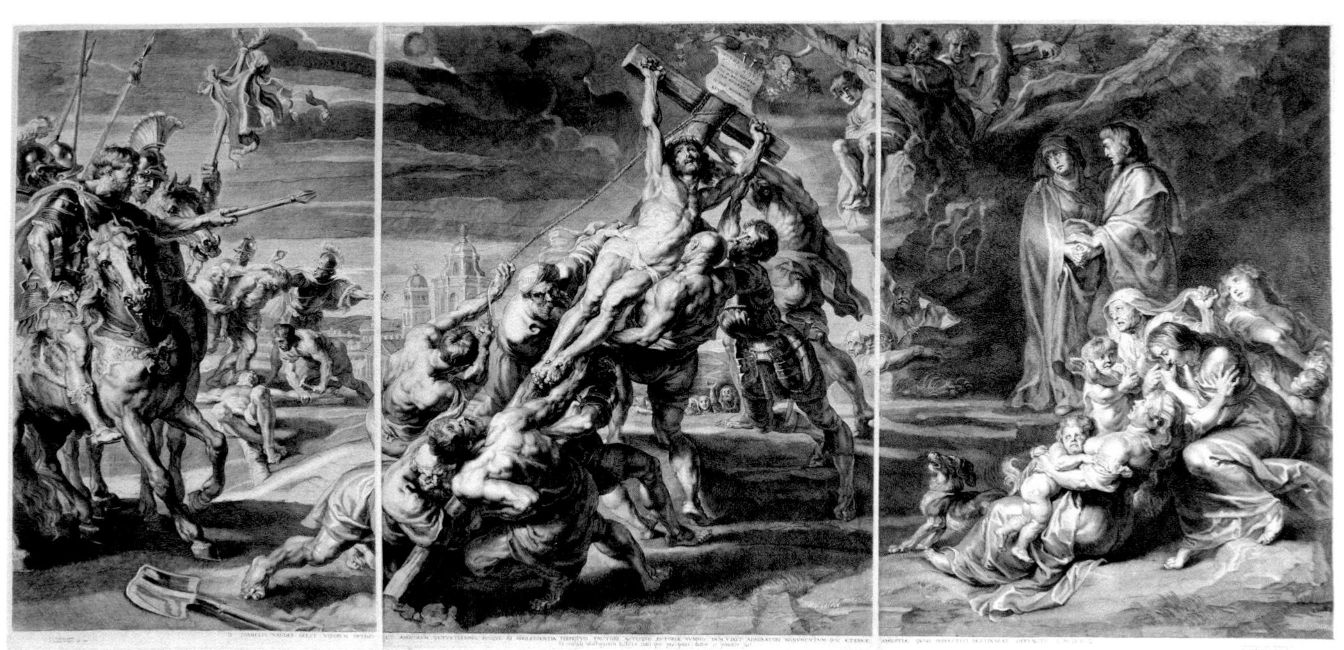

24 JAN WITDOECK

Elevation of the Cross, after a painting by Peter Paul Rubens 1638

Engraving on three sheets, fourth state of five, overall: 24 7/8 × 50 9/16 in. (63.2 × 128.5 cm). Hollstein 5 (2002.2584.1/3–3/3) bucks, and kids from what appears to be the Dutch Landrace breed, eschews symbolic and moralistic overtones in favor of naturalism and picturesque form; it also asserts a distinctly Dutch agricultural aesthetic.[88] De Bye's sensitive portrayal of these creatures' spirited expressions and uninhibited poses probably intrigued Steinberg, who collected many series of animal prints and whose keen observation of body language was so integral to his research.

> JAN WITDOECK
> *Elevation of the Cross*
> PLATE 24

Unlike Rembrandt, his contemporary, the prolific Flemish painter Peter Paul Rubens (1577–1640) seems to have executed only one print himself; however, more than eighteen hundred prints were made after his designs.[89] During his lifetime, Rubens carefully oversaw this process, regularly employing at least one printmaker in his Antwerp studio to reproduce his works. Among the forty-three prints after Rubens in Steinberg's collection at the Blanton, Jan Witdoeck's *Elevation of the Cross* (1638) and Conrad Lauwers's *Elijah in the Desert Fed by an Angel* (1660–85), along with Soutman's *Last Supper* (1620–30; fig. 21), are the largest. Witdoeck's *Elevation of the Cross* reprises one of Rubens's greatest religious works—the triptych now in Antwerp Cathedral. To aid his engraver, Rubens created an oil sketch in which he adjusted the composition and the figures, linking the three panels of the triptych in a contiguous scene.[90] The dimensions of the sketch are almost identical to those of the final engraving, which stretches across three copperplates. In all the versions, the central, unfolding drama of Christ's body being raised on the cross is analogous to the priest's elevation of the bread and wine during Mass and the subsequent transformation of these elements into Christ's body and blood (transubstantiation).

> CONRAD LAUWERS
> *Elijah in the Desert Fed by an Angel*
> PLATE 25

Renewed support for the doctrine of transubstantiation under the Counter-Reformation (in the face of Protestant rejection of most of the traditional sacraments) also became the theme of Rubens's twenty-part tapestry series known as *The Triumph of the Eucharist*.[91] Commissioned in about 1625 by the Infanta Isabella Clara Eugenia, Governor of the Spanish Netherlands, for the convent of the Descalzas Reales in Madrid, the series ingeniously depicts scenes of Old Testament prefigurations, allegories, Christian figures, and triumphal processions in the form of tapestries hung between Solomonic and Tuscan columns—that is, as tapestries within tapestries. In Conrad Lauwers's engraving showing *Elijah in the Desert Fed by an Angel* (1660–85) after Rubens's preparatory oil sketch, the Eucharist is prefigured by an angel's miraculous provision of food and drink for the prophet Elijah, as recounted in 1 Kings 19:3–8.[92] The figures here are so robustly modeled that they appear to stand out from, and even firmly upon, a woven-tapestry background, which appears, in turn, to be suspended from ropes in a shallow niche and recessed between Solomonic columns. This feat of perspective represents a multilayered realism akin to the material transformations believed to occur in the Eucharist itself. Further, the large format of both prints, which pushes the medium to its limits in approximating the visual impact of the originals, epitomizes the boldness of the theological

25 CONRAD LAUWERS
Elijah in the Desert Fed by an Angel, after a painting by Peter Paul Rubens 1660–85
Engraving, 25¼ × 20 in. (61.5 × 50.8 cm). Hollstein 1 (1997.33)

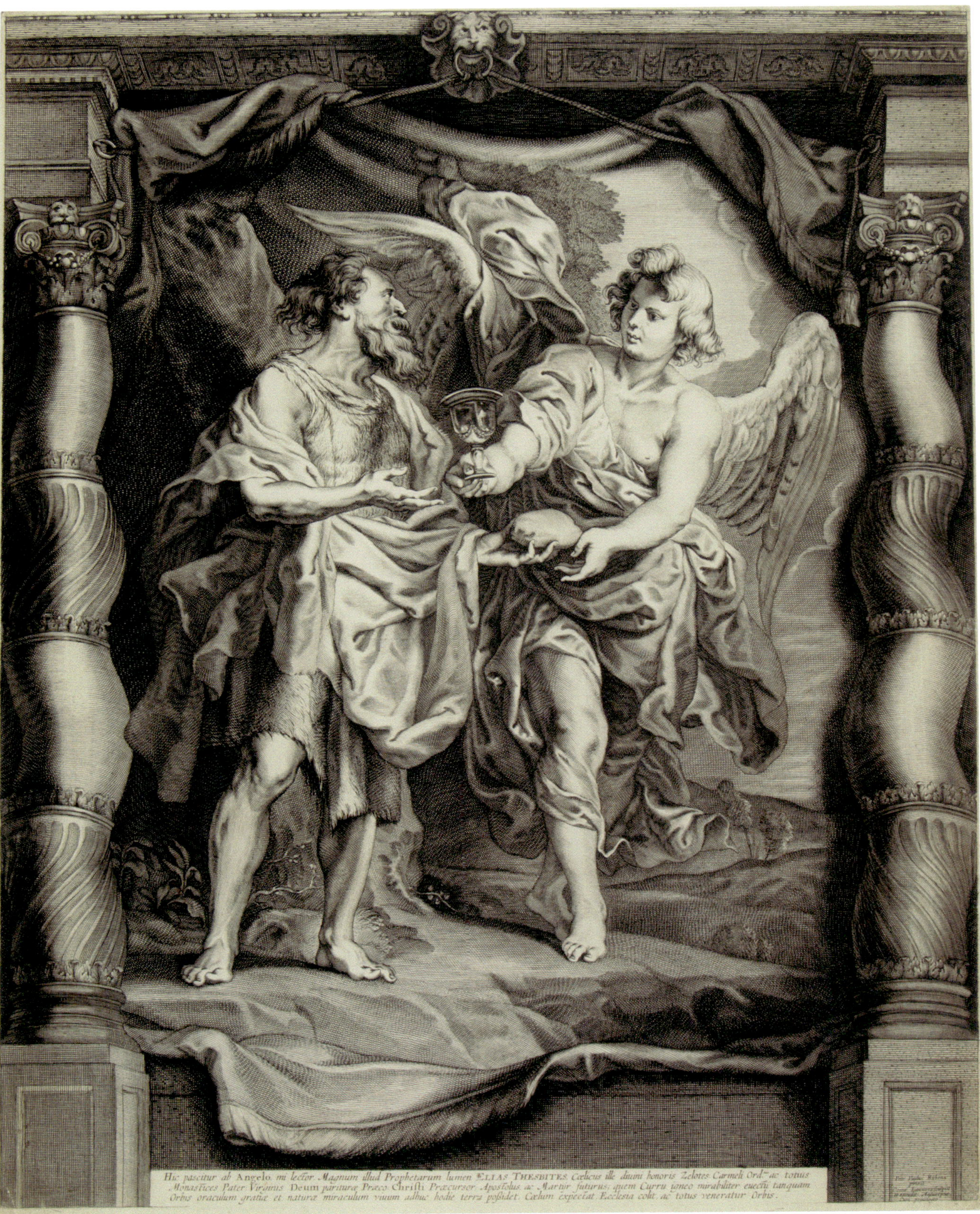
Hic pascitur ab Angelo, mi lector, Magnum illud Prophetarum lumen ELIAS THESBITES, Cœlicus ille diuini honoris Zelotes Carmeli Ord.ⁱˢ ac totius
Monastices Pater Virginis Deum parituræ Præco Christi Præcursor Apostolus ac Martyr futurus; quem Curru igneo mirabiliter euectū tanquam
Orbis oraculum gratiæ et naturæ miraculum viuum adhuc hodie terra poßidet. Cœlum expectat Ecclesia colit, ac totus veneratur Orbis.

claims of the Counter-Reformation, while the replicative nature of printmaking itself serves to propagate the faith, an objective codified in the formal establishment of the Catholic Church's missionary arm, the Propaganda Fide, in 1622.

> JACQUES CALLOT
> *The Temptation of St. Anthony*
> PLATE 26

Due to the prolonged conflict between the Netherlands and Spain, many artists from the Low Countries fled to France, bringing their exceptional skills in etching and engraving with them. They cannot, however, be solely credited for the eclipse of the Netherlands by Paris as Europe's printmaking center by the mid-seventeenth century.[93] This can also be attributed to the early flowering of etching at Fontainebleau and the further dissemination of those designs through the work of Parisian engravers like René Boyvin. Steinberg's collection at the Blanton includes nearly 150 prints by another Frenchman, Jacques Callot (1592–1635), one of the most influential intaglio printers of the seventeenth century.[94] Born in Nancy and trained in Rome, he was employed by the Medici family to produce drawings and prints of the court's festivities and theatrical productions. After returning to his hometown in 1621, Callot continued working for other royal courts, and his prolific output includes religious subjects, single figures from various levels of society, contemporary battles, and scenes of war. In one of his final prints, *The Temptation of St. Anthony* (1635), he presents the tormenting of the hermit saint as a stage drama, reminiscent of the intermission performances during musical productions at the Medici court. Towering cliffs on the right and left serve as parted curtains, while the harbor backdrop recedes in a series of lightly bitten lines.[95] Suspended by a chain, a large devil presides over the scene, with further devils tumbling from his mouth into the swirling clouds and the chaotic landscape below. There, the somewhat comic scatalogical motifs, among them devils passing gas and dripping excrement on each other's heads (at upper left) turn sadistic as pointed implements such as arrows, pikes, lances, and even snouts impale and penetrate human and animal victims alike. Fire, destruction, and violence reign in a tableau that recalls the torments of hell invented by painter Hieronymus Bosch (ca. 1450–1516), whose designs were known in print by the mid-sixteenth century.[96]

The tonal virtuosity of this print was established by two of Callot's technical innovations, which would have long-lasting consequences for the future of printmaking. Inspired by lute varnishes, the artist's recipe for a protective hard ground for etching reduced foul biting, which occurs when the acid that incises designs into the copperplate bleeds through the typically soft wax ground, resulting in fuzzy lines and imperfections. His invention of an oval-shaped etching needle, an échoppe, that produces the swelling and tapering lines characteristic of engraving, further reduced the amount of training necessary to successfully produce crisp images. When printmaker and theorist Abraham Bosse (1602–1676) published Callot's recipe in his *Traité des manières de graver en taille douce* (Treatise on Line Engraving, 1645), the first-ever etching manual, he encouraged many other artists to turn their hands to etching as well.[97]

> ABRAHAM BOSSE
> *Gentleman Holding a Stick* from *Le Jardin de la Noblesse Françoise* (The Garden of the French Nobility)
> PLATE 27

Bosse was born in Tours and made frequent visits to Paris throughout the 1620s, where he lodged with Netherlandish émigré and fellow Protestant printmaker Melchior Tavernier. During that time, Bosse etched Jean de Saint-Igny's designs for *Le Jardin de la Noblesse Françoise* (The Garden of the French Nobility, 1629) and Tavernier published it. Bosse settled permanently in Paris in 1632 and was hired to teach perspective at the Académie royale de peinture et de sculpture after its founding in 1648.[98] His treatises on

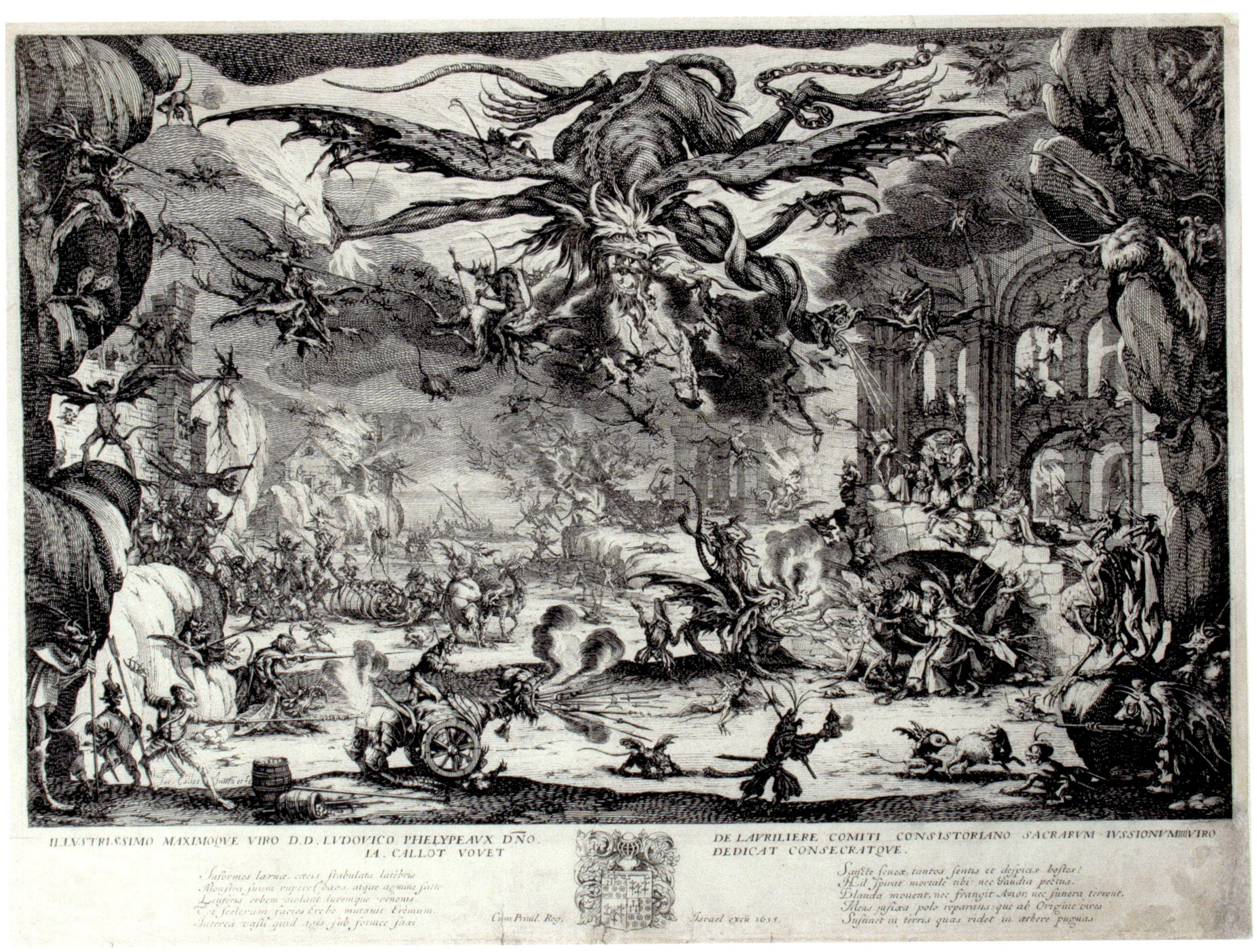

26 JACQUES CALLOT

The Temptation of St. Anthony 1635

Etching, fourth state of five, 14 1/16 × 18 1/4 in. (35.7 × 46.3 cm). Lieure 1416 (2002.1849)

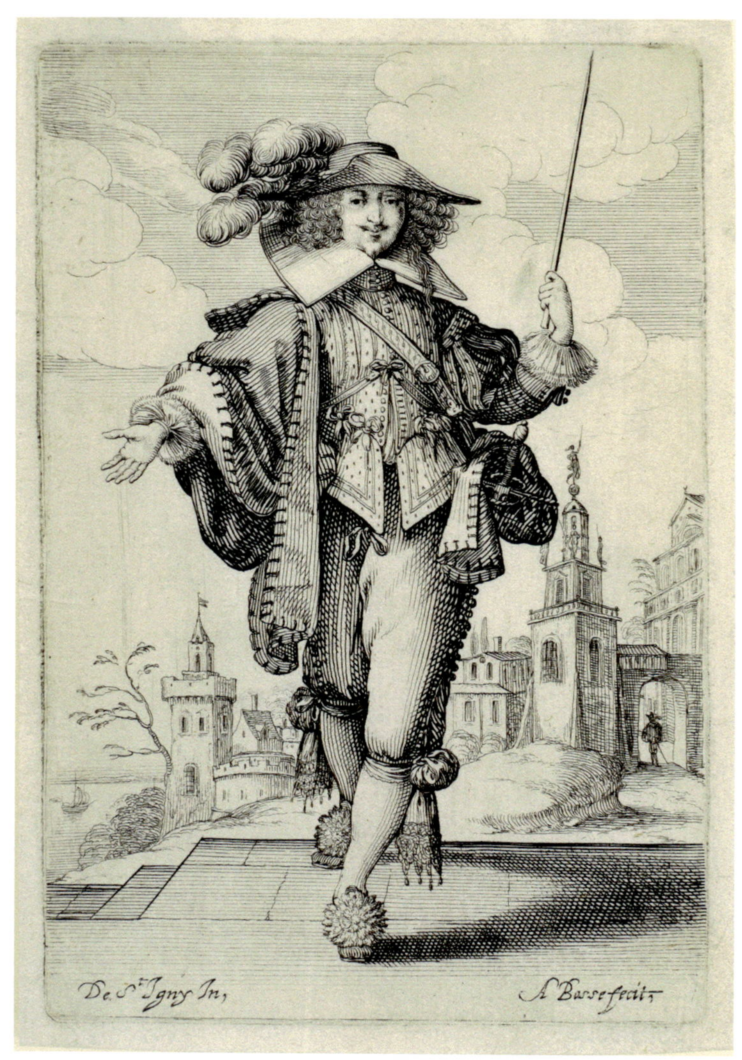

27 ABRAHAM BOSSE

Gentleman Holding a Stick from *Le Jardin de la Noblesse Françoise* (The Garden of the French Nobility), after a design by Jean de Saint-Igny 1629

Etching, first state of two, $5\frac{9}{16} \times 3\frac{9}{16}$ in. (14.2 × 9 cm). Lothe 173 (2002.362) scientific and technical subjects, including his *Moyen universel de pratiquer la perspective sur les tableaux ou surfaces irrégulières* (Universal means of practicing perspective on flat or irregular surfaces, 1653) place him in the ranks of scholar-practitioners like Albrecht Dürer, who also wrote books on perspective and proportion. Bosse produced some fifteen hundred prints, primarily showing images of contemporary society, ranging from the bourgeois professions to life at court. The documentary-like precision with which he depicts domestic interiors and commercial premises, styles of clothing, and all manner of social customs offers the promise of a "slice of life," which collector and connoisseur Pierre-Jean Mariette praised as being "in such a sincere and true manner that it is impossible to wish for anything more interesting."[99] As in *Gentleman Holding a Stick* from *Le Jardin de la Noblesse Françoise*, Bosse's representations of his countrymen in various costumes—with every plume, pleat, and *pouffe* meticulously recorded—reveal his keen, and even cutting, eye. Although Louis XIII would ban such sumptuous attire in 1633, Bosse's later etchings testify to the ultimate futility of the royal edict.[100]

ROBERT NANTEUIL
Antoine Dulieu
PLATE 28

ROBERT NANTEUIL AND GÉRARD EDELINCK
Moses with the Tablets of the Law
PLATE 29

The court officials and aristocrats who formed part of the country's rapidly expanding bureaucracy under Louis XIV were well served by the increasingly refined technical skills of French engravers, from whom they soon began to commission portraits.[101] Among the most proficient and successful of these artists was Robert Nanteuil (1623–1678), whose approximately 220 portrait engravings include no fewer than eleven of King Louis XIV.[102] Nanteuil was eventually rewarded by a large royal pension, and the king's esteem for the engraver informed his 1660 edict elevating printmaking from a manual to a liberal art; the first printmakers entered the Royal Academy in 1663.[103] Two engravings in Steinberg's collection, *Antoine Dulieu* (1667) and *Moses with the Tablets of the Law* (1699), epitomize Nanteuil's facility with the burin.

Antoine Dulieu, who had served as a high-ranking magistrate and officer in the court of Louis XIII, appears in formal dress, and the engraver has meticulously described the plush folds of his robe and the delicate, woolly curls of his hair. As with most of his prints, Nanteuil first drew the sitter from life, as indicated by the phrase "ad vivum" in the signature. The artist's remarkable command of texture is also evident in his reproduction of the painting *Moses with the Tablets of the Law* by his mentor Philippe de Champaigne (1602–1674). The print was finished by the equally accomplished engraver Gérard Edelinck (1640–1707) after Nanteuil's death, and his subtle shading lends an impressive verisimilitude to Moses's weathered face and wrinkled hand; the patriarch's fingers, in an illusionistic effect, appear to reach over the top of the stone plinth into the viewer's space. The softness of Moses's beard, the subtly articulated pattern woven into his vestments, and the elaborate calligraphic script of the Ten Commandments convincingly distinguish the surfaces of hair, brocade, and carved stone. However, the vividness of engravings by artists like Nanteuil and Edelinck represents both a pinnacle and a dead end. As Emily Peters suggests, "Nanteuil employed a system that sought to hide its linear vocabulary altogether. While Goltzius and Mellan emphasized the artificiality of line, and Rubens its imitation of paint, Nanteuil's line was deployed to imitate life. Nanteuil could claim, therefore, that his portraits paid homage to their noble subjects by providing true likenesses, free from the artist's hand."[104] Although engravers incrementally perfected Nanteuil's system until the nineteenth century, many artists of the next generation pursued a greater freedom of expression, drawing attention to the hand that Nanteuil and his colleagues had sought to obscure.[105]

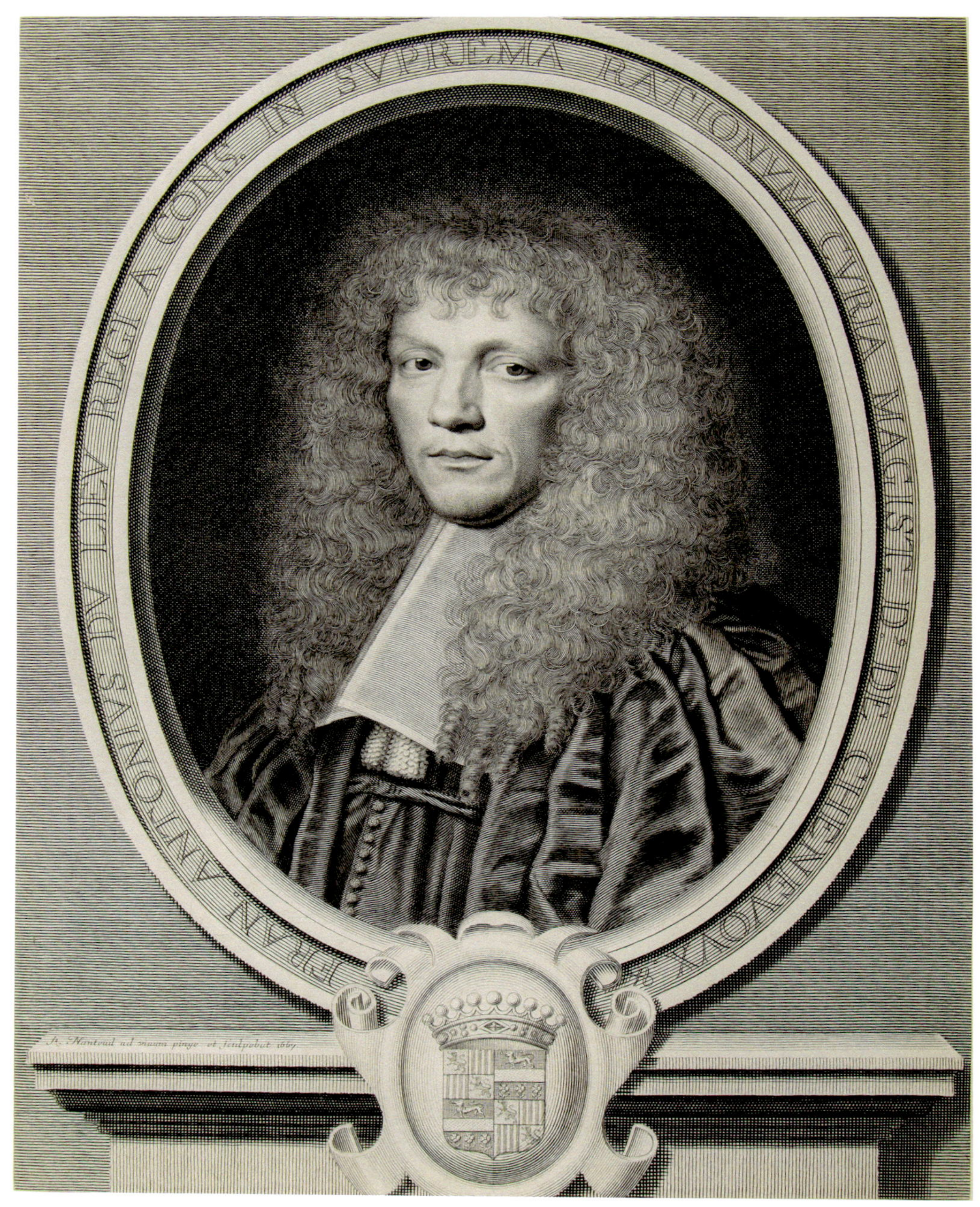

28 ROBERT NANTEUIL

Antoine Dulieu 1667

Engraving, first state of two, 15½ × 12⅛ in. (39.3 × 30.8 cm). Petitjean and Wickert 63, Adamczak 205 (2002.1466)

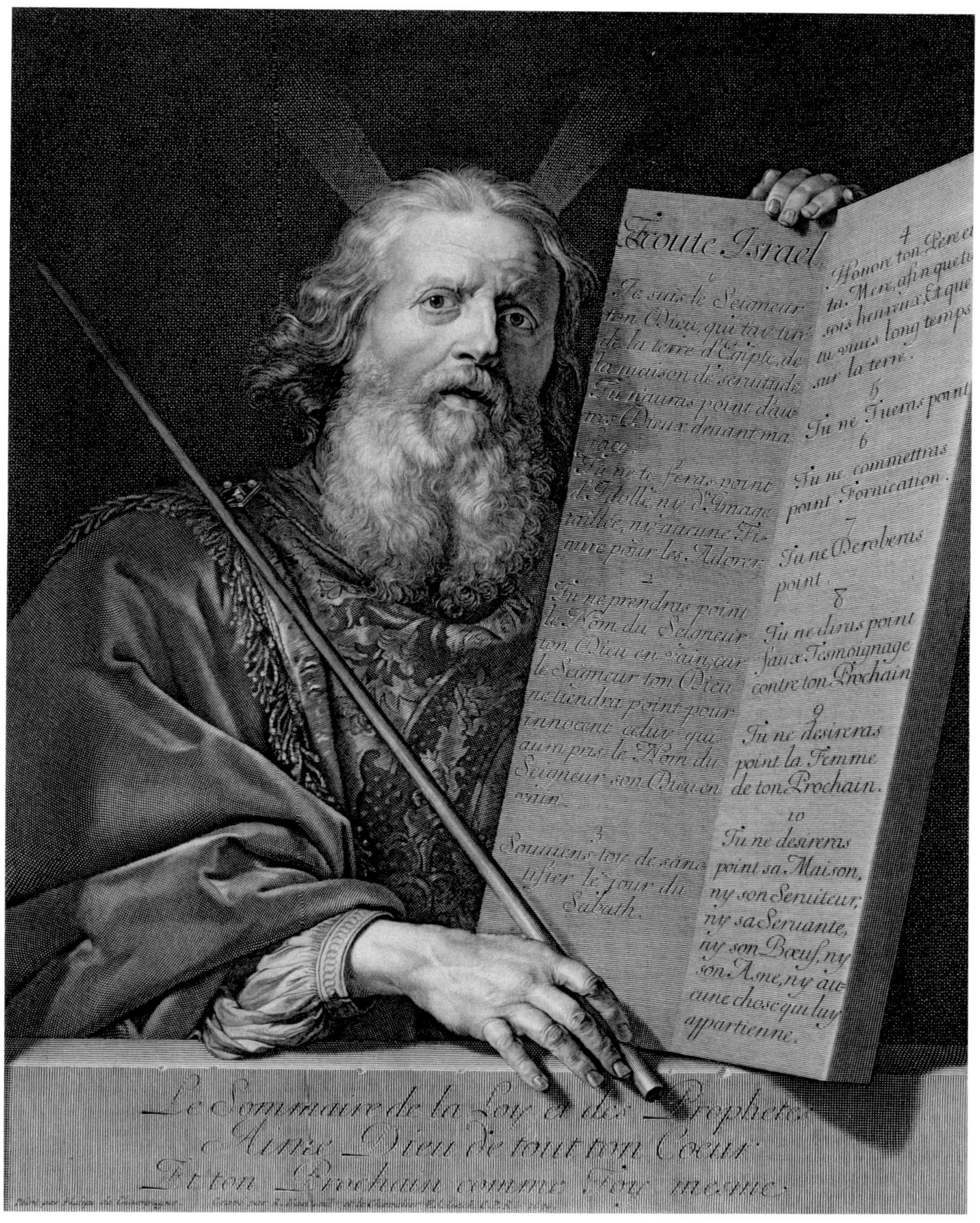

29 ROBERT NANTEUIL AND GÉRARD EDELINCK

Moses with the Tablets of the Law, after a painting by Philippe de Champaigne 1699

Engraving, second or third state of three, $20\frac{11}{16} \times 16\frac{1}{8}$ in. (52.6 × 41 cm, trimmed). Petitjean and Wickert Ap.1, Adamczak 257 (2002.1918)

CLAUDE LORRAIN
Harbor Scene with Rising Sun
PLATE 30

Etching, especially as practiced in the freehanded manner of Rembrandt rather than in the engraving-like style of Callot, appealed to many French and Italian artists of the seventeenth century. Steinberg's collection at the Blanton contains eleven prints by French landscape artist Claude Lorrain (1604–1682), who also found the etching needle particularly well suited to the depiction of the irregular and fluid forms of nature. In Italy, where he spent the greater part of his life, Claude was acclaimed for his paintings of classically composed landscapes, also the subject of most of his forty or so etchings. *Harbor Scene with Rising Sun* (1634), widely considered one of his masterpieces, reflects the emerging contemporary taste for landscape, for light effects, and for drawing-like plates by painter-etchers.[106] In this depiction of a harbor, one of his favorite motifs, Claude captures the paradox of the brightness of a sunrise combined with a star shining so brilliantly as to obscure itself. The figures in the foreground are densely articulated with clusters of irregularly hatched lines. The depth of this frontal tonality renders the shadowed areas of the seascape more richly detailed than the areas blotted out by sunlight. Produced late in his career, this work showcases Claude at the height of his capabilities as an etcher—with the staged biting so apparent in the delicacy of the strokes depicting sunbeams contrasting with the width of those depicting the shoreline, and his comfort with the etching needle pronounced in the highly detailed yet hazily atmospheric forms of the distant architecture and ships.

GIOVANNI BENEDETTO CASTIGLIONE
Noah and the Animals Entering the Ark
PLATE 31

Giovanni Benedetto Castiglione (1609–1664) similarly exploited the etching technique to define the varied textures of natural forms in his representations of rural landscapes and animals, which come together in his frequent depictions of Noah's Ark.[107] Both in this etching, *Noah and the Animals Entering the Ark* (ca. 1650), and in a painting on the same theme in the Blanton's collection, Castiglione reveals his debt to Rembrandt with his masterful control of the dramatic contrasts between light and shade throughout the composition.[108] At the center, pairs of creatures bound from the finely etched foliage, making for the shore where the ark is just faintly visible in the left background. Meanwhile, their human companions blend into the dense woodland on the right. The magnificent lone horse in the foreground, whose anatomy is delineated merely by stippled dots, provides a humorous contrast to the earthiness of the ewe seen crouching to urinate at the lower right. Here, the natural world, rather than the religious figures of Noah's family, emerges as the primary subject. Castiglione also produced this particular composition as a **monotype**, a technique that he had actually invented in the 1640s.[109] Throughout his career, Castiglione tended to borrow motifs and compositions from other artists and to reuse his own compositions, transposing them from one medium to another, so as to concentrate on their execution.[110] Both his light-filled, draftsman-like style and his pastoral subjects exerted a powerful influence on printmakers through the end of the eighteenth century.

STEFANO DELLA BELLA
Clovis Abducting Clotilde
PLATE 32

The incredibly prolific Florentine artist Stefano della Bella (1610–1664) learned etching from Callot's colleague Remigio Cantagallina (ca. 1582–1656), and in his early years made drawings after many of Callot's prints.[111] With patronage from the Medici court, Della Bella set out for new centers of artistic production. Upon arrival in Rome in 1633, he made numerous open-air sketches of monuments, public spectacles, the landscape, and the daily activity of the cosmopolitan city. Between 1639 and 1650, Della Bella relocated

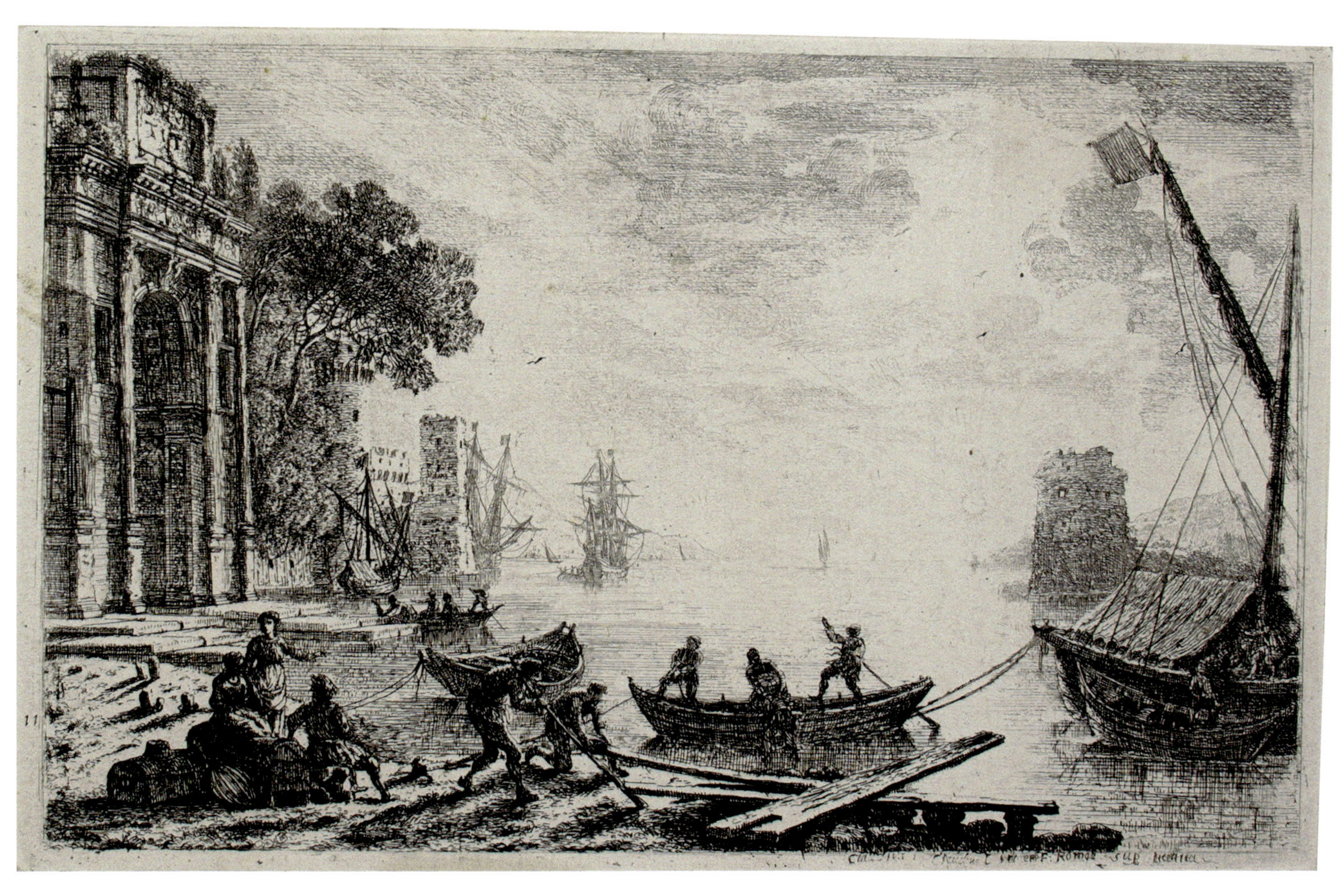

30 CLAUDE LORRAIN

Harbor Scene with Rising Sun 1634

Etching, fourth state of eight, 4⅞ × 7½ in. (12.7 × 19 cm). Mannocci 15 (2002.385)

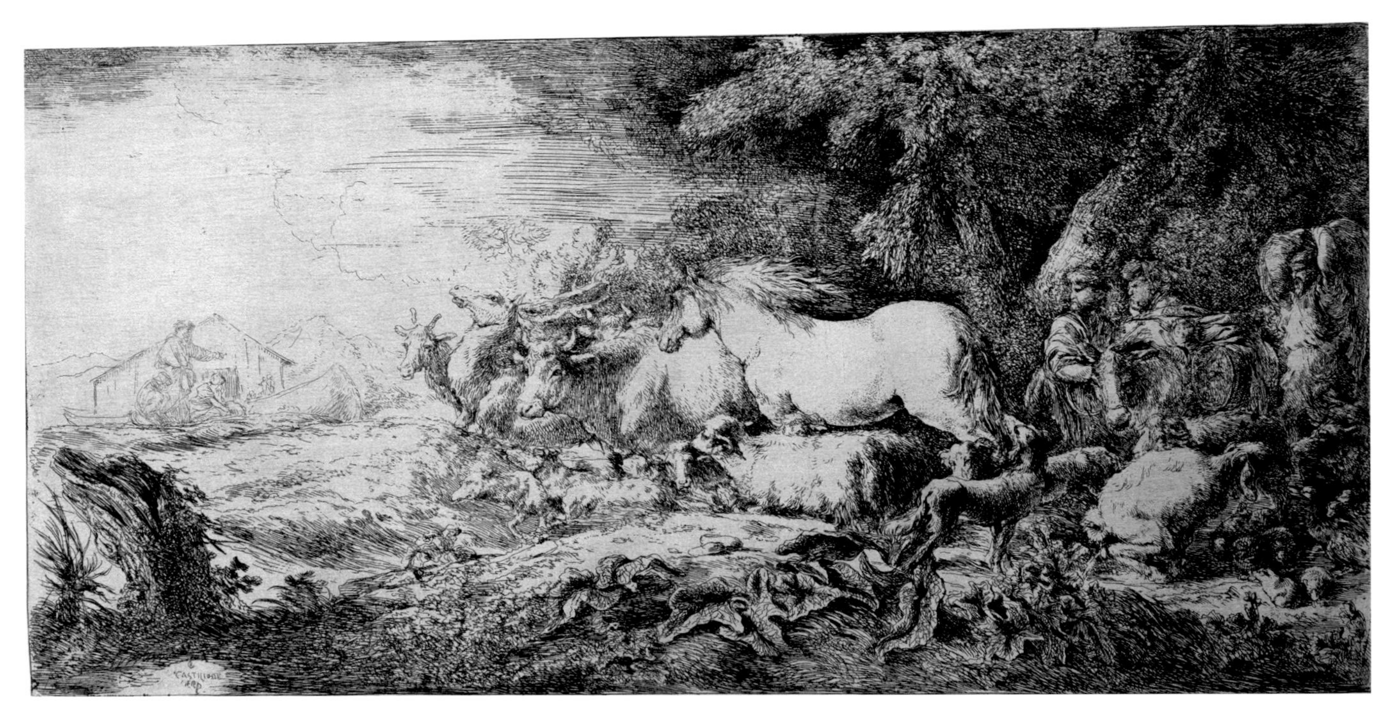

31 GIOVANNI BENEDETTO CASTIGLIONE

Noah and the Animals Entering the Ark CA. 1650

Etching, only state, 8 × $15\frac{11}{16}$ in. (20.3 × 39.9 cm). Bellini (1982) 61 (2002.1768)

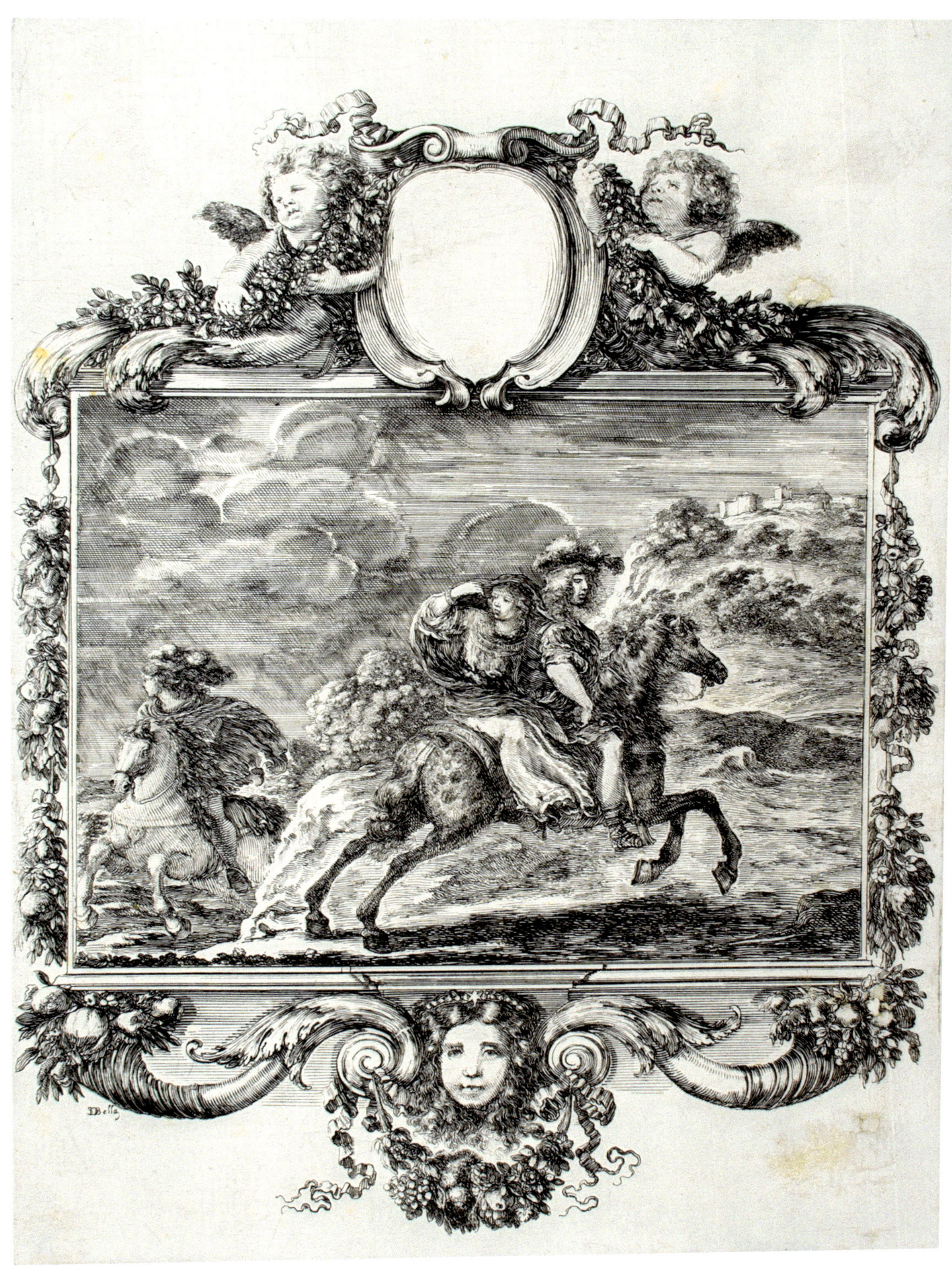

32 STEFANO DELLA BELLA

Clovis Abducting Clotilde 1652–57

Etching, third state of three, 10 7/16 × 8 1/4 in. (27.1 × 20.9 cm). De Vesme and Massar 80.211, Talbierska IV.47 (2002.1389)

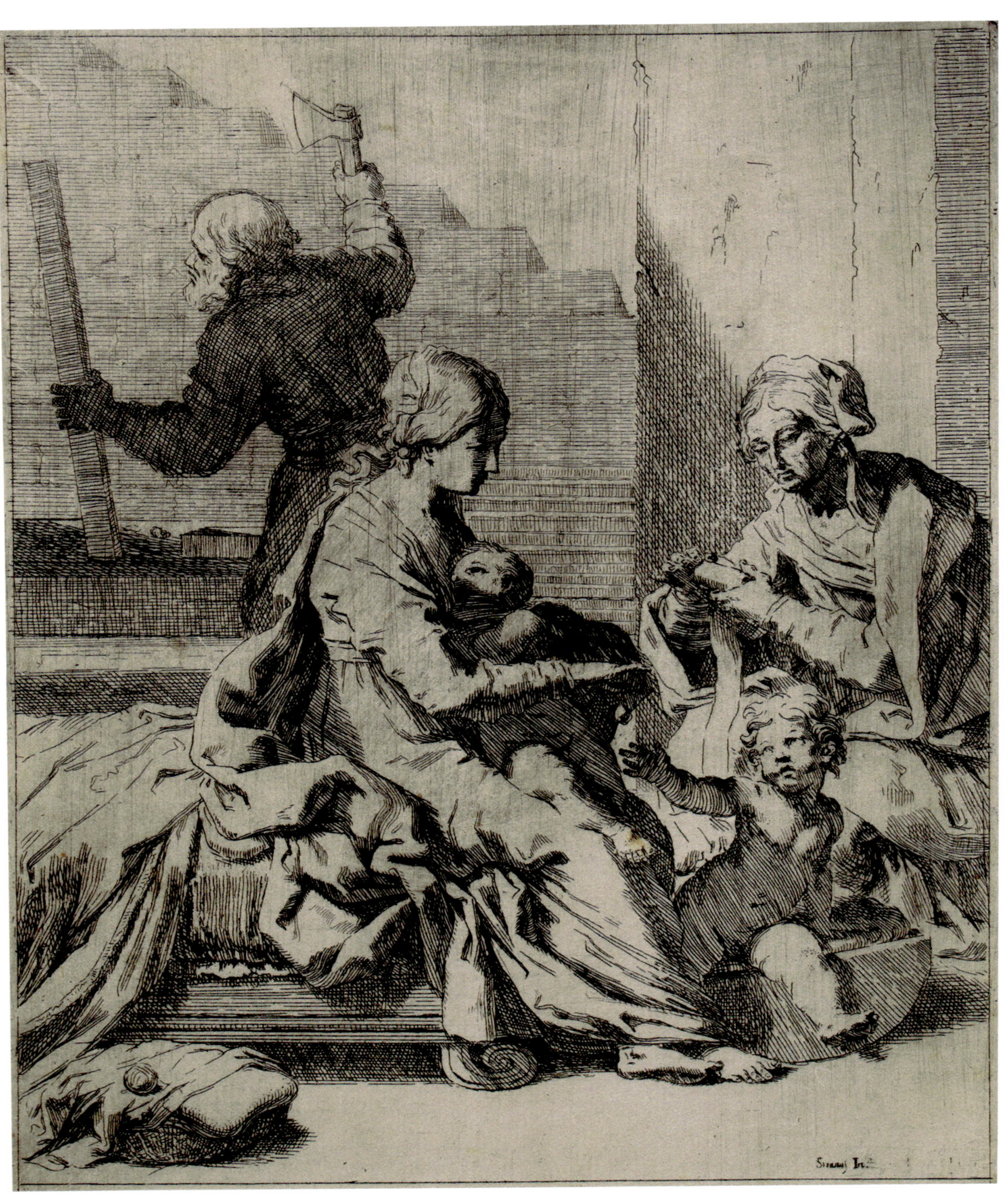

33 ELISABETTA SIRANI

Holy Family with St. Elizabeth and St. John 1655–65

Etching, third state of three, 10 3/16 × 8 3/8 in. (25.9 × 21.4 cm). Bellini (1976) 8 (2002.237) to Paris, where he continued to draw the urban scene and produced most of the 1,052 etchings that make up his printed oeuvre. Ornamental designs, festival scenes, battle scenes, landscapes, topographical views, playing cards, and hunting parties are among the subjects he captured in etchings that came to resemble his free-flowing drawings. *Clovis Abducting Clotilde* (1652–57), possibly made to accompany a poem on the Merovingian king that was published in France in 1657, typifies the artist's mature style with its frenzied lines and densely staged composition.[112] The elaborate framing device with garlands of fruit, flowers, and foliage, soft cherubic figures, and a central escutcheon recall the highly inventive decorative friezes Della Bella produced for Parisian printers. An earlier state of this print demonstrates his efforts to introduce a range of tonalities to his plates by brushing them with an acid wash, much as Rembrandt did, but this element disappears in later states.

Although Della Bella's prints remained popular with collectors until the eighteenth century, they then fell out favor.[113] In 1954, in his catalogue of Della Bella's drawings at Windsor Castle, Anthony Blunt wrote, "It would be foolish to claim him as a great artist, but he ranks high among the *petits maîtres*."[114] However, during the 1970s, Steinberg's friend and fellow print collector Phyllis Dearborn Massar played a significant role in creating a renewed appreciation for the artist as a protodocumentarian, one that persists today.

ELISABETTA SIRANI
Holy Family with St. Elizabeth and St. John
PLATE 33

Steinberg's collection contains several examples of the work of early modern female artists who had accessed training through the one avenue commonly available to them—their fathers' studios. Under the tutelage of Giovanni Andrea Sirani, his daughter Elisabetta Sirani (1638–1665) also benefited from relatively liberal attitudes towards girls' education in her hometown of Bologna, a university city that had a tradition of female artists extending back to Caterina de'Vigri (St. Catherine of Bologna) in the mid-fifteenth century.[115] Sirani herself founded Europe's first school of painting for women outside the convents.[116] She achieved international acclaim within her lifetime and was the first woman in Bologna to specialize in history painting, then considered the most prestigious genre.[117] Biblical subjects make up the largest category in her oeuvre. In *Holy Family with St. Elizabeth and St. John* (1655–65), one of only ten etchings by her, Sirani depicts the Virgin nursing the Christ child while offering a small fruit to the cherubic John the Baptist as his mother, Elizabeth, winds swaddling clothes nearby. In this intimate and down-to-earth scene, the artist further describes the shadowy folds of Mary's robes with elegant, precise hatching and uses chiaroscuro to accentuate the weathered planes of Elizabeth's face. Joseph, brandishing his carpenter's tools, stands with his back to the central scene against a much less distinctive background.

THE EIGHTEENTH CENTURY

GIOVANNI DOMENICO TIEPOLO
Old Man with a Helmet
PLATE 34

The continuing influence of Rembrandt and his contemporaries on Italian painter-etchers of the eighteenth century is represented by Giovanni Domenico Tiepolo's (1727–1804) *Raccolta di Teste* (Collection of Heads, 1773–74).[118] The artist and his father, Giovanni Battista Tiepolo (1696–1770), effectively dominated Venetian painting during the eighteenth century. Giovanni Domenico's sixty-plate series, based on paintings by his father, features etched portraits of unidentified male figures, most of whom sport full beards, weighty cloaks, and distinctive head coverings.[119] When the printmaker and collector Antonio Maria Zanetti (1680–1767) encountered the set, he observed that, "if Rembrandt and Castiglione returned from the grave,

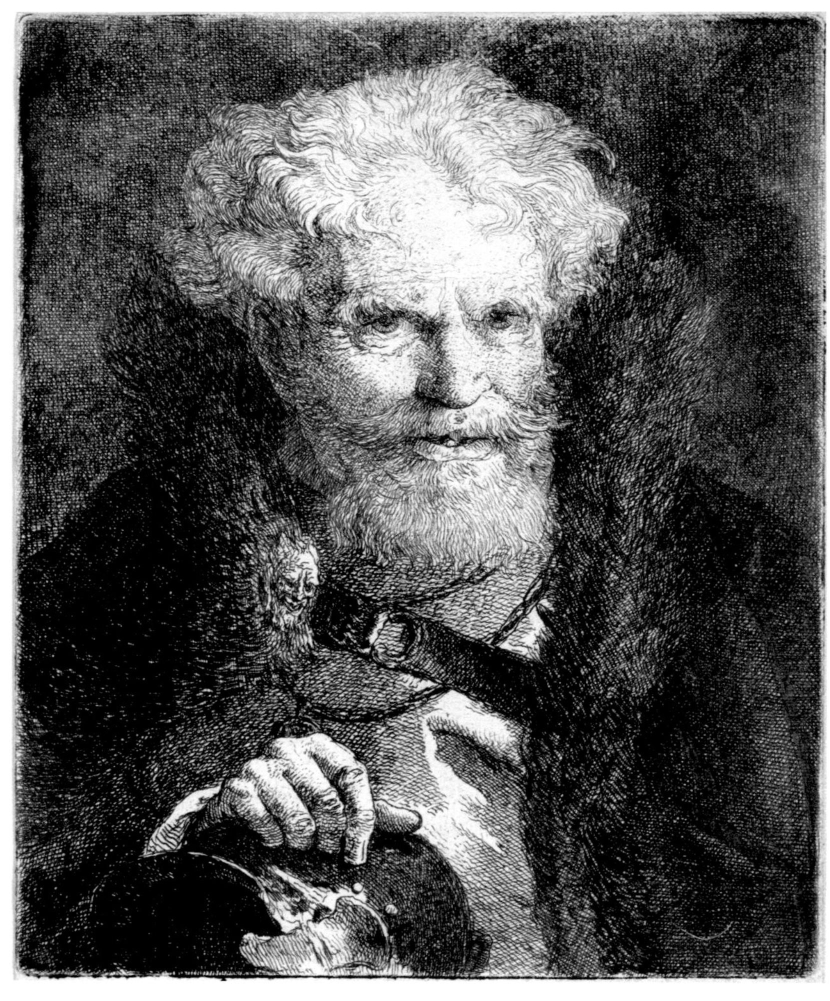

34 GIOVANNI DOMENICO TIEPOLO

Old Man with a Helmet, after a painting by Giovanni Battista Tiepolo CA. 1757

Later published in the *Raccolta di Teste* (Collection of Heads) 1773–74

Etching, first state of two, $5\frac{5}{8} \times 4\frac{1}{2}$ in. (14.3 × 11.5 cm). Rizzi 179 (2002.245) they would kiss the person who made them."[120] *Old Man with a Helmet* (ca. 1757) from this series reflects the influence of those paragons of printmaking with its dramatic chiaroscuro effects and the light, loose treatment of the man's wispy hair and crinkly eyelids. All kinds of *tronies* appear in Rembrandt's paintings and etchings as well as in Castiglione's two series showing busts of men "in oriental head-dress."[121] As these titles suggest, the *tronie* called for invention and whimsical imagination, in which subjects might be presented as types with distinctive expressions or as exoticized specimens. Here, a clasp in the form of a wizened, satyr-like visage attached to the figure's fur collar provides an uncanny contrast to the appraising but more genial gaze of the elderly warrior. Most impressions of the *Raccolta di Teste* come from the first published edition of 1773–74. Steinberg's impression, rich, uneven, and very individual in its inking, may be a rare proof, pulled by the artist himself.

JEAN-JACQUES DE BOISSIEU
Studies of Heads
PLATE 35

Eagerly collected by French connoisseurs of the eighteenth century, the etchings of the Tiepolos, alongside those of fellow Italians Castiglione, Della Bella, and Salvator Rosa, became reference points for a new circle of artists and amateurs who began to eschew the formality of the highly finished engravings of French printmakers like Nanteuil in favor of freely handled etchings. This also reflected a commitment to etching as an independent art form comparable to drawing and capable of conveying artistic genius.[122] Some French printmakers, distancing themselves from colleagues chiefly concerned with printing precise reproductions of paintings for the commercial market, also began to champion an aesthetic of sketch-like spontaneity, partly inspired by the light handling and experimental tendencies visible in the work of Rembrandt.[123] Derived from Rembrandt's oeuvre, the genre of the sketch plate, on which figures are represented at various scales and states of finish, probably arose as a site of experimentation with the etching needle but ultimately allowed the artist to demonstrate ingenuity and technical prowess.[124] The informal appearance of such sketch plates, however, did not always reflect the printmaker's actual process. In *Studies of Heads* (1770), an etching by self-taught artist Jean-Jacques de Boissieu (1736–1810), for example, the six small, loosely described heads at the lower right replaced a single, larger, more finished head that Boissieu had originally placed there and later burnished out.[125]

JEAN-HONORÉ FRAGONARD
Nymph Stepping over the Hands of Two Satyrs
PLATE 36

In 1666, Louis XIV had introduced the Prix de Rome, which sent France's most promising young painters, sculptors, and architects to Rome for four years of study. Jean-Honoré Fragonard (1732–1806) produced four etchings of *Bacchanales* (1763) while he was there, pointing to his study of classical antiquities and his growing interest in landscape.[126] In the series, he channels the light touch and loose, expressive lines of Castiglione and the Tiepolos, whose etchings he would have seen in the collection of his teacher François Boucher (1703–1770) even before his journey to Italy.[127] Fragonard conveys a dazzling variety of textures with the etching needle. His treatment of the foliage, from the dense cross-hatching of the shadows in the underbrush to the exuberant squiggles of the canopies of leaves and the patches of the paper left blank to evoke the gleam of sunlight on the overhanging fronds, recalls the lush verdure of Castiglione's prints (pl. 31) and might even be understood as a pastiche of his work.[128] Throughout the series, the satyrs and nymphs seem to emerge from the stone and into their leafy surroundings, sustaining the atmosphere of dreamlike fantasy suggested by the siting of the reliefs amid a tangle of greenery, an overgrown fragment of a forgotten past. In *Nymph Stepping over the Hands of Two Satyrs*, the artist blends landscape with classical allusion and illusion in

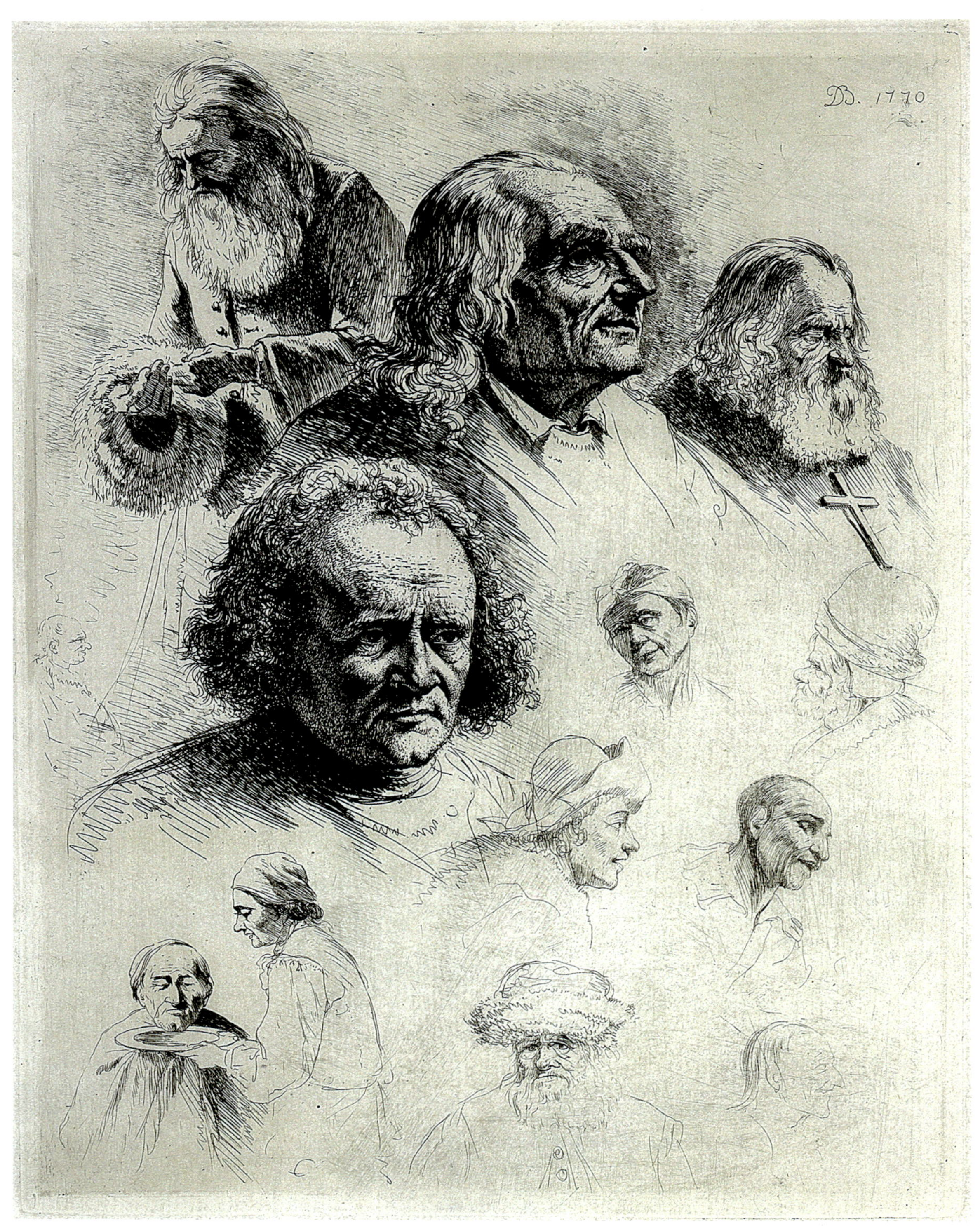

35 JEAN-JACQUES DE BOISSIEU

Studies of Heads 1770

Etching, third state of three, $9\frac{1}{8} \times 6\frac{15}{16}$ in. (23.2 × 17.7 cm). Perez 49 (2002.653)

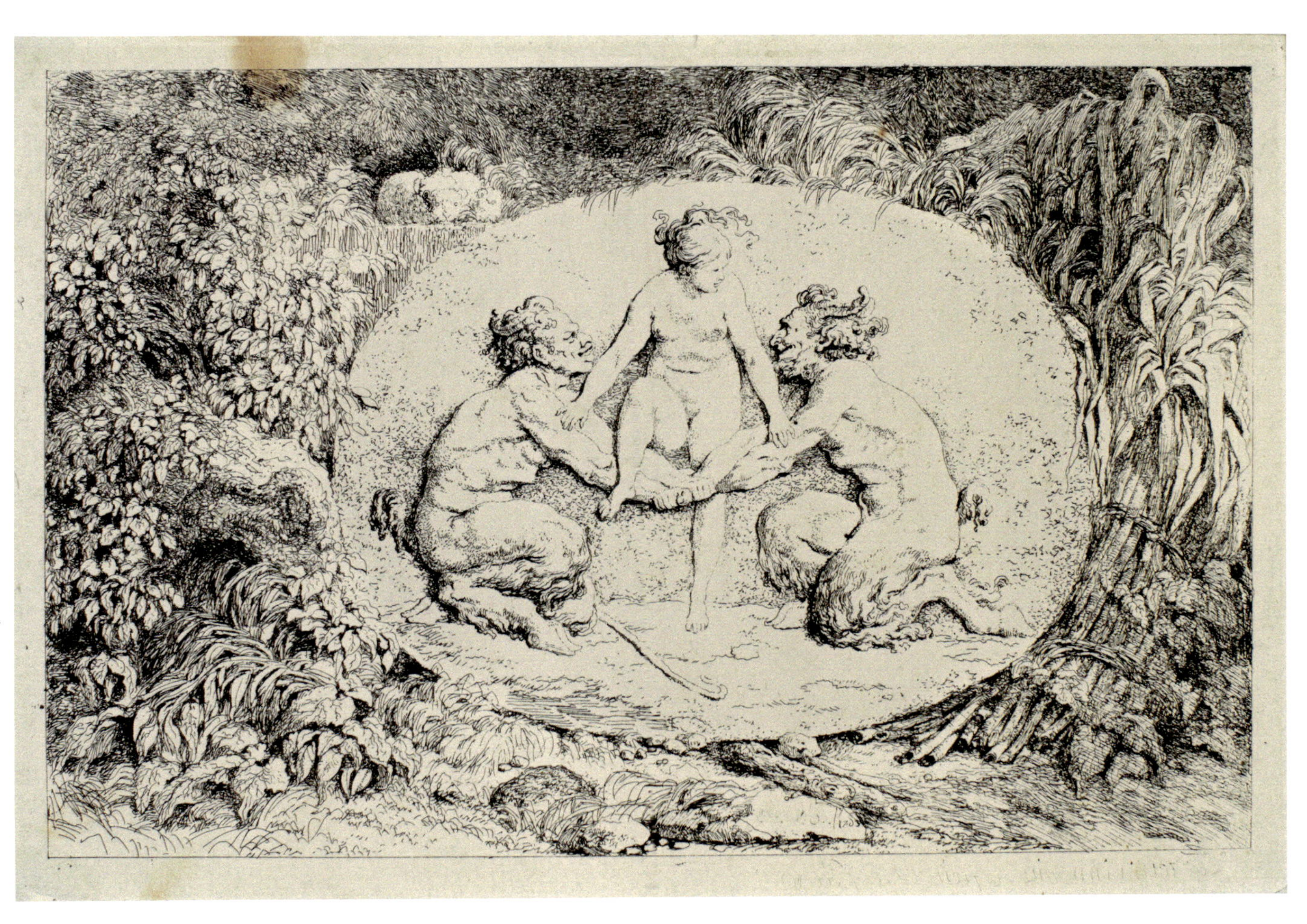

36 JEAN-HONORÉ FRAGONARD

Nymph Stepping over the Hands of Two Satyrs, plate 1 from *Bacchanales* 1763

Etching, first state of two, 5 11/16 × 8 1/4 in. (14.4 × 21 cm). Wildenstein 3 (2002.2591) a composition loosely related to an ancient sarcophagus relief from the Villa Mattei in Rome;[129] the design reflects the playful practices of appropriation, adaptation, and selective copying championed by the etchers of the time.[130]

GIOVANNI BATTISTA PIRANESI
Avanzi del Tempio del Dio Canopo nella Villa Adriana in Tivoli (Remains of the Temple of the God Canopus at Hadrian's Villa, Tivoli) from *Vedute di Roma* (Views of Rome)
PLATE 37

Italian printmakers were, perhaps inevitably, also captivated by visions of antiquity during this period. Trained in architecture and influenced by time spent in the studio of Giovanni Battista Tiepolo, a fellow Venetian, Giovanni Battista Piranesi (1720–1778) would become the foremost interpreter of Rome's monuments, both past and present.[131] During his first visit to Rome in the early 1740s, sketching expeditions with companions from the French Academy nurtured his infatuation with the city's history, resulting in his first published folios of imaginary views of classically inspired buildings and architectural fragments.[132] Within the decade, Piranesi had turned his attention to specific, identified sites, albeit in his evocative and theatrical style. As he adopted a larger format and incorporated scholarly commentary into the captions and accompanying texts (published under his name but most likely composed in collaboration with other scholars, as was standard practice at the time), his works become more documentary in nature.[133]

In his etching of *Avanzi del Tempio del Dio Canopo nella Villa Adriana in Tivoli* (Remains of the Temple of the God Canopus at Hadrian's Villa in Tivoli) from *Vedute di Roma* (Views of Rome, ca. 1769), Piranesi exaggerates the colossal scale of this picturesque ruin by placing tiny contemporary figures in the scene. Two chunks of fallen ceiling from the ruin's overgrown half dome lie between the viewer and the vaulted interior, creating a sense of removal from the remains of the past, while the letters A through D, faintly visible against the walls, refer to a key at the bottom of the page, suggesting that the past is systematically decipherable. Piranesi's archeological views play on this tension between the melancholy of ravaged grandeur and the positivism of scientific discovery. The commentary identifies materials and decorative elements and also argues for a new identification of this structure as a temple dedicated to Neptune, rather than Canopus. With publications that combine magnificently etched views (sometimes with up to twelve applications of acid to achieve such varied tonalities)[134] and scholarly text, Piranesi sought a place for himself in the European antiquarian intellectual community, framing his printmaking activities as primarily motivated by a scholarly interest in the classical past rather than merely decorative or commercial exercises.[135] In any case, these works brought him considerable financial success. An influx of tourists to Rome during this period, particularly wealthy British Grand Tourists, eagerly acquired prints as souvenirs of their travels, as had Regensburg's pilgrims two centuries before (pl. 2).

JOHN CLERK OF ELDIN
Pont y Prydd (Bridge of Beauty)
PLATE 38

Among Piranesi's closest foreign associates was the Scottish architect Robert Adam (1728–1792), who arrived in Rome in 1755 and soon began exploring its antiquities under Piranesi's tutelage; Piranesi dedicated his publication *Campus Martius antiquae urbis* (Campus Martius of the ancient city, 1762) to Adam, thus promoting the architect's reputation.[136] When Adam returned to England in 1758, he resumed artistic collaborations with his brother-in-law, John Clerk of Eldin (1728–1812), an Edinburgh merchant and amateur artist.[137] Adam, Clerk, and Paul Sandby, a founding member of the Royal Academy in London and an early practitioner of the aquatint technique, had been going on sketching expeditions together in the Scottish countryside since the 1740s.[138] Scottish enthusiasm for

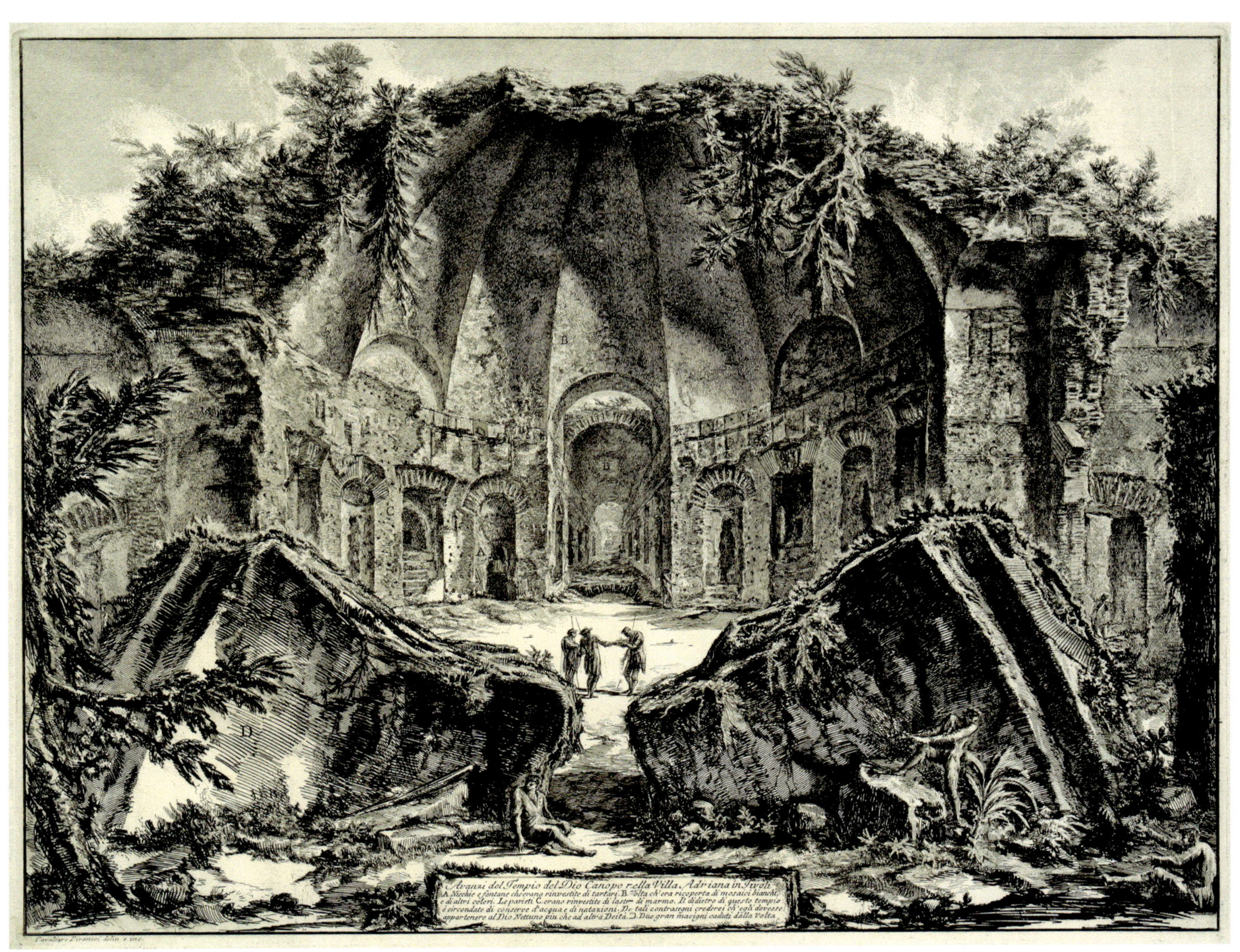

37 GIOVANNI BATTISTA PIRANESI

Avanzi del Tempio del Dio Canopo nella Villa Adriana in Tivoli (Remains of the Temple of the God Canopus at Hadrian's Villa in Tivoli) from *Vedute di Roma* (Views of Rome) CA. 1769

Etching, second state of four, 18 × 23⅛ in. (45.7 × 58.7 cm). Hind 90, Wilton-Ely 223 (2002.1670)

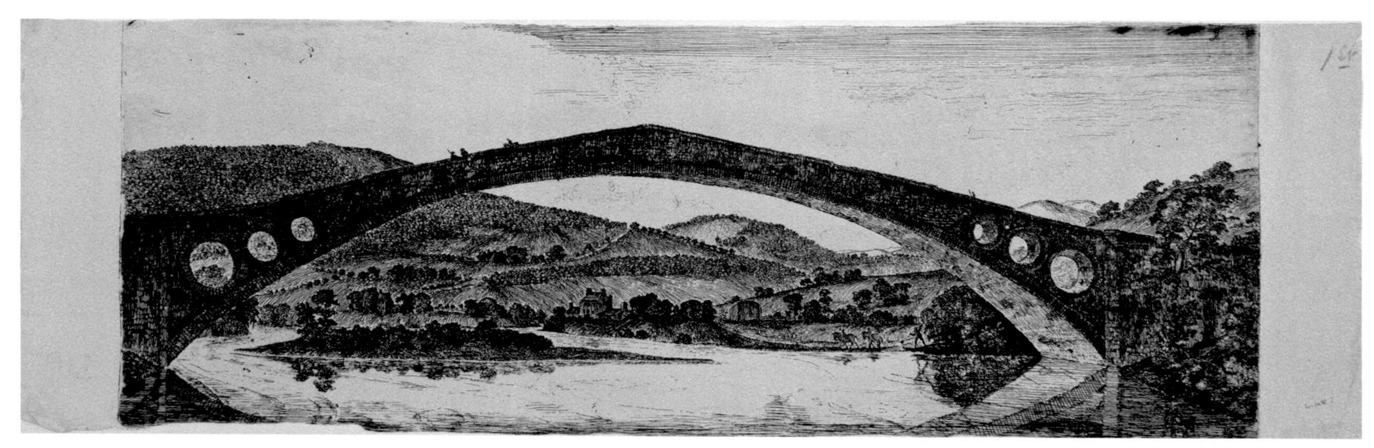

38 JOHN CLERK OF ELDIN

Pont y Prydd (Bridge of Beauty) 1772–78

Etching, first state of five, 4 7/16 × 11 3/4 in. (11.3 × 29.8 cm). Lumsden 48, Bertram 64 (2002.1234) landscape as a genre had never been higher, particularly among the rising population of amateur artists, most working in the fashionable medium of drawing.[139] Scottish landscape etching, however, remained rare.[140] Intrigued by the mechanical process as well as by the prospect of reproducing his drawings in print, Clerk took up etching in around 1770, and within eight years produced more than one hundred compositions, including two after Claude Lorrain.[141] In contrast to Clerk's typical scenes of castles and ruins, *Pont y Prydd* (Bridge of Beauty, 1772–78) illustrates a major structural achievement: the largest single-arch bridge in Wales, which he traveled to draw before making his print.[142] With its subtle elegance—the wooded hills in the distance echo the bridge's unusual curvature—and the artist's neat, careful recording of the different textures and arrangements of stone that make up the bridge, *Pont y Prydd* reflects both the scientific curiosity and the longing for the picturesque that characterized the contemporary fascination with landscape, both local and foreign.

> CORNELIS PLOOS VAN AMSTEL
> *The Virgin Adoring the Christ Child*
> PLATE 39

In response to the increasing interest of collectors in drawings during the eighteenth century, printmakers sought to mimic the effects of chalk, ink, and watercolor by texturizing their plates with various tools, and began working in the new **aquatint** and **mezzotint** techniques to this end.[143] The addition of colored inks and the layering of multiple plates allowed artists to further approximate the appearance of drawing in print. In his reproductions of drawings by various Netherlandish artists, Cornelis Ploos van Amstel (1726–1798), another somewhat obscure figure in Steinberg's collection, often employed all of these processes. A timber merchant, artist, collector, and director of the Amsterdam Drawing Academy, Ploos also applied his own transfer method, which involved tracing a drawing whose verso had been treated with a rough powder that, when impressed into a hard-ground coating on the plate, produced a chalk-like line.[144] For his reproduction of Abraham Bloemaert's *The Virgin Adoring the Christ Child* (1769), he created two plates: one with the etched lines and roulette printed in black, and a second mezzotint plate printed in ochre.[145] The third color—white—is represented by reserves of exposed paper. By replicating the collector's mark of a previous owner at the lower right, Ploos draws attention to Bloemaert's drawing as a unique, historical object in itself rather than as a design to be transferred and adapted, as in previous models of collaborative reproductive printmaking. That many of Ploos's prints are copies of drawings in his own collection, numbering more than seven thousand,[146] places his oeuvre within the larger context of the *recueil*, a compendium of prints intended to reproduce either a famous collection of paintings and drawings or all the works of a particular artist.[147] Such publications enhanced the status of wealthy collectors and promoted the work of prominent artists while effectively circulating new artistic ideas.

> ANGELICA KAUFFMANN
> *La Penserosa*
> PLATE 40

The vogue in late eighteenth-century England for "furniture prints" was largely related to the ability of artists to produce prints resembling drawings and watercolors using the latest techniques. Such prints were typically framed and hung—often in pairs to provide balanced interior design—rather than hidden between the pages of a collector's album.[148] The oval-formatted *La Penserosa* (1779) and its pendant, *L'Allegra* (also in Steinberg's collection), typify the genre and showcase the sensitive etching and aquatint skills of Swiss-born painter Angelica Kauffmann (1741–1807), one of two female founding members of the Royal Academy of Arts in London in 1768. Kauffmann began her artistic training with her father, the muralist Johann Joseph Kauffmann, and received her

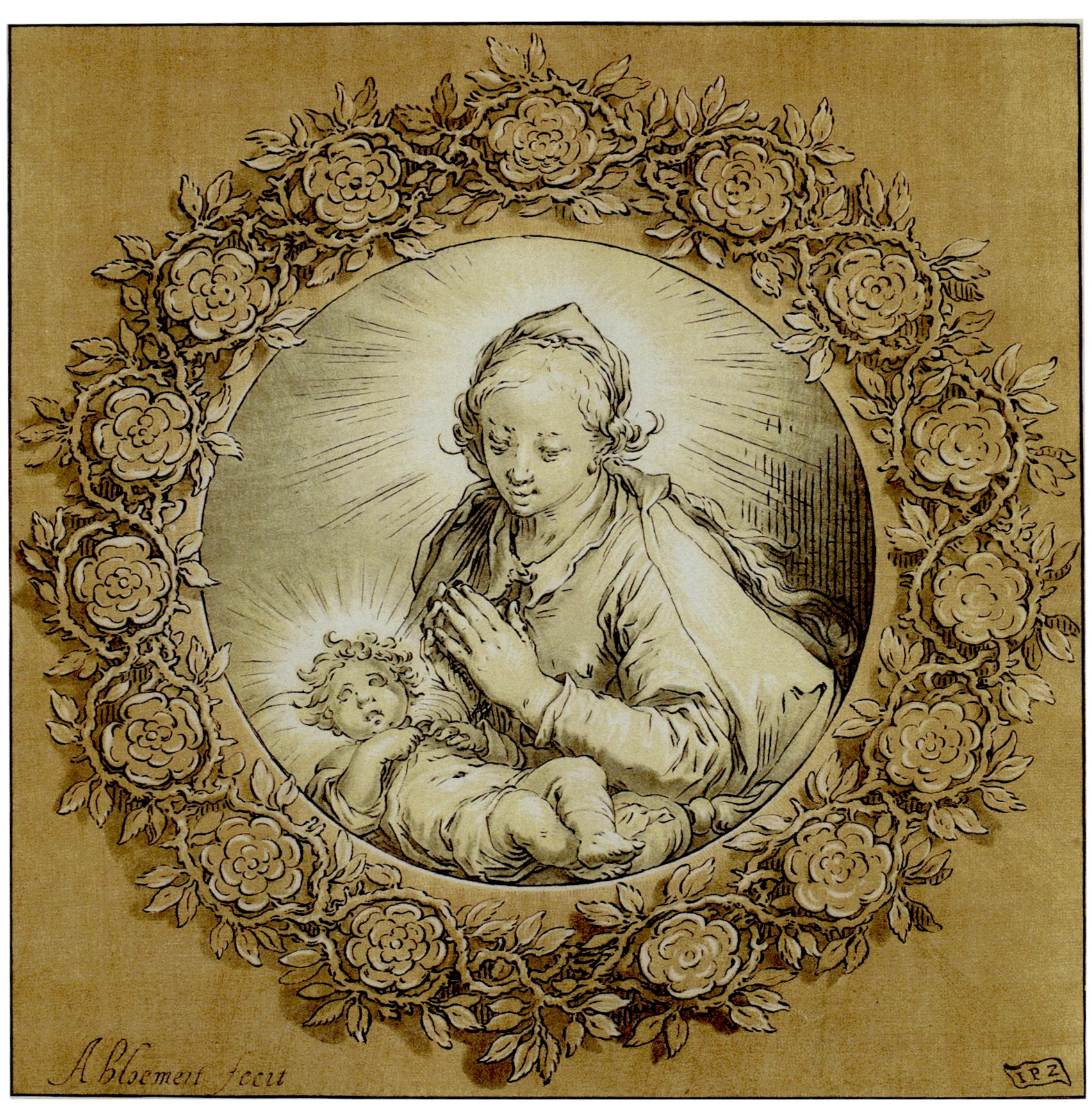

39 CORNELIS PLOOS VAN AMSTEL

The Virgin Adoring the Christ Child, after a drawing by Abraham Bloemaert 1769

Etching and roulette in Ploos van Amstel's transfer technique printed in black and mezzotint printed in ochre, from two plates, only state, 6⅞ × 6⅝ in. (17.4 × 16.8 cm). Laurentius 16 (2002.1096)

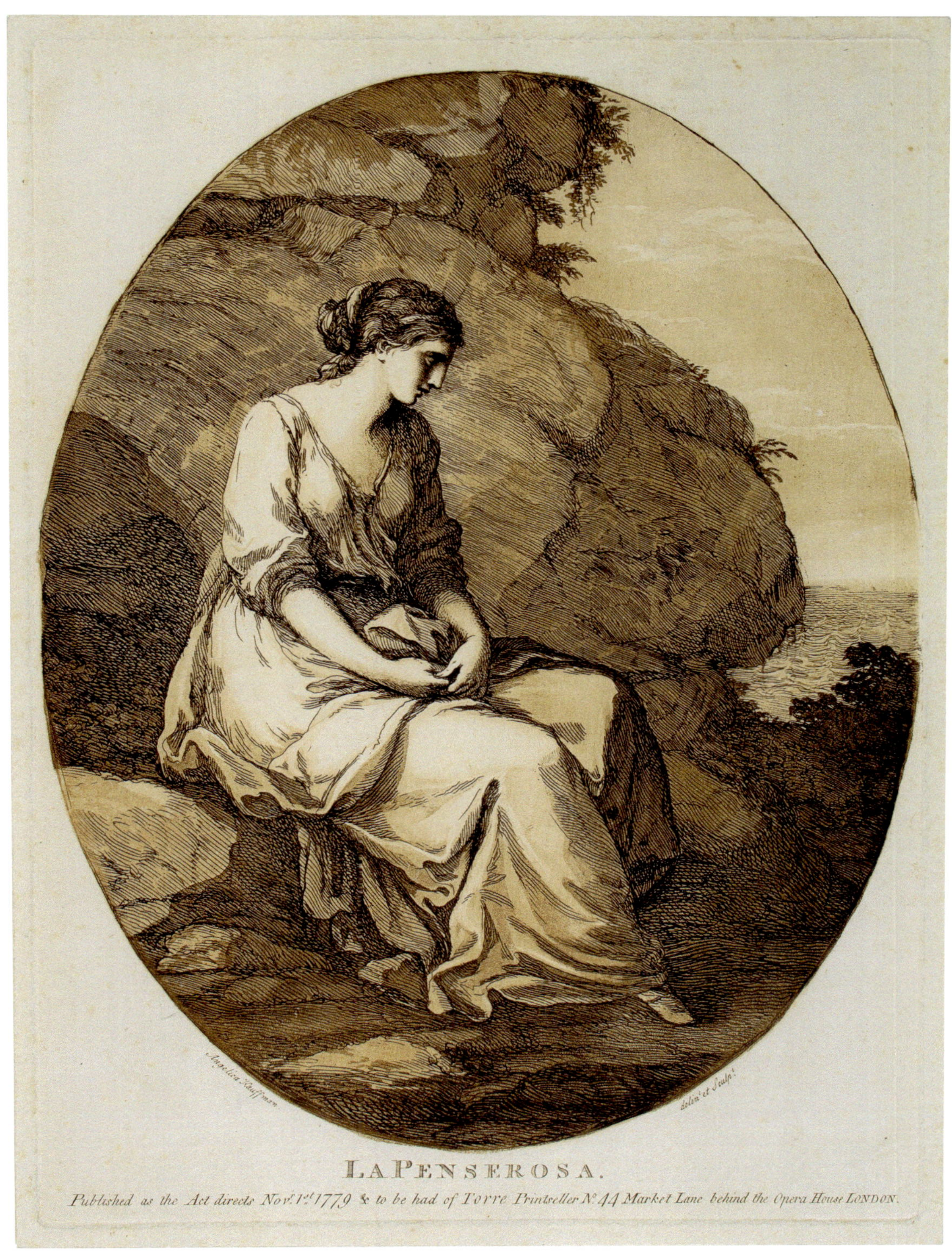

40 ANGELICA KAUFFMANN

La Penserosa 1779

Color etching and aquatint printed in black and brown, first state of two (?). 11 × 8 in. (27.9 × 20.3 cm). Andresen 19 (2002.1224) first portrait commissions in her early teens.[149] Working as her father's assistant, Kauffmann traveled throughout Switzerland, Austria, and Italy in the early 1760s, which gave her the opportunity—exceedingly rare for women in her time—to study key works from antiquity and the Renaissance. In 1762, she began making small etchings in Florence, bringing her plates with her when she moved to London in 1766. There she further solidified her reputation as a portraitist and history painter. Before she permanently left London for Rome in 1781, Kauffmann sold her plates, most of which were purchased by the publisher John Boydell, who added aquatint to some before reprinting them.[150]

La Penserosa and *L'Allegra* are based on John Milton's "Il Penseroso" (1632) and "L' Allegro" (1645), allegorical meditations on the melancholy and joy that drive the creative process. In "Il Penseroso," the speaker, presumably male, summons a contemplative muse:

> But hail thou goddess, sage and holy
> Hail divinest Melancholy,
> Whose saintly visage is too bright
> To hit the sense of human sight . . .

Kauffmann shifts the title to the feminine *Penserosa*, inviting the viewer to read the central figure in this work not as the muse but as the poet, offering an articulation of female authorship rare for the period.[151] Kauffmann, of course, embodied this rarity herself, and by 1781 was so successful that an engraver was quoted by the Danish ambassador as saying that, "the whole world is angelicamad."[152] The high demand for Kauffmann's work led her to collaborate with several reproductive printmakers whose numerous mezzotints and stipple engravings after her designs made her the most reproduced painter in England.[153] Her designs not only appeared on such decorative objects as furniture, porcelain, and textiles, but these reproductive prints were also avidly collected by connoisseurs both in England and abroad.[154]

GILLES-LOUIS CHRÉTIEN
Physionotrace portrait of an unidentified female
PLATE 41

While artists like Kauffmann painted portraits for elite patrons, others found a lucrative market and ample room for innovation by pleasing a more modest clientele. Steinberg acquired quite a number of these more popular prints, works that also reflect his own eclectic tastes as a collector. This portrait, whose sitter remains unidentified, is a product of the physionotrace, a prephotographic process invented by musician and entrepreneur Gilles-Louis Chrétien (1757–1811) around 1784. To capture the image, one of Chrétien's colleagues traced the subject's profile with a pantograph, a device that makes it possible to draw in two scales at once.[155] Chrétien then etched the miniaturized version onto a copperplate. Wealthier clients, like the one in his *Physionotrace portrait of an unidentified female* (ca. 1789), paid extra to have color added to their images, achieved "à la poupée" by dabbing colored ink on the plate by hand with a wad of cloth. Within four days of the initial session, a client received the full-scale drawing, twelve small prints, and, for an additional fee, the copperplate itself.[156] With its mechanized methodology, the physionotrace appealed to the growing interest of the French public in physiognomy, a pseudoscience devoted to the deduction of character traits based on facial features. Due to its small cost, the short sitting time it required, its much-touted verisimilitude (surpassing even Nanteuil's ability to minimize the hand of the artist), and its resemblance to more expensive works in oil, crayon, or pencil, the physionotrace enjoyed a heyday between 1788 and 1830.[157] It spread from France to Germany and the United States before 1839, when the emergence of the daguerreotype—the first commercial photographic process—rendered it obsolete.

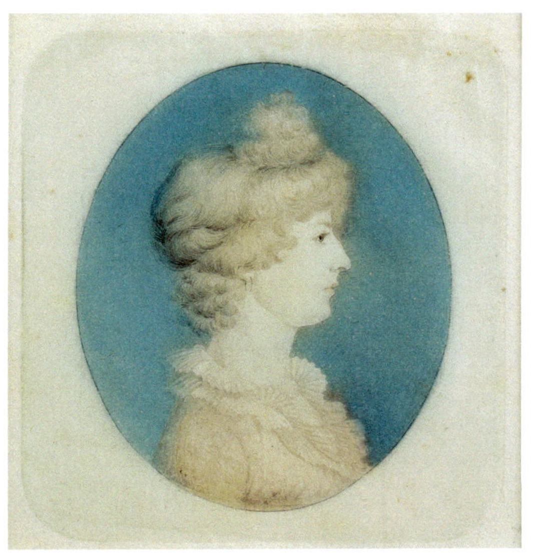

41 GILLES-LOUIS CHRÉTIEN

Physionotrace portrait of an unidentified female CA. 1789

Color etching and aquatint, inked à la poupée, only state, 2 15/16 × 2 11/16 in. (7.5 × 6.8 cm). (2002.699)

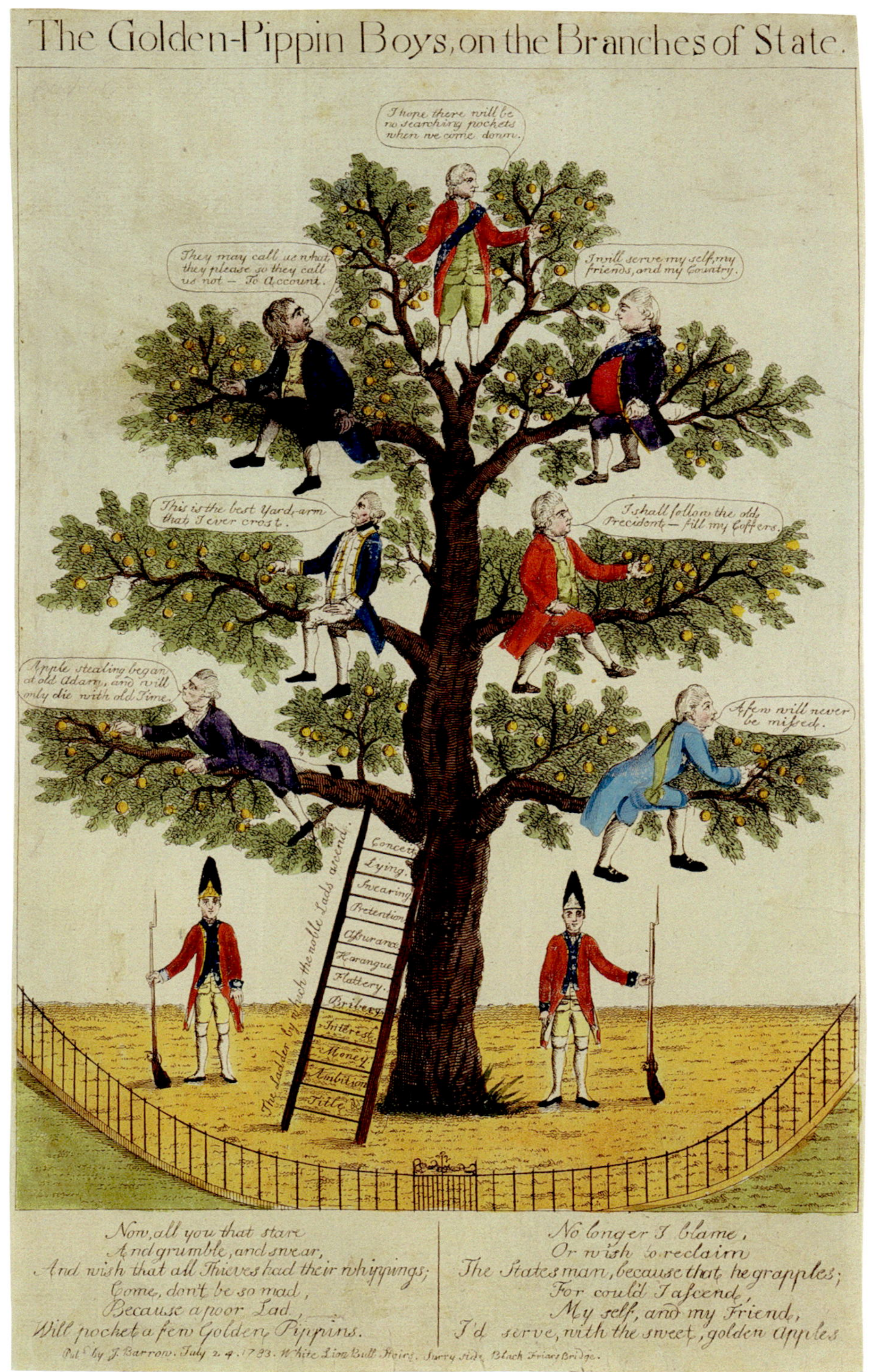

42 UNKNOWN BRITISH ARTIST

The Golden-Pippin Boys on the Branches of State 1783

Etching with hand coloring, only state, 13¾ × 8⁵⁄₁₆ in. (35 × 21.1 cm). George 6251 (2002.1218)

UNKNOWN BRITISH ARTIST
The Golden-Pippin Boys on the Branches of State
PLATE 42

English printmakers and publishers, lacking the kind of state sponsorship for print production that had existed in France since the late seventeenth century, began marketing their works to a broader audience through newspapers, subscription services, and printed catalogues.[158] By 1780, London had overtaken Paris as the capital of the European print market. Among the prints displayed in the windows of London's print shops, satirical images addressing the city's political and social life were particularly popular.[159] In the hand-colored etching ***The Golden-Pippin Boys on the Branches of State*** (1783), an anonymous British satirist depicts statesmen and noblemen perched in the branches of a tall tree, stealing golden apples and expressing in speech bubbles their barely concealed greed, self-interest, and corruption.[160] Flanked by armed guards, a ladder rests against the tree trunk, each of its rungs bearing a tactic or trait required to ascend to political power: "ambition," "bribery," "flattery," "lying," "conceit." Although their corruption and their excuses for it are timeless enough (one cites "the old precident [*sic*]" while another claims "A few will never be missed"), these shameless gentlemen represent specific people, including Prime Minister Frederick North (who led Britain through most of the American War of Independence) and the prominent Whig statesman Charles James Fox; they were archenemies and two of the period's most frequently targeted figures.[161] The man leaning out over the lowest of the branches on the left, adding a biblical flavor to his apologism ("Apple Stealing began at old Adam, and will only die with old Time"), is the philosopher, economist, and Member of Parliament Edmund Burke.[162] Offended parties usually considered prosecution too costly to pursue, and politicians who took a hostile stance against caricaturists risked finding themselves the subjects of the next print. Given this, and its relative press freedom, Britain enjoyed a golden age of graphic satire between 1770 and 1830.[163]

THE NINETEENTH CENTURY

HONORÉ DAUMIER
Nayades de la Seine (Naiads of the Seine)
PLATE 43

The nineteenth century in France saw the rise of such illustrated newspapers as Charles Philipon's *Le Charivari*, to which Honoré Daumier (1808–1879) contributed more than four thousand caricatures. Such publications offered a new generation of artists an outlet for providing up-to-the-minute commentary on contemporary life with a humorous or satirical twist. **Lithography**, the newly invented printmaking process that allowed artists to create prints nearly as easily as drawings, greatly facilitated these efforts.[164]

Daumier first made his name with political cartoons lampooning the repressive government of King Louis-Philippe, and received a six-month prison sentence for an 1831 depiction of the king as Rabelais's Gargantua; he and the artists of *Le Charivari* continued to produce their famous caricatures of the king in the guise of a pear (*poire* also translates as "fool").[165] When stricter censorship was enacted under the July Monarchy's September Laws of 1835, Daumier, in accordance with *Le Charivari*'s new strategy, shifted his focus to satirical images of the emerging bourgeoisie, a class that also constituted his primary audience during this period.[166] His caricature ***Nayades de la Seine*** (Naiads of the Seine, *Le Charivari*, July 14, 1847) showing Parisian bathers reflects new standards of hygiene and the encouragement of bathing as a healthy form of recreation conducive to cleanliness.[167] Swimming schools sprang up along the Seine in the early nineteenth century, along with public baths ranging from the inexpensive *bains à quatr'sous* to the luxurious spas favored by wealthy citizens.[168] Daumier found boundless potential for comedy in the awkward enactment

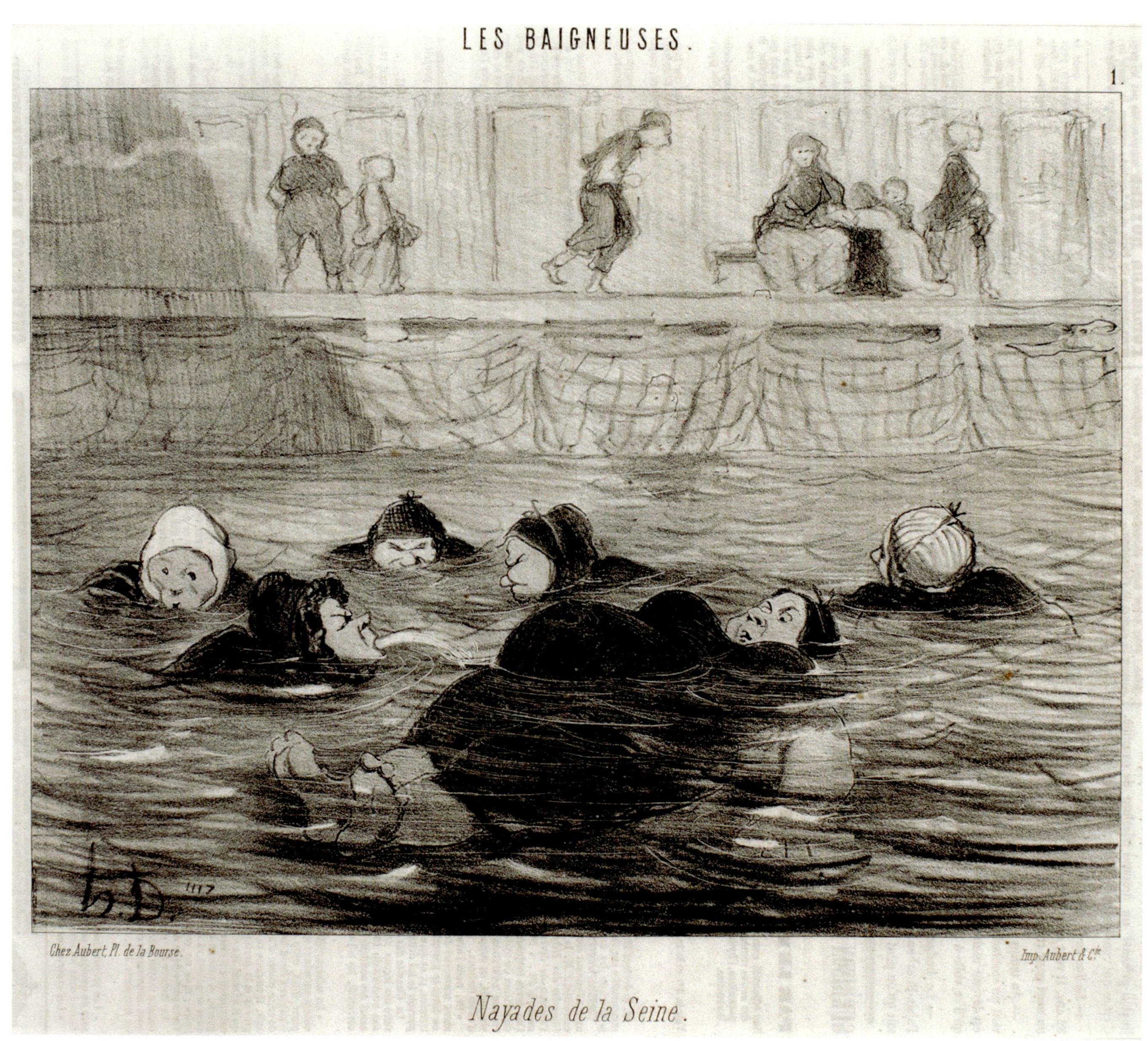

43 HONORÉ DAUMIER

Nayades de la Seine (Naiads of the Seine), plate 1 from *Les Baigneuses* (The Bathers), published in *Le Charivari* JULY 14, 1847

Lithograph on newsprint, second state of two, 7⁹⁄₁₆ × 9½ in. (19.2 × 24.1 cm). Daumier Register 1629 (2002.1567) of this highly visible middle-class fixation, making it the subject of two series, *Les Baigneurs* (1839–1842) and *Les Baigneuses* (1847), showing bathing men and women. Here, Daumier cheekily likens a group of heavy-set women cooling off in the Seine, clad in long bathing dresses and caps, to naiads, the dainty water spirits of classical mythology. He achieved a range of tones through the use of lithographic crayons in varying degrees of softness, which he then scraped away in thin, arcing lines that delineate the water's surface from its depths.

UNKNOWN FRENCH ARTIST
PUBLISHED BY IMAGERIE D'ÉPINAL, PELLERIN & CIE
La Robe de N.-S. Jésus-Christ, no. 1851
PLATE 44

The brightly hand-colored wood engravings (and later, lithographs) produced by the French printing house Imagerie d'Épinal, Pellerin & Cie in the Vosges in northeastern France were intended for viewers of more conventional tastes than those who enjoyed the biting wit and cosmopolitanism of Daumier's satires. When designer, illustrator, and printmaker Jean-Charles Pellerin (1756–1836) founded the house in Épinal in 1796, he capitalized on the long-established paper industry of the Vosges region and its historic production of printed playing cards and decorative papers.[169] Imagerie d'Épinal prints featured religious themes, military exploits, historical events, moralizing stories, and games, appealing to adults and children alike. Through four generations, the Pellerins expanded their repertoire of subjects—offering nearly two thousand titles in their 1914 sales catalogue—as well as their printing capacity, with each matrix producing between three hundred thousand and five hundred thousand impressions by the late nineteenth century.[170] Networks of *colporteurs* (traveling peddlers) sold Épinal prints, along with rosaries, candles, and other small devotional items throughout the French provinces.[171] Despite their prolific production runs, Épinal prints survive in small numbers because they were cut up, pasted on walls, and used for instruction, rather than preserved in the pages of albums or framed.

Typical of Épinal's pious subjects, *La Robe de N.-S. Jésus-Christ* (ca. 1844) commemorates the 1844 display of a relic known as the Holy Coat. The seamless robe, believed to have been worn by Christ just before the Crucifixion and brought to Europe from the Holy Land in 326 C.E. by St. Helena, is housed in St. Peter's Cathedral in Trier in southwestern Germany, which continues to be a site of pilgrimage for this reason. Like Ostendorfer's woodcut, *A Pilgrimage to the Church of the Beautiful Virgin at Regensburg* (pl. 2), this lithograph served both to commemorate a significant religious event and as a devotional aid. The eye-catching colors were stenciled by hand, a process usually carried out by children, who made up more than half of Épinal's employees in 1845.[172]

FRANCIS SEYMOUR HADEN
An Early Riser
PLATE 45

In an era that saw the expansion of commercial lithography, the popularization of photography, and the final flowering of highly technical reproductive engraving, artists in Britain and France founded societies that promoted etching as a creative technique unique in its ability to channel the hand and mind of the artist.[173] The Société des aquafortistes was established in Paris in 1862, while the Etching Club, formed in London in 1838, was succeeded there by the Society for Painter-Etchers in 1880. A cofounder of the latter organization, surgeon and artist Francis Seymour Haden (1818–1910) also championed etching through his own printmaking as well as in his exhibitions of prints by Rembrandt with related lectures and publications.[174] He mainly produced landscapes and riverscapes, influenced by the work of his brother-in-law, the American painter and etcher James McNeill Whistler, and by prints in his personal collection by artists like Adriaen van Ostade and Rembrandt.[175] The draftsman-like immediacy of his etchings partly relates to his practice of

PELLERIN & Cie, imp.-édit. **LA ROBE DE N.-S.-JÉSUS-CHRIST.** IMAGERIE D'EPINAL, N° 1851

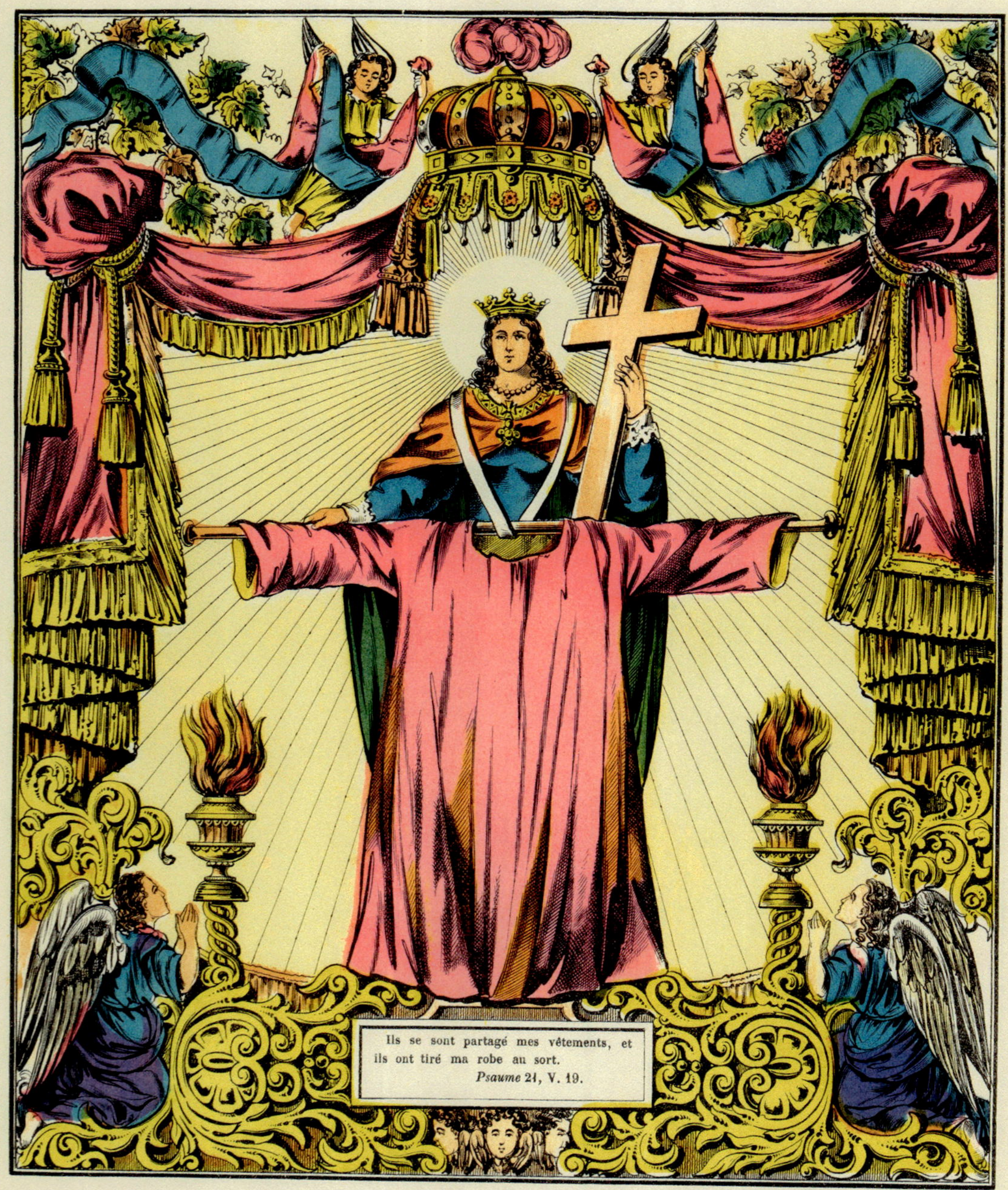

Cette Robe est conforme à celle qui a été apportée de la Terre-Sainte en 326, par Sainte Hélène, et qui a été exposée depuis le 18 août 1844 jusqu'au 29 septembre de la même année, dans la cathédrale de Trèves.

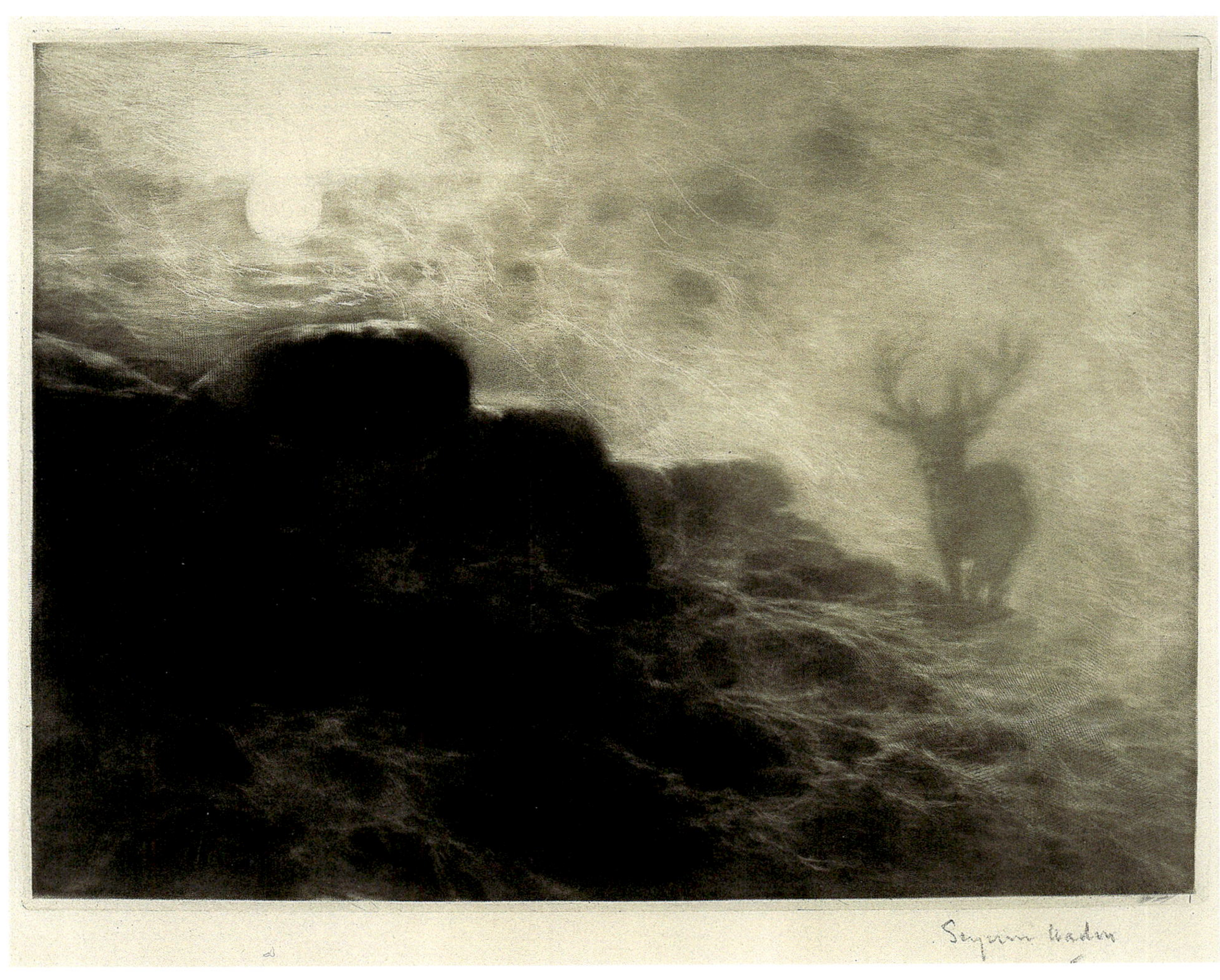

44

UNKNOWN FRENCH ARTIST
PUBLISHED BY IMAGERIE D'ÉPINAL, PELLERIN & CIE

La Robe de N.-S. Jésus-Christ, no. 1851 CA. 1844

Lithograph with hand-stenciled color on newsprint, 13 7/16 × 10 1/8 in. (34.2 × 25.6 cm). (2002.717)

45

FRANCIS SEYMOUR HADEN

An Early Riser 1897

Mezzotint, third state of four, signed in graphite, 8 3/4 × 11 11/16 in. (22.3 × 29.7 cm). Schneiderman 226 (2002.1810) sketching directly onto copperplates outdoors and his practice of working from photographs to capture the transitory effects of nature.[176] Captivated by the painterly quality of mezzotint, which he declared printmaking's "Omega" (with "intellectual etching" as the "Alpha"), Haden also experimented en plein air with mezzotint drawing, which involved scraping away at charcoal-covered paper that he brought on sketching expeditions.[177] In *An Early Riser* (1897), he depicts a fleeting encounter with a stag silhouetted against the morning fog, soon to be burnt off by the rising sun. Weblike mists swirl across dark boulders and rise through the sky in an atmospheric tour-de-force, pointing to the artist's fascination with the momentary effects of light.

> FÉLIX BUHOT
> *La Falaise: Baie de Saint-Malo* (The Cliff: Bay of Saint-Malo)
> PLATE 46

Weather conditions held a similar allure for the painter and etcher Félix Buhot (1847–1898), who described his own etchings in a letter to Haden as "paintings on copper."[178] By combining all sorts of intaglio techniques, selecting papers of various weights and colors that he sometimes soaked in turpentine, coffee, or tea, and printing in different colored inks, he developed a highly experimental approach to etching that he called "an art of improvisation."[179] Although some printmakers resented the advent of photography, Buhot incorporated this new medium into his repertoire.[180] Photography posed much less of a threat to a printmaker like Buhot, acclaimed for the expressiveness and sensitivity of his prints, than it did to printmakers whose livelihood and prestige rested on the realism of their work.

A photomechanical reproduction of a watercolor by Buhot's father-in-law, Henry Johnston, provides the basis for the central composition of *La Falaise: Baie de Saint-Malo* (The Cliff: Bay of Saint-Malo, 1889–90), one of many prints that Buhot reworked over a period of years, here layering etching, roulette, aquatint, spit bite, drypoint, and burnishing, and even using a pumice stone to achieve the rich, black tones of the cliff's flanks.[181] Inspired by Japanese prints (which began arriving in Paris shortly after Japan opened to trade with the West in 1853), French manuscript illumination, and the contemporary taste for *remarques*—all of which feature marginal images and notations bracketed from the central image—Buhot surrounded many of his compositions with etched vignettes, which he called "symphonic margins."[182] In the separately printed frame of *La Falaise*, twisting vines, boats at sea, birds in flight, religious figures, everyday characters, and other motifs settle like a mist of daydreams around the view of the cliff, enveloping its central melody within a lush yet subtle soundscape. Light green-gray ink imbues these marginal illustrations with a sense of ephemerality, while warm bistre ink imparts solidity to the landscape. Buhot's monogrammed owl stamp in the lower margin, impressed in red like the artists' seals on Japanese prints, is a further reference to his interest in *Japonisme*. His moody, impressionistic prints were lauded at the Paris Salon and published in prominent periodicals and books; he became one of the most celebrated printmakers of his day, both in France and in the United States.

> MAURICE DELCOURT
> *La Place Saint Georges*
> PLATE 47

Maurice Delcourt's (1877–1916) *La Place Saint Georges* (1899), a scene set in a Parisian square, is even more indebted to the aesthetic of Japanese ukiyo-e ("pictures of the floating world") woodcuts, sharing with them an emphasis on outline, the juxtaposition of bold, flat planes of color, and a close-up, flattened perspective.[183] Produced between the seventeenth and nineteenth centuries, ukiyo-e represent the pleasures and entertainments of daily life. Delcourt's bustling urban scene similarly portrays two fashionably garbed women pausing to allow a young girl dressed for First Communion

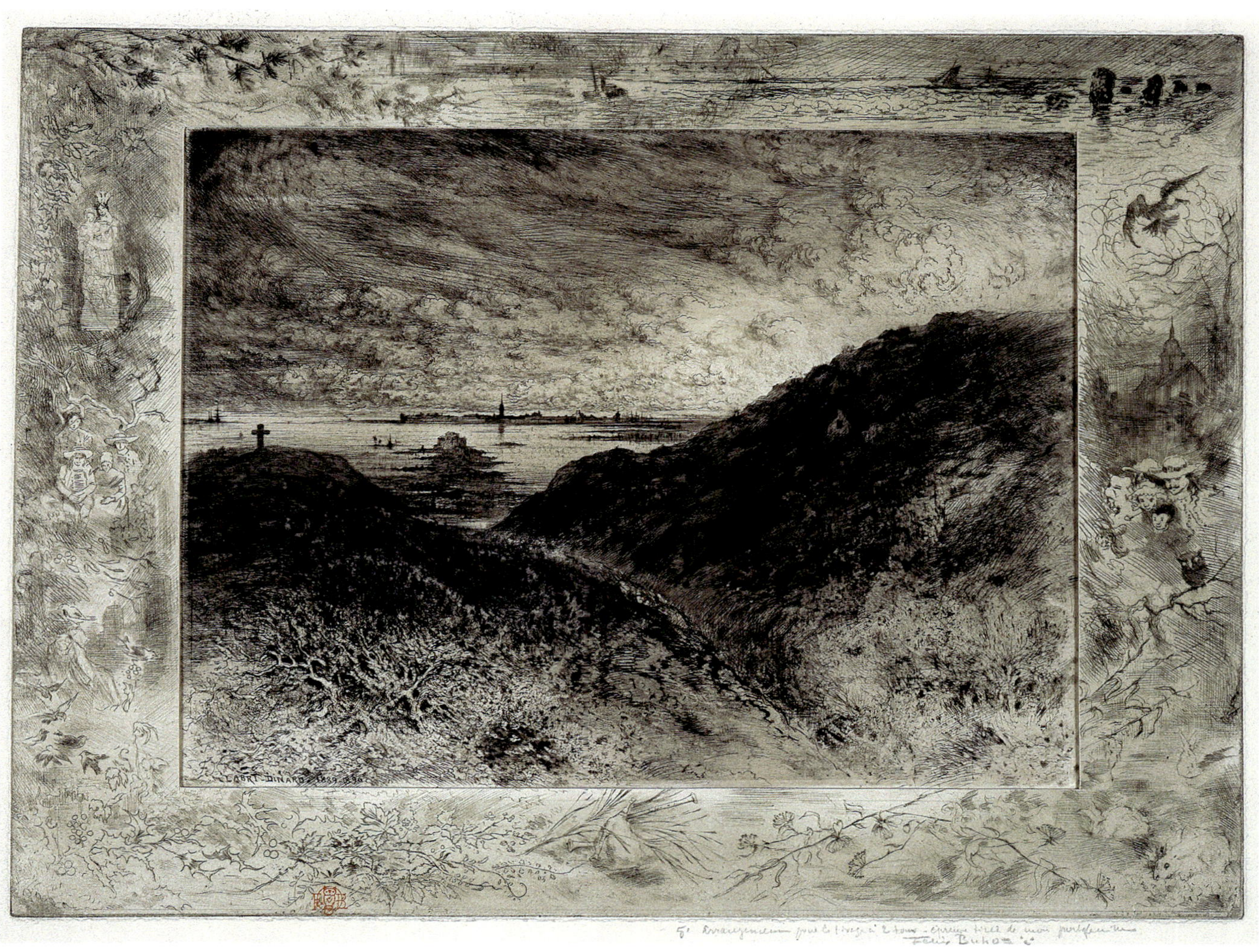

46 FÉLIX BUHOT

La Falaise: Baie de Saint-Malo (The Cliff: Bay of Saint-Malo) 1889–90

Central image: photogravure with etching, drypoint, roulette, spit bite, aquatint, and burnishing printed in bistre ink, fifth state of five, 10⅝ × 14⁹⁄₁₆ in. (27 × 37 cm). Frame: etching, aquatint, drypoint, and roulette printed in gray-green ink, second state of two, inscribed in graphite in lower margin "5e arrangement pour le tirage à 2 tous épreuve tirée de mon portefeuille" and signed, 11⅞ × 15¾ in. (30.2 × 40 cm). Bourcard and Goodfriend 165 (2002.1973)

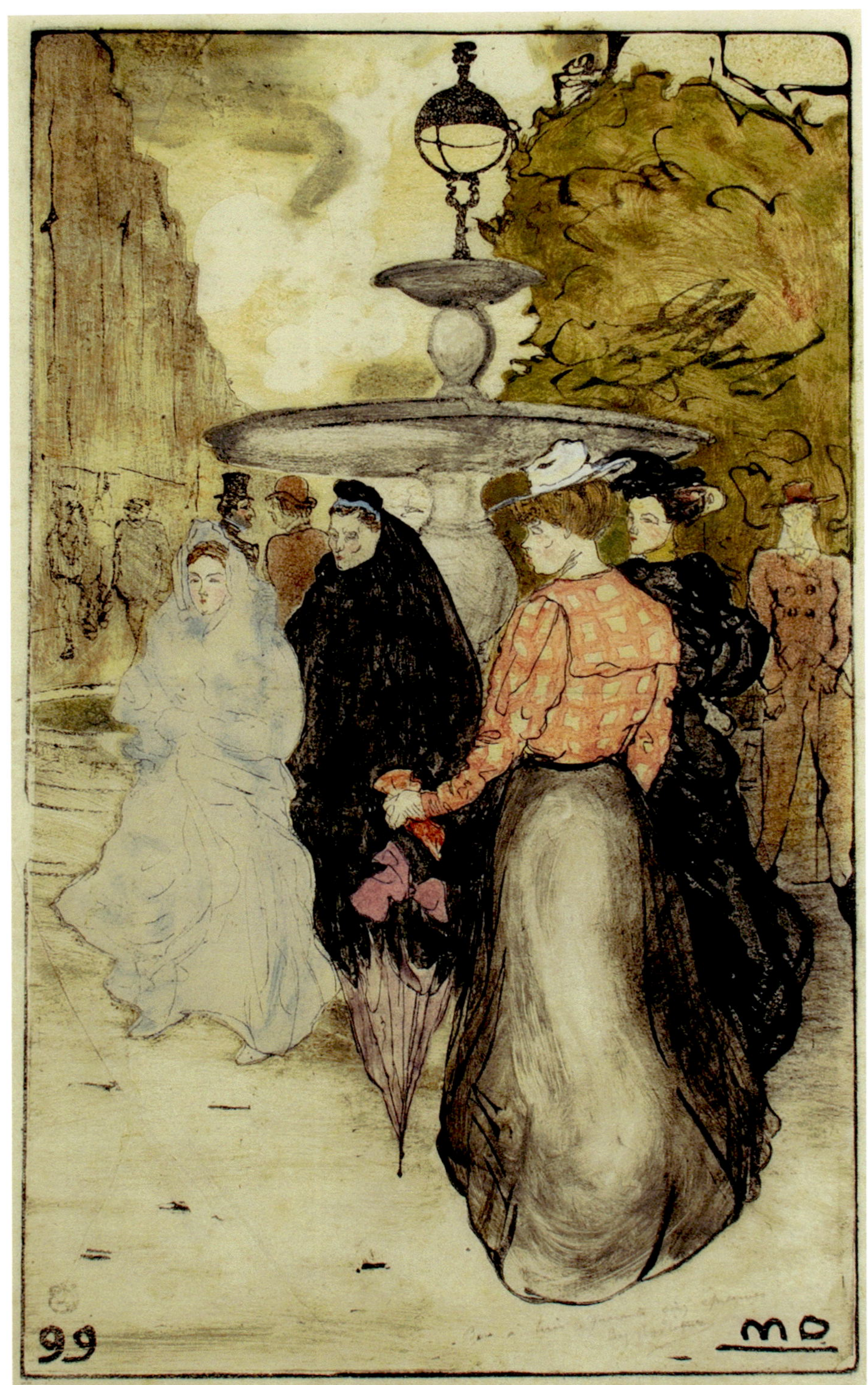

47 MAURICE DELCOURT

La Place Saint Georges 1899

Color woodcut printed from endgrain boxwood blocks in black and gelatin-based colors on thin Japan paper, inscribed "bon à tirer" from edition of 45, 12¾ × 7⁹⁄₁₆ in. (32.4 × 19.2 cm). IFF–19 6.5 (2002.1581)

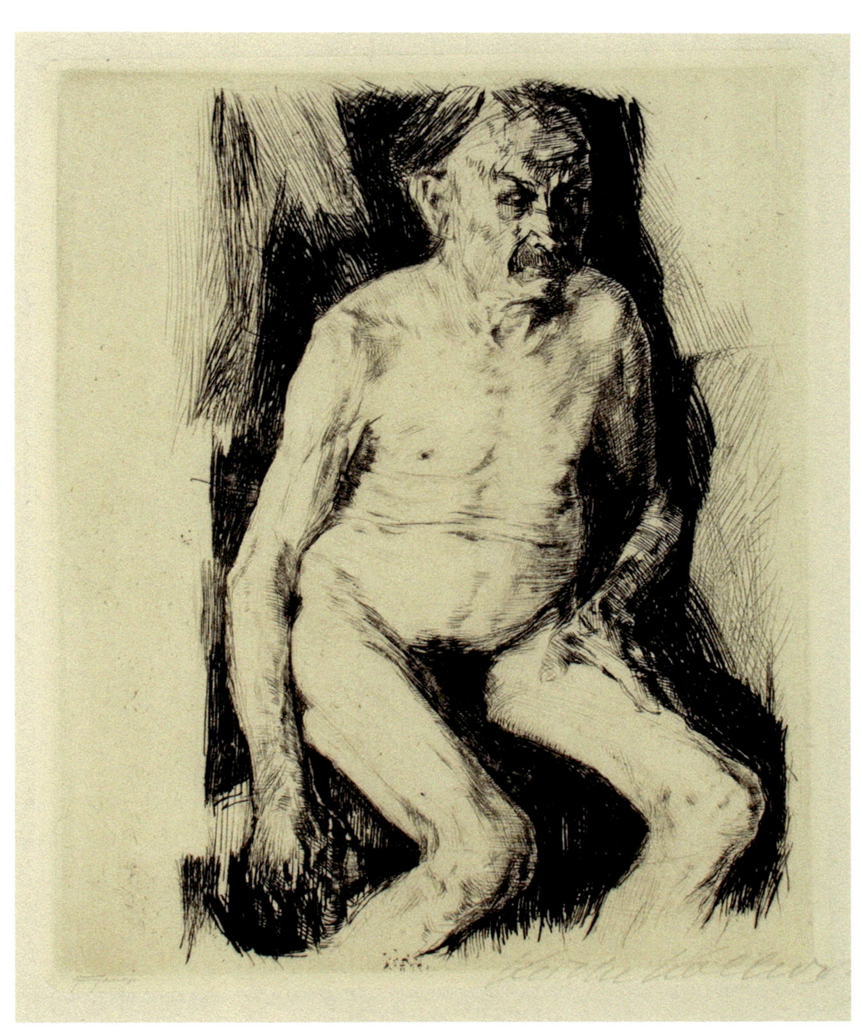

48 KÄTHE KOLLWITZ

Sitzender männlicher Akt (Seated Male Nude) 1891

Etching and drypoint, second state of two, signed in graphite, 6¼ × 5¹⁄₁₆ in. (15.7 × 12.8 cm). Knesebeck 4 IIb/f (2002.1573) and her mother to pass by, while others are engaged in their daily activities in the background. The slightly cropped figure at right and an overall sense of stilled motion give the image the quality of a photographic snapshot. Delcourt printed his woodcut—the traditional process for Japanese prints—by layering colored blocks inked with gelatin over a black line block on thin, translucent paper from Japan; such specialized papers had long appealed to European artists, including Rembrandt. This print was originally distributed through L'Estampe Nouvelle, a print society founded in 1897 that circulated to its members by subscription a publication containing original contemporary prints.[184]

> KÄTHE KOLLWITZ
> *Sitzender männlicher Akt* (Seated Male Nude)
> PLATE 48

In contrast to Delcourt's scene of passing encounters between elegant Parisians, Käthe Kollwitz's intimate *Sitzender männlicher Akt* (Seated Male Nude, 1891) emphasizes human fragility. Kollwitz (1867–1945) believed that it was her duty as an artist "to voice the sufferings of humankind."[185] At seventeen, she moved to Berlin and enrolled in a women's art school to learn painting and etching, eventually expanding her practice to include woodcut and sculpture. Throughout her career, she leveraged her work as a form of social critique, and after the devastation of World War I, she was especially drawn to lithography and woodcut as mediums that allowed her to address a broad public through political posters, pamphlets, and periodicals.[186] In an art world dominated by men, Kollwitz developed a visual vocabulary centered on women, the working classes, and the experience of grief (she had lost a son in the war). In 1919, she became the first woman elected to the Prussian Academy of Arts and given the title of professor, and in 1928 she was named the director of the Master Class for Graphic Arts at the Berlin Academy of Art.

Kollwitz created this etching in 1891, the year she married the physician Karl Kollwitz, who treated many poor and working-class patients at his clinic. She established her studio in the same building, and this male figure may have been based on someone she encountered there. Though anonymous, the vulnerability and specificity of this old man are movingly conveyed through delicate drypoint and etched lines. Steinberg actually met Kollwitz while growing up in Berlin, and she was the subject of his first "published" article, which he wrote for the children's magazine he cofounded at the age of twelve.[187] Like Kollwitz, Steinberg was captivated by the expressive potential of the human figure, both in his own artmaking and in his scholarship.

THE TWENTIETH CENTURY

> GEORGE GROSZ
> *Die Spinne* (The Spider)
> PLATE 49

George Grosz (1893–1959), like many of his artistic contemporaries, challenged social norms through the expressive distortion of form.[188] His drypoint ***Die Spinne*** (The Spider, 1914) takes its title from Hanns Heinz Ewers's 1908 short story about a medical student who investigates the suicides of three men who have hanged themselves in the same Paris hotel room on three successive Fridays; each body is discovered in the presence of a large, black spider.[189] Confident in his ability to solve the mystery, the student, Richard Bracquemont, begins his residency at the hotel, where he gradually becomes enchanted by an enigmatic black-clad woman he calls Clarimonde, who sits at her window in a building across the street, spinning thread. The distanced interaction grows more and more intense, and it does not end well for Bracquemont, who is later found dead, wide-eyed with fear and clenching a big, black spider between his teeth.

In his visual adaptation of the story, Grosz shifts the point of view, illustrating the woman's quarters as she gazes out the window, plotting to ensnare her victims. Less overtly political than some of his later work, this relatively early print suggests a sense of anxiety and exhibits the rebellious formal contortions and perspectival play associated with German Expressionist painting and printmaking. To amplify the eerie mood of Ewers's tale, Grosz renders both the figure and her environment with weblike drypoint lines and adds dark shading through plate tone (selectively leaving ink on the plate during wiping). Further, by inserting a layer of gauze between the plate and the paper before printing, he creates a textural background reminiscent of a spiderweb. Grosz's intaglio prints are rare—he soon switched to lithography—and Steinberg's is one of only seven known impressions of this work.[190]

HENRI MATISSE
Profile of Madame Derain, I
PLATE 50

Produced in the same year as ***Die Spinne***, Matisse's austere monotype ***Profile of Madame Derain, I*** (1914) depicts the wife of his friend and fellow artist André Derain. Henri Matisse (1869–1954) is celebrated as one of the leading Fauves or "wild beasts" who exhibited at the Salon d'Automne in Paris in the fall of 1905. Here, the absence of the bright color for which his work is known emphasizes the artist's remarkable finesse in capturing the likeness and spirit of his sitter through the economical use of thin, tapering lines. He employed the subtractive "dark-field" technique, first spreading ink over the entire plate, then drawing with a rolled piece of paper or cardboard to selectively remove some of it.[191] When printed, Mme. Derain's face appears as a series of delicate, white strokes, glowing on a rich, black ground. Afterward, someone—possibly Matisse himself—applied a fingerprint on the reverse of the sheet, as if to underscore the work's uniqueness. A prolific but sporadic printmaker, Matisse created sixty-nine monotypes between 1914 and 1917 with the help of his daughter Marguerite, and never returned to the form again.[192] Portraits, figures, and still lifes comprise most of the artist's monotype subjects and represent "playful permutations" of similar themes in his paintings and sculpture of the same period.[193] These timeless topics were nevertheless connected to pressing historical circumstances; Matisse spent the money he earned from selling many of his monotypes on food and supplies for French soldiers captured during World War I.[194] The majority of his more than eight hundred prints are etchings, drypoints, lithographs, linocuts, and ***pochoirs*** (hand-colored stencils), primarily produced in professional print-publishing workshops.[195]

JOSEF ALBERS
Porta Negra from *Soft Edge–Hard Edge*
PLATE 51

Matisse's exploration of color, line, and abstraction take a more geometric turn in the work of German-born artist, designer, and teacher Josef Albers (1888–1976), whose drive toward "pictorial economy" reflected a search for "maximum psychological effect" from minimum visual information.[196] An instructor at the progressive Bauhaus school, which sought to rethink the material world through the unification of all the arts, Albers emigrated to the United States when the school was shuttered by the Nazis in 1933, the same year Steinberg's family fled Berlin for London. Albers took up a teaching position at the newly founded Black Mountain College in North Carolina, whose faculty and students include some of the most influential artists of the twentieth century. In 1950, he became chair of Yale University's Department of Design, where he began a long and fruitful printmaking relationship with protégés Norman Ives and Sewell Sillman, who incorporated as Ives-Sillman in 1956. [197] A few years later, he began supplying designs that the company translated into print, a collaborative model dating back to the workshops and publishers of the Renaissance. Their first edition, produced in 1961, built on Albers's decades-long study of color interaction in his painting series ***Homage to the Square*** (1950–75).[198] Ives-Sillman specialized in **screenprinting**, a process developed in the 1930s that became especially popular among artists of the sixties.

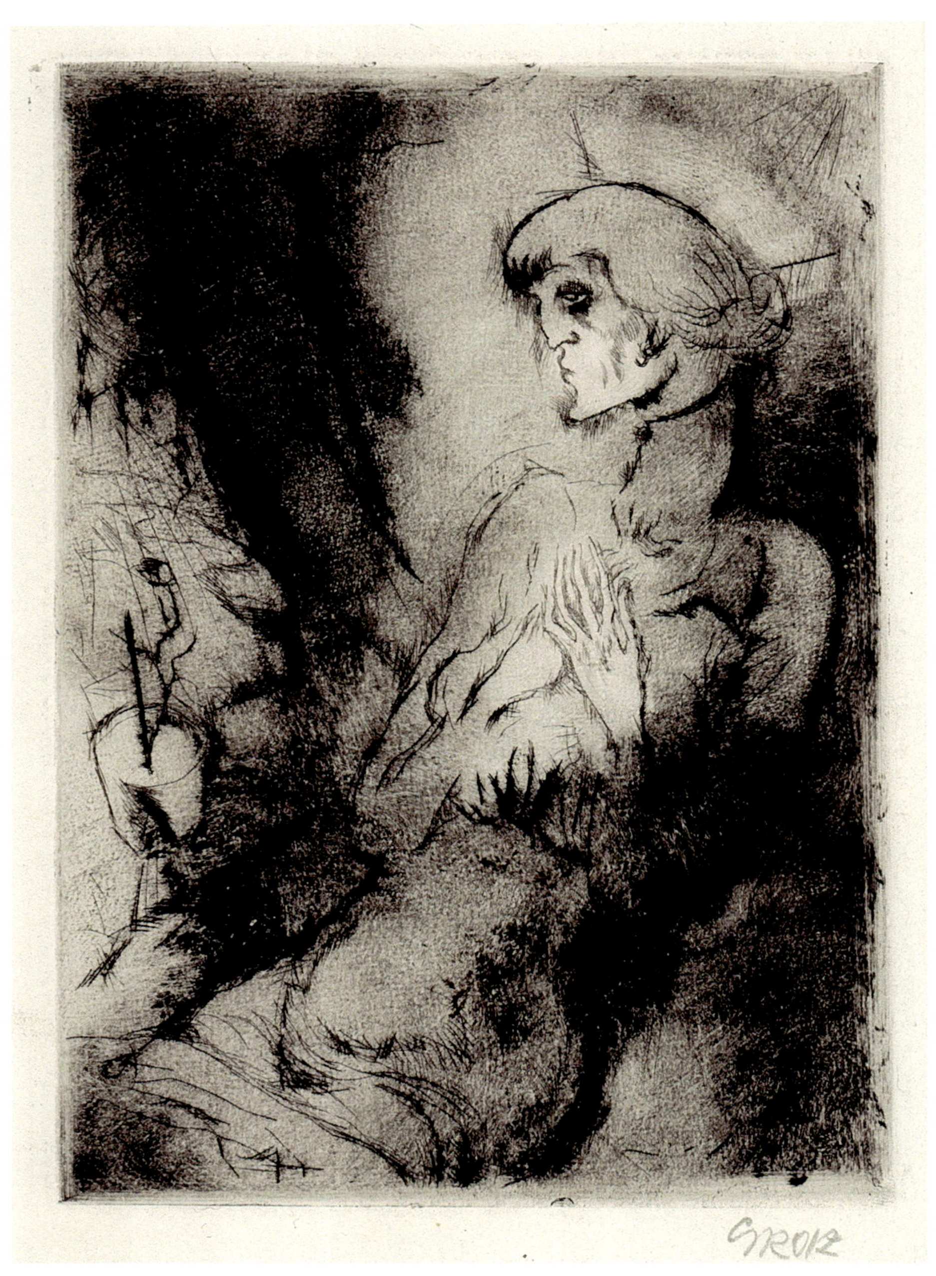

49 GEORGE GROSZ

Die Spinne (The Spider) 1914

Drypoint, second state of two, signed in graphite, 6⅝ × 4¾ in. (16.8 × 12.1 cm). Dückers E12 (2002.1570)

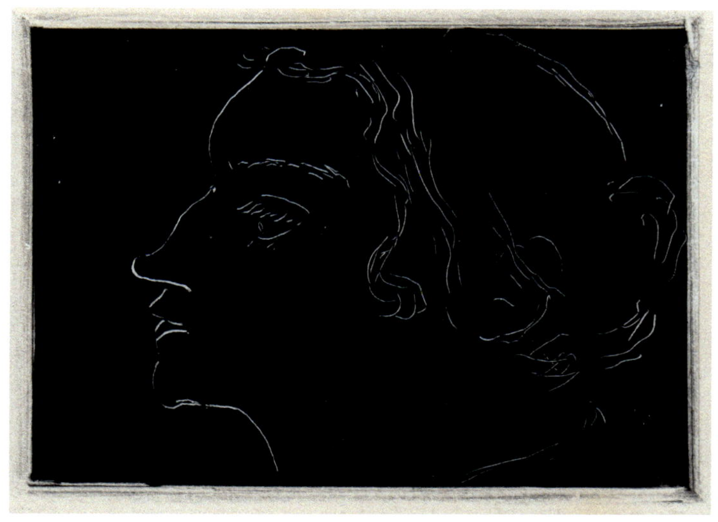

50 HENRI MATISSE

Profile of Madame Derain, I 1914

Monotype, 2 7/16 × 3 3/8 in. (6.2 × 8.6 cm). Dutuit-Matisse I 337 (2002.1577) © 2023 Succession H. Matisse / Artists Rights Society (ARS), New York

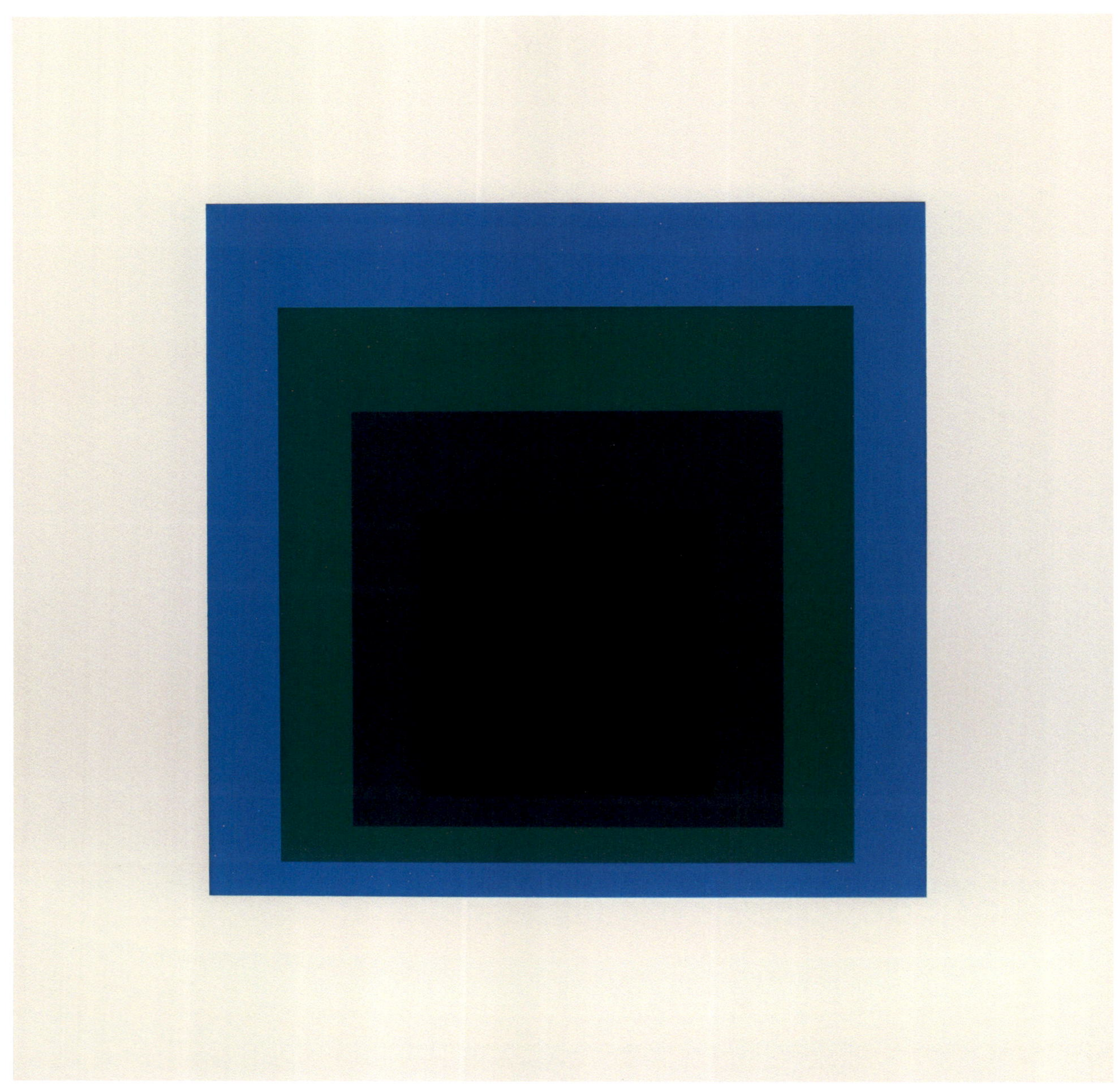

51 JOSEF ALBERS

Porta Negra from *Soft Edge–Hard Edge* 1965

Color screenprint, unsigned edition of 250, 11 × 11 in. (28 × 28 cm). Danilowitz 165.5 (2002.2800) © The Josef and Anni Albers Foundation / Artists Rights Society (ARS), New York, 2022.

Ives-Sillman used the same screens to produce Albers's serial explorations of color relationships within a set of nested squares, changing the color of the inks to create the sense that each square was advancing or receding depending on its affinity to the adjacent color.[199]

Sillman and Ives also helped organize Albers's first retrospective at the Yale University Art Gallery in 1956.[200] Impressed by Steinberg's reviews of recent New York exhibitions, Albers personally invited him to see this show, and Steinberg subsequently acquired the screenprints *Porta Negra* (1965), *Profundo* (1965), and *Nacre* (1965) from the *Soft Edge–Hard Edge* portfolio. In his notes on *Porta Negra*, Steinberg transcribed a poem by Albers titled "On My Painting":

> "When I paint / I think and see / first and most—color / but color as motion // Color not only accompanying / form of lateral extension / and after being moved / remaining arrested // But of perpetual inner movement / as aggression—to and from the spectator / besides interaction and interdependence / with shape and hue and light // Color in a direct and frontal focus / and when closely felt / as breathing and pulsating / —from within"[201]

RAY JOHNSON
Untitled (Nose of Nero)
PLATE 52

Ray Johnson (1927–1995) studied under Albers at Black Mountain College in the late forties and was the founder of the New York Correspondance School of mail art. He began his lifelong practice of sending illustrated letters, objects, and collages to friends through the postal service as a high schooler in Michigan. By the early sixties, he had expanded these activities to the point that one of his correspondents, the artist Ed Plunkett, suggested a name for the practice in playful reference to art schools and correspondence courses offering degrees by mail. Johnson accepted Plunkett's idea, but he purposely misspelled "correspondence" to convey improvisation and movement.[202]

In his collage *Untitled* (*Nose of Nero*, ca. 1968), which Johnson mailed to Steinberg, the artist assembled paper cutouts that include a reproduction of Salvador Dalí's 1947 painting *Dematerialization Near the Nose of Nero*, in which the nose of a marble bust of the Roman emperor drifts from his face in a surreal dreamscape.[203] Dalí was a frequent point of reference for Johnson in other collage works, and in 1979, the artists actually met at the (in)famous New York nightclub Studio 54.[204] At right is a magazine cutout of a marble bust of the Roman emperor Nerva, also with a missing nose, which Johnson extends by cutting into the black ground surrounding the head. He also enhances these materials with handwritten text, his signature "bunny heads," and a punning "Roy Johnsong" stamp. Here Johnson combines type, magazine cutouts, and stickers, material undergirded by centuries of innovation in print technology. He inverts hierarchies by appropriating objects produced in multiple and turning them into singular originals, which circumvent the art market by arriving unbidden in the recipient's mailbox. Further reliant on such quotidian printed matter as postage stamps, these assemblages add a new, contemporary dimension to the role of prints as disseminators of visual ideas.

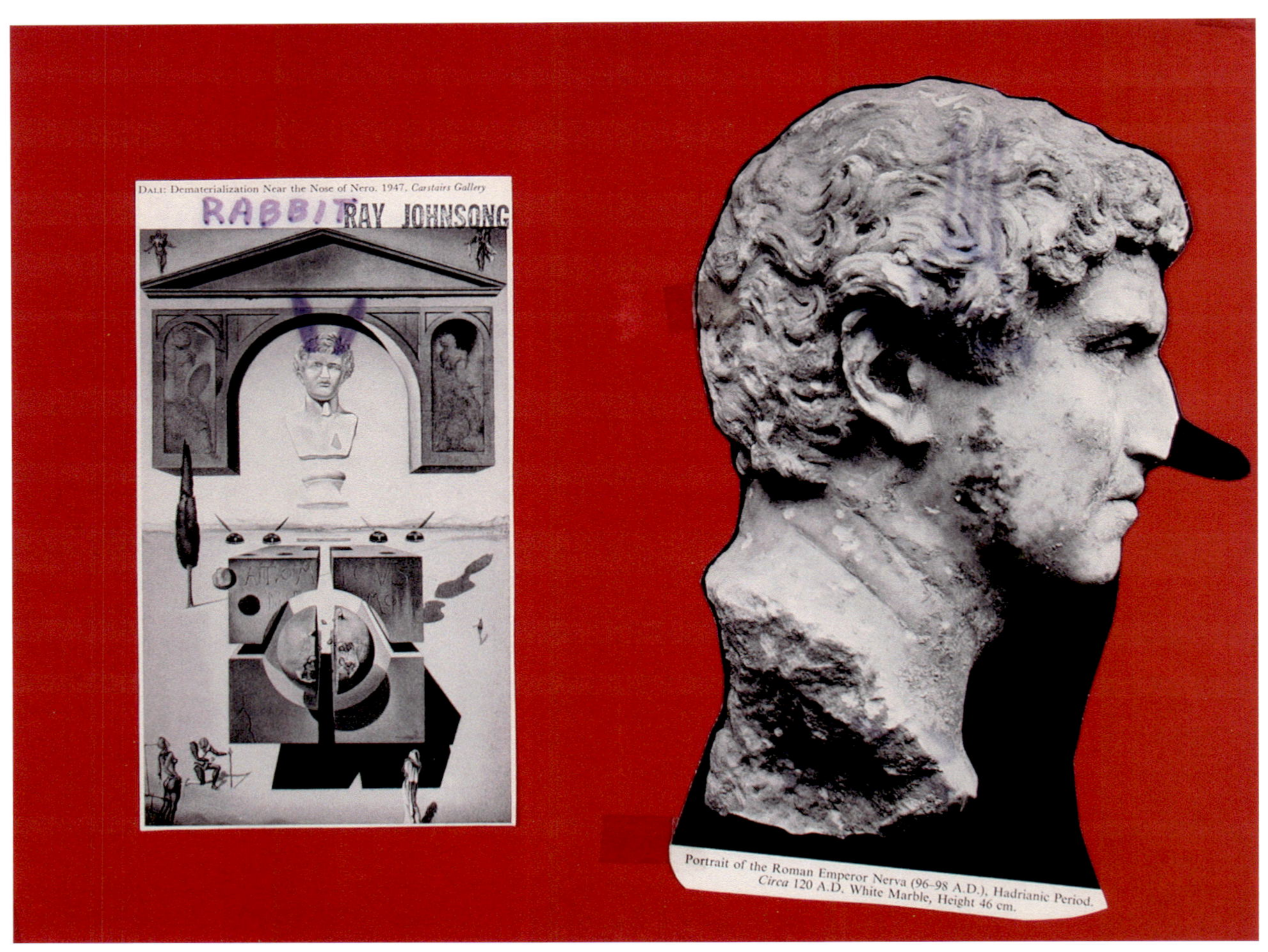

52 RAY JOHNSON

Untitled (*Nose of Nero*) CA. 1968

Collage of cut offset lithographs with purple ink and ink stamp in black taped on red paper, 10¹⁄₁₆ × 13⅛ in. (25.5 × 33.3 cm). (2002.2943) © Ray Johnson Estate / Artists Rights Society (ARS), New York.

NOTES

1 Anthony Griffiths, *The Print Before Photography: An Introduction to European Printmaking 1550–1820* (London: British Museum, 2016), 15–16.

2 Ad Stijnman, *Engraving and Etching, 1400–2000: A History of the Development of Manual Intaglio Printmaking Processes* (London: Archetype Publications, 2012), 34, 39.

3 Christof Metzger, *Daniel Hopfer: Ein Augsburger Meister der Renaissance: Eisenradierungen—Holzschnitte—Zeichnungen—Waffenätzungen* (Munich: Staatliche Graphische Sammlung, 2009); Nadine Orenstein and Ad Stijnman, "Bitten with Spirit: Etching Materials and Techniques in the Sixteenth Century," in *The Renaissance of Etching* (New York: Metropolitan Museum of Art, 2019), 15–23.

4 Steinberg, "What I Like About Prints," *Art in Print* 7, no. 5 (January–February 2018): 21.

5 Sandra Hindman and James H. Marrow, eds., *Books of Hours Reconsidered*, Studies in Medieval and Early Renaissance Art History (London: Harvey Miller, 2013); Virginia Reinburg, *French Books of Hours: Making an Archive of Prayer, c. 1400–1600* (Cambridge: Cambridge University Press, 2012).

6 I am grateful to John McQuillen for the identification of the publisher and for dating the leaf.

7 David Landau and Peter W. Parshall, *The Renaissance Print, 1470–1550* (New Haven, CT: Yale University Press, 1994), 230–231; Walter L. Strauss, *The German Single-Leaf Woodcut, 1550–1600: A Pictorial Catalogue* (New York: Abaris Books, 1975), 1–9.

8 For discussions of the print in its historical context, see Landau and Parshall, *The Renaissance Print*, 337–42 and Christopher S. Wood, "Ritual and the Virgin on the Column: The Cult of the Schöne Maria in Regensburg," *Journal of Ritual Studies* 6, no. 1 (1992): 87–107.

9 Charles W. Talbot and Christiane Andersson, eds., *From a Mighty Fortress: Prints, Drawings, and Books in the Age of Luther, 1483–1546* (Detroit, MI: Detroit Institute of Arts, 1983), 323–325, no. 184.

10 Lead and silver pilgrim badges and Albrecht Altdorfer's numerous woodcuts of the Beautiful Virgin served many of these same functions. For badges, see Talbot and Andersson, *From a Mighty Fortress*, 323 and for woodcuts, see Landau and Parshall, *The Renaissance Print*, 339–340.

11 Wood, "Ritual and the Virgin," 104n2.

12 For Schön's woodcut without text, see Ursula Mielke and Rainer Schoch, *Hollstein's German Engravings, Etchings and Woodcuts, 1400–1700: Erhard Schön*, (Rotterdam: Sound & Vision, 2000), vol. 47, 44–45, no. 15, which includes references to earlier literature addressing the Sachs poem that was paired with the woodcut. See also W. A. Coupe, "Political and Religious Cartoons of the Thirty Years' War," *Journal of the Warburg and Courtauld Institutes* 25, nos. 1/2 (January–June 1962): 77–78, pl. 15a.

13 Heinrich Röttinger, *Erhard Schön und Niklas Stör, der Pseudo-Schön; zwei Untersuchungen zur Geschichte des alten Nürnberger Holzschnittes* (Strasbourg: J. H. E. Heitz, 1925), 146; Coupe, "Cartoons," 78.

14 The impression published in Eugen Diederichs, *Deutsches leben der Vergangenheit in Bildern; ein Atlas mit 1760 Nachbildungen alter Kupfer- und Holzschnitte aus dem 15ten–18ten Jahrhunderts* (Jena: E. Diederichs, 1908), 201, pl. 681, is now in The Leo Steinberg Collection.

15 Freyda Spira, "Between Court and City: Artistic Productions in Renaissance Augsburg," in *Imperial Augsburg: Renaissance Prints and Drawings 1475–1540* (Washington, DC: National Gallery of Art, 2012), 45–49.

16 Landau and Parshall, *The Renaissance Print*, 3.

17 See Michael J. Waters, "Candelabra-Columns and the Lombard Architecture of Sculptural Assemblage," in *The Art of Sculpture in Fifteenth-Century Italy*, eds. Amy R. Bloch and Daniel M. Zolli (Cambridge: Cambridge University Press, 2020), 344–366 for contemporaneous examples of the varied uses of candelabra forms in Italy.

18 1963 purchases: NA.2021.2, inv.914–917. Three remain in the Blanton's collection: 2002.831, 2002.832, 2002.833. 1990 purchase: NA.2021.6, inv. 90.21, 2002.2327.

19 Rainer Schoch, Matthias Mende, and Anna Scherbaum, *Albrecht Dürer: Das druckgraphische Werk*, 3 vols. (Munich: Prestel, 2001); Giulia Bartrum,

Albrecht Dürer and His Legacy: The Graphic Work of a Renaissance Artist (Princeton, NJ: Princeton University Press, 2002), 266–282. For a recent attempt at recreating a Dürer engraving, see Andrew Raftery and Angela Campbell, "Remaking Dürer: Investigating the Master Engravings by Masterful Engraving," *Art in Print* 2, no. 4 (November–December 2012): 15–21.

20 Peter Parshall discusses the tension between nature and imagination in Dürer's writings in "Graphic Knowledge: Albrecht Dürer and the Imagination," *The Art Bulletin* 95, no. 3 (September 2013): 393–410.

21 For the significance of Dürer's monogram in establishing his artistic identity, see Joseph Leo Koerner, "Albrecht Dürer: A Sixteenth-Century Influenza," in *Albrecht Dürer and His Legacy: The Graphic Work of a Renaissance Artist* (Princeton, NJ: Princeton University Press, 2002), 18–38.

22 Schoch et al., *Das druckgraphische Werk*, 2:145–148; Femke Speelberg, "Fashion & Virtue: Textile Patterns and the Print Revolution 1520–1620," *The Metropolitan Museum of Art Bulletin* 73, no. 2 (Fall 2015): 11–13.

23 Arnold Nesselrath, "Raphael's Gift to Dürer," *Master Drawings* 31, no. 4 (Winter 1993): 376–389.

24 Innis H. Shoemaker, *The Engravings of Marcantonio Raimondi* (Lawrence, KS: Spencer Museum of Art, 1981), xiv.

25 Shoemaker, *Marcantonio Raimondi*, 3; Lisa Pon discusses this concept in relation to the works of Marcantonio in *Raphael, Dürer, and Marcantonio Raimondi: Copying and the Italian Renaissance Print* (New Haven, CT: Yale University Press, 2004), 27–38; Landau and Parshall chart the transformation from a collaborative to a reproductive model in the first half of the sixteenth century in Italy in *The Renaissance Print*, 103–168.

26 Steinberg, "What I Like About Prints," 7. Marcantonio likely worked from a preparatory drawing for Raphael's fresco of this subject in the Vatican loggia. See Nicole Dacos, *The Loggia of Raphael: A Vatican Art Treasure* (New York: Abbeville, 2008), 188, pl. 140, 213–216, pls. 155, 233; Gudrun Knaus, *Invenit, Incisit, Imitavit: Die Kupferstiche von Marcantonio Raimondi als Schlüssel zur weltweiten Raffael-Rezeption 1510–1700* (Berlin: De Gruyter, 2016), 127–39; and Shoemaker, *Marcantonio Raimondi*, 166–168.

27 See Stefania Massari, *Incisori mantovani del '500: Giovan Battista, Adamo, Diana Scultori e Giorgio Ghisi: dalle collezioni del Gabinetto nazionale delle stampe e della Calcografia nazionale* (Rome: De Luca, 1981), 23.

28 On the designer, see Patricia Emison, "Truth and *Bizzarria* in an Engraving of *Lo stregozzo*," *The Art Bulletin* 81, no. 4 (December 1999): 626–627, 631, 634n19; on the engraver: 627–628, 635n31.

29 Edward Peters and Alan Charles Kors, *Witchcraft in Europe, 400–1700: A Documentary History*, 2nd ed. (Philadelphia: University of Pennsylvania Press, 2001).

30 Mantegna's print is illustrated in Jay A. Levenson, Konrad Oberhuber, and Jacquelyn Sheehan, *Early Italian Engravings from the National Gallery of Art* (Washington, DC: National Gallery of Art, 1973), 188, cat. no. 75; on Dürer and Michelangelo, see Emison, "Truth and *Bizzarria* in an Engraving of *Lo stregozzo*": 625–627. Emison's suggestion that the crouching demon is modeled on the figure of God seen from behind in *The Creation of the Sun* in the Sistine Ceiling makes this visual quotation particularly subversive.

31 Apsley House, London.

32 Catherine Jenkins, *Prints at the Court of Fontainebleau, c. 1542–47*, Studies in Prints and Printmaking 7 (Ouderkerk aan den IJssel: Sound & Vision, 2017), 25.

33 Catherine Jenkins, "Etching in Renaissance France," in *The Renaissance of Etching* (New York: Metropolitan Museum of Art, 2019), 235–236, cat. no. 113.

34 John-Paul Stonard, *Germany Divided: Baselitz and His Generation: From the Duerckheim Collection* (London: British Museum, 2014), 14, fig. 9.

35 Erik Hinterding et al., "Acquisitions: Prints and Drawings," *The Rijksmuseum Bulletin* 64, no. 4 (2016): 404–405, 418.

36 Henri Zerner, *Renaissance Art in France: The Invention of Classicism* (Paris: Flammarion, 2003), 67–153; *L'École de Fontainebleau* (Paris: Éditions des Musées nationaux, 1972); Rebecca Zorach, *Blood, Milk, Ink, Gold: Abundance and Excess in the French Renaissance* (Chicago: University of Chicago Press, 2005).

37 Jenkins, *Prints at the Court of Fontainebleau.*

38 Ibid., part 1, 26–28, part 2, 129–269.

39 Ibid., part 2, AF71, 219.

40 Zerner, *Renaissance Art in France*, 139–140. On the series, see Jacques Levron, *René Boyvin, graveur angevin du XVIe siècle, avec le catalogue de son œuvre & la reproduction de 114 estampes* (Angers: Jacques Petit, 1941), 66–67, nos. 16–41, pls. XIX–XLIV.

41 The hair and beard of the seated scholar at upper right are particularly reminiscent of the prophet Zechariah in the Sistine Chapel. On Michelangelo's influence, see Jenkins, *Prints at the Court of Fontainebleau*, 67–72. Steinberg's impression of this plate does not have the accompanying text panel below the image; a complete transcription of the text is in Alexandre-Pierre-François Robert-Dumesnil, *Le Peintre-graveur français, ou Catalogue raisonné des estampes gravées par les peintres et les dessinateurs de l'école français* (Paris: Gabriel Warée, 1835–1871), vol. 8, 42, no. 56.

42 Femke Speelberg, "'Ordine con più ornamento': Reconsidering the Origins of Strapwork Ornament in Relation to the Emancipation of the Ornamental Frame," in *Questions d'ornements*, ed. Ralph Dekoninck, Caroline Heering, and Michel Lefftz (Turnhout: Brepols, 2013), 154–165.

43 Steinberg, "What I Like About Prints," 9.

44 Jan van der Stock, *Printing Images in Antwerp: The Introduction of Printmaking in a City: Fifteenth Century to 1585*, trans. Beverley Jackson, Studies in Prints and Printmaking 2 (Rotterdam: Sound & Vision Interactive, 1998); for publishing houses, see especially chapter 4, 143–172.

45 Jan van der Stock, "Hieronymus Cock and Volcxken Diericx: Print Publishers in Antwerp," in *Hieronymus Cock: The Renaissance in Print* (Brussels: Mercatorfonds, 2013), 14–21.

46 Timothy A. Riggs, *Hieronymus Cock, Printmaker and Publisher* (New York: Garland, 1977), 29–30; Ger Luijten, "Hieronymus Cock and the Italian Printmakers and Publishers of His Day," in *Hieronymus Cock: The Renaissance in Print* (Brussels: Mercatorfonds, 2013), 34–35.

47 Heiner Borggrefe, Thomas Fusenig, and Barbara Uppenkamp, eds., *Hans Vredeman de Vries und die Renaissance im Norden* (Munich: Hirmer, 2002), 253, and nos. 87–88.

48 Peter Fuhring, "Hieronymus Cock and the Impact of His Published Architectural and Ornamental Prints," in *Hieronymus Cock: The Renaissance in Print* (Brussels: Mercatorfonds, 2013), 36–41.

49 On etching at Aux Quatre Vents and the Van Doetecums' techniques, see Riggs, *Hieronymus Cock*, 125–155. See also Henk Nalis, Ger Luijten, and Christiaan Schuckman, *The New Hollstein Dutch & Flemish Etchings, Engravings and Woodcuts, 1450–1700: The van Doetecum Family* (Rotterdam: Sound & Vision, 1998), vol. 1, xi–xxi.

50 Ria Fabri, "Perspectives in Wood: Hans Vredeman de Vries and the Designs for Intarsia and Civil Furniture," in *Hans Vredeman de Vries and the Artes Mechanicae Revisited*, Architectura Moderna 3 (Turnhout: Brepols, 2005), 153–168.

51 Bernadine Ann Barnes, *Michelangelo in Print: Reproductions as Response in the Sixteenth Century* (Farnham: Ashgate, 2010).

52 Barnes, *Michelangelo in Print*, 38.

53 On the series, including the dating, see Alida Moltedo, *La Sistina riprodotta: gli affreschi di Michelangelo dalle stampe del Cinquecento alle campagne fotografiche Anderson* (Rome: Fratelli Palombi, 1991), 73–79; Suzanne Boorsch, Michal Lewis, and R. E. Lewis, *The Engravings of Giorgio Ghisi* (New York: Metropolitan Museum of Art, 1985), 151–153, 164–165; Barnes, *Michelangelo in Print*, 38–41.

54 David Rosand and Michelangelo Muraro, *Titian and the Venetian Woodcut* (Washington, DC: International Exhibitions Foundation, 1976), 8–27.

55 Ibid., 177–178.

56 Konrad Oberhuber, "Titian Woodcuts and Drawings: Some Problems," in *Tiziano e Venezia*, ed. F. Benvenuti (Vicenza: Neri Pozza, 1980), 523–528; David Landau reassigns several to Giovanni Britto in "Printmaking in Venice and the Veneto," in *The Genius of Venice, 1500–1600* (London: J. Martineau and C. Hope, 1983), 333–335.

57 Manfred Sellink and Huigen Leeflang, *The New Hollstein Dutch & Flemish Etchings, Engravings and Woodcuts, 1450–1700: Cornelis Cort* (Rotterdam: Sound & Vision, 2000), vol. 1, xxiii–xxiv; on the

arrangement with Titian, see Michael Bury, *The Print in Italy, 1550–1620* (London: British Museum, 2001), 70–71.

58 On Venetian privileges, see Bury, *The Print in Italy*, 175–176; and on their significance for Titian and his contemporaries, see Landau and Parshall, *The Renaissance Print*, 361–362.

59 Sellink and Leeflang, *The New Hollstein: Cornelis Cort*, vol. 1, xxiv for the development of Cort's swelling line; also Edward H. Wouk, "'Con la perfettione et le bellezze chi si vede nelle figure. . . .': Cornelis Cort and the Transformation of Engraving in Europe, c. 1565," in *Myth, Allegory, and Faith: The Kirk Edward Long Collection of Mannerist Prints*, ed. Bernard Barryte (Stanford, CA: Iris & B. Gerald Cantor Center for Visual Arts, 2015), 243–246.

60 Louise S. Richards, "Federico Barocci as a Printmaker," in *The Graphic Art of Federico Barocci: Selected Drawings and Prints* (New Haven, CT: Yale University Art Gallery, 1978), 93–101; Sue Welsh Reed and Richard W. Wallace, *Italian Etchers of the Renaissance & Baroque* (Boston: Museum of Fine Arts, 1989), 89–90.

61 According to Landau and Parshall, Marcantonio was the first Italian printmaker to do so; *The Renaissance Print*, 264–266. On *Il Perdono*, see Richards, "Federico Barocci," 102–105 and Reed and Wallace, *Italian Etchers*, 93–95.

62 Richards, "Federico Barocci," 98.

63 Reed and Wallace note that delicate drypoint lines evident in the earliest impressions quickly disappeared during the printing process; *Italian Etchers*, 93.

64 Bury, *The Print in Italy*, 81–82; Marilyn Aronberg Lavin, "Signed, Sealed, and Delivered: Federico Barocci's Indulgenced Print of the 'Perdono,'" *Artibus et Historiae* 35, no. 69 (2014): 209–212.

65 Huigen Leeflang et al., *Hendrick Goltzius (1558–1617): Drawings, Prints and Paintings* (Zwolle: Waanders, 2003), 16, 33–34.

66 Nadine Orenstein, "Hendrick Goltzius (1558–1617)," *Heilbrunn Timeline of Art History*, Metropolitan Museum of Art, New York, October 2003, http://www.metmuseum.org/toah/hd/golt/hd_golt.htm.

67 William Breazeale, "Goltzius's *Birth and Early Life of Christ:* Transformation and Renown," in *Passion and Virtuosity: Hendrick Goltzius and the Art of Engraving* (San Diego, CA: University of San Diego, 2013), 12–25 draws on the seminal essays by Walter Melion: "Hendrick Goltzius's Project of Reproductive Engraving," *Art History* 13, no. 4 (December 1990): 458–487; "Karel van Mander's 'Life of Goltzius': Defining the Paradigm of Protean Virtuosity in Haarlem around 1600," *Studies in the History of Art* 27 (1989): 113–133; and "Piety and Pictorial Manner in Hendrick Goltzius's *Early Life of the Virgin*," in *Hendrick Goltzius and the Classical Tradition* (Los Angeles: Fisher Gallery, University of Southern California, 1992), 44–51.

68 Walter Strauss suggests that Goltzius saw Barocci's *Madonna of the Cat* painting while in Rome; *Hendrik Goltzius 1558–1617: The Complete Engravings and Woodcuts* (New York: Abaris Books, 1977), 574.

69 Gary Schwartz and Jan Bok Marten, *Pieter Saenredam: The Painter and His Time* (New York: Abbeville, 1990), 15–27. Schwartz claims here that after Goltzius gave up engraving in 1600, "there was no better reproductive engraver in Holland than Saenredam" (21).

70 Amy Namowitz Worthen, "Calligraphic Inscriptions on Dutch Mannerist Prints," *Netherlands Yearbook for History of Art/Nederlands Kunsthistorisch Jaarboek* 42–43, no. 1 (January 1991): 282–283; in the Kupferstich-Kabinett, Dresden, inv. no. C 1972-271.

71 On one such competition, see Worthen, "Calligraphic Inscriptions," 268–269; and on Dutch writing manuals, 267–273.

72 In "Calligraphic Inscriptions," Worthen describes Saenredam's method of engraving closely spaced lines so that they appear to comprise a single pen stroke (277) and also suggests that the trained notary and print publisher Jacques Razet supplied the calligraphic design (290–297).

73 The change in designation from "Netherlandish" to "Dutch" later in this entry is based on the 1609 signing of the Twelve Years' Truce between Spain and the Republic of the United Netherlands that demarcated the division between the northern (Dutch) and southern (Flemish) Netherlands.

74 Robert Fucci argues that Van de Velde was unusual in providing Latin captions for landscapes; "Landscape into History: The Early Printed Landscape Series by Jan van de Velde II (1593–1641)" (PhD diss., Columbia University, 2018), Academic Commons, https://academiccommons.columbia.edu/doi/10.7916/D8PP0J50, 167, 170.

75 See, for example, a 1588 version by his former teacher, Jacob Matham, after a design by Hendrick Goltzius in Léna Widerkehr and Huigen Leeflang, *The New Hollstein: Dutch & Flemish Etchings, Engravings and Woodcuts 1450–1700: Jacob Matham*, vol. 3, 101, no. 348.

76 Egbert Haverkamp-Begemann, *William Buytewech* (Amsterdam: Menno Hertzberger, 1959), 16.

77 For context on this shift in subject matter, see David Freedberg, *Dutch Landscape Prints of the Seventeenth Century* (London: British Museum, 1980) and Larry Silver, *Peasant Scenes and Landscapes: The Rise of Pictorial Genres in the Antwerp Art Market* (Philadelphia: University of Pennsylvania Press, 2012).

78 Erik Hinterding, Jaco Rutgers, and Ger Luijten, *The New Hollstein Dutch & Flemish Etchings, Engravings and Woodcuts, 1450–1700: Rembrandt*, 7 vols. (Ouderkerk aan den IJssel: Sound & Vision, 2013).

79 On Rembrandt's techniques and the use of watermarks to support the theory that Rembrandt printed his own plates, see Erik Hinterding, *Rembrandt as an Etcher*, trans. Michael Hoyle (Ouderkerk aan den IJssel: Sound & Vision, 2006) and Christopher White, *Rembrandt as an Etcher: A Study of the Artist at Work*, 2nd ed. (New Haven, CT: Yale University Press, 1999), 5–18.

80 Erik Hinterding, "The History of Rembrandt's Copperplates, with a Catalogue of Those That Survive," *Simiolus: Netherlands Quarterly for the History of Art* 22, no. 4 (1993): 253–315.

81 Edmé-François Gersaint, *Catalogue raisonné de toutes les pièces qui forment l'œuvre de Rembrandt, composé par feu M. Gersaint, et mis au jour avec les augmentations nécessaires, par les sieurs Helle et Glomy* (Paris: Hochereau l'ainé, 1751).

82 Steinberg, "What I Like About Prints," 27. The plate for this print is in the collection of the Museum of Fine Arts, Boston.

83 S. W. Pelletier, Leonard J. Slatkes, and Linda A. Stone-Ferrier, *Adriaen van Ostade: Etchings of Peasant Life in Holland's Golden Age*, ed. Patricia Phagan (Athens: Georgia Museum of Art, University of Georgia, 1994).

84 In a chapter on family life in Ostade's prints, Nanette Salomon addresses issues of class and gender in *Shifting Priorities: Gender and Genre in Seventeenth-Century Dutch Painting* (Stanford, CA: Stanford University Press, 2004), 93–105. The literature on Netherlandish peasant scenes is voluminous; for a concise overview of the debates as they relate to Pieter Bruegel, see Walter S. Gibson, *Pieter Bruegel the Elder* (Lawrence, KS: Spencer Museum of Art, 1991), 10–52.

85 Ben Broos, "Paulus Potter as Draughtsman and Etcher," in *Paulus Potter: Paintings, Drawings and Etchings* (The Hague: Mauritshuis, 1994), 52.

86 Walter L. Strauss and Leonard J. Slatkes, eds., *The Illustrated Bartsch* (New York: Abaris Books, 1978), vol. 1, 56–109. De Bye also etched after his own designs and Broos suggests that he augmented some of the series after Potter with his own compositions.

87 Boudewijn Bakker, "The Netherlands Drawn from Life: An Introduction," trans. Claire C. Whitner, *Journal of Historians of Netherlandish Art* 10, no. 2 (Summer 2018): 1–29.

88 For example, Karel van Mander's *Handbook of Allegory* of 1616 associates goats with good hearing, licentiousness, and prostitution; Wolfgang Stechow, *Northern Renaissance Art, 1400–1600: Sources and Documents* (Evanston, IL: Northwestern University Press, 1989), 71.

89 C. G. Voorhelm Schneevogt, *Catalogue des estampes gravées d'après P. P. Rubens: avec l'indication des collections où se trouvent les tableaux et les gravures* (Haarlem: Les Héritiers Loosjes, 1873); Frank van den Wijngaert's *Inventaris der Rubeniaansche prentkunst* (Antwerp: De Sikkel, 1940) records 779 prints after Rubens produced in the seventeenth century. For recent treatments of this subject, see Nico van Hout, ed., *Rubens et l'art de la gravure* (Amsterdam:

Ludion, 2004) and Jaco Rutgers, "Rubens's Early Involvement in Printmaking," in *Early Rubens*, ed. Sasha Suda and Kirk Nickel (New York: DelMonico Books-Prestel, 2019), 102–114.

90 On the oil sketch at the Art Gallery of Ontario and its relationship to the engraving, see Julius S. Held, *The Oil Sketches of Peter Paul Rubens: A Critical Catalogue* (Princeton, NJ: Princeton University Press, 1980), vol. 1, 482–484, no. 351, pl. 346.

91 Nora de Poorter, *The Eucharist Series*, Corpus Rubenianum, pt. 2, 2 vols. (London: Harvey Miller, 1978); Charles Scribner III, *The Triumph of the Eucharist: Tapestries Designed by Rubens* (Ann Arbor: UMI Research Press, 1982); Alexander Vergara and Anne T. Woollett, eds., *Spectacular Rubens: The Triumph of the Eucharist* (Los Angeles: J. Paul Getty Museum, 2014).

92 On the different versions of this composition and its copies, see de Poorter, *The Eucharist Series*, Corpus Rubenanium, pt. 2, vol. 1, 300–307, nos. 9–9c, Lauwers's print is 9b, copy 5; on engravings after the tapestry series more generally, 213–222.

93 Sue Welsh Reed addresses the evolution of French intaglio printmaking between 1610 and 1660 in *French Prints from the Age of the Musketeers* (Boston: Museum of Fine Arts, 1998).

94 Jules Lieure, *Jacques Callot* (San Francisco: Alan Wofsy Fine Art, 1989); Diane Russell, *Jacques Callot: Prints and Related Drawings* (Washington, DC: National Gallery of Art, 1975); Paulette Choné et al., *Jacques Callot 1592–1635* (Paris: Éditions de la Réunion des musées nationaux, 1992).

95 Maxime Préaud discusses Callot's techniques in his two versions of this subject in "'Saint Antoine', morsures et remorsures" in *Jacques Callot 1592–1635*, 415–429.

96 See Elizabeth Wyckoff on the "Boschian print phenomenon" in "Hieronymus Cock and the Invention of the Print Market in Antwerp," in *Beyond Bosch: the Afterlife of a Renaissance Master in Print* (St. Louis, MO: St. Louis Art Museum, 2015), 35.

97 José Lothe, *L'œuvre gravé d'Abraham Bosse: graveur parisien du XVIIe siècle* (Paris: Paris Musées, 2008); Reed, *French Prints from the Age of the Musketeers*, 242; and Carl Goldstein, "Looking in the Mirror of Abraham Bosse," in *French Prints from the Age of the Musketeers*, 21–27 and many entries in the catalogue.

98 By 1661, however, he had been expelled for disagreements with Charles LeBrun, the king's favorite painter. For an analysis of Bosse's fraught relationship with the Académie, see Sheila McTighe, "Abraham Bosse and the Language of Artisans: Genre and Perspective in the Académie royale de peinture et de sculpture, 1648–1670," *Oxford Art Journal* 21, no. 1 (1998): 1–26.

99 "d'une façon tout à fait naive et si vraye que l'on ne peut guerre rien desirer de plus interressant" in Pierre-Jean Mariette et al., *Catalogues de la collection d'estampes de Jean V, roi de Portugal* (Paris: Fundação Calouste Gulbenkian; Bibliothèque nationale de France; Lisbon: Fundação da Casa de Bragança, 1996–2003), vol. 2, 132.

100 On Bosse, see Millia Davenport, *The Book of Costume* (New York: Crown, 1976), vol. 1, 512–514.

101 John C. Rule, "Louis XIV, Roi-Bureaucrate," in *Louis XIV and the Craft of Kingship* (Columbus: Ohio State University Press, 1969), 3–101.

102 Audrey Adamczak, *Robert Nanteuil, ca. 1623–1678* (Paris: Arthena, 2011); for Nantueil's fees, see also Rémi Mathis, "The Portrait" in *Kingdom of Images: French Prints in the Age of Louis XIV, 1660–1715* (Los Angeles: Getty Research Institute, 2015), 181.

103 Maxime Préaud, "Printmaking under Louis XIV," in *Kingdom of Images*, 9–14.

104 Emily J. Peters, "Systems and Swells: The Collective Lineage of Engraved Lines, 1480–1650" in *The Brilliant Line: Following the Early Modern Engraver 1480–1650* (Providence: Museum of Art, Rhode Island School of Design, 2009), 45. On Nanteuil's collaboration with Abraham Bosse to modulate lines and hatching around various surfaces, see Adamczak, *Robert Nanteuil*, 37–39.

105 From Edelinck through the engravers of the mid-nineteenth century, see Stephen Bann, *Parallel Lines: Printmakers, Painters and Photographers in Nineteenth-Century France* (New Haven, CT: Yale University Press, 2001), esp. 174–208.

106 Lino Mannocci, *The Etchings of Claude Lorrain* (New Haven, CT: Yale University Press, 1988), 113–221, no. 15.

107 Paolo Bellini, *L'Opera incisa di Giovanni Benedetto Castiglione* (Milan: Ripartizione cultura e spettacolo, 1982), 162–164, no. 61; Timothy J. Standring and Martin Clayton, *Castiglione: Lost Genius* (London: Royal Collection Trust, 2013).

108 For more on the influence of Rembrandt, see Standring and Clayton, *Castiglione: Lost Genius*, 51n27, 65. The Blanton's painting is *Noah Leading the Animals into the Ark*, ca. 1640, oil on antique laid paper mounted on cradled wood, 15⁹⁄₁₆ × 22⁹⁄₁₆ in. (39.5 × 57.3 cm), The Suida-Manning Collection, 2017.1024.

109 On the invention and revival of monotype, see Linda C. Hults, *The Print in the Western World* (Madison: University of Wisconsin Press, 1996), 565–576; on this monotype by Castiglione, see Carmen Bambach and Nadine Orenstein, *Genoa: Drawings and Prints, 1530–1800* (New York: Metropolitan Museum of Art, 1996), cat. nos. 55, 57.

110 Standring and Clayton, *Castiglione: Lost Genius*, 93.

111 Alexandre De Vesme and Phyllis Dearborn Massar, *Stefano Della Bella: Catalogue Raisonné* (New York: Collectors' Editions, 1971), vol. 1, 32.

112 The subject and date are not entirely settled; see Jolanta Talbierska, *Stefano Della Bella (1610–1664): Etchings from the Collection of the Print Room of the Warsaw University Library* (Warsaw: Noriton, 2001), 188, IV.47. For the preparatory drawing, see Anthony Blunt, *The Drawings of G. B. Castiglione and Stefano Della Bella, in the Collection of Her Majesty the Queen at Windsor Castle* (London: Phaidon, 1954), 94, cat. no. 15, pl. 5.

113 Phyllis Dearborn Massar, *Presenting Stefano Della Bella, Seventeenth-Century Printmaker* (New York: Metropolitan Museum of Art, 1971), 7.

114 Blunt, *G. B. Castiglione and Stefano Della Bella*, 89.

115 Babette Bohn, "The Antique Heroines of Elisabetta Sirani," *Renaissance Studies* 16, no. 1 (March 2002): 52–79; Adelina Modesti, *Elisabetta Sirani 'Virtuosa': Women's Cultural Production in Early Modern Bologna* (Turnhout: Brepols, 2015); Babette Bohn, *Women Artists, Their Patrons, and Their Publics in Early Modern Bologna* (University Park, PA: Penn State University Press, 2021). On Vigri, see Bohn, *Women Artists*, 26–27.

116 Bohn, "Antique Heroines," 59.

117 Ibid.

118 The dating of individual works within the series is unclear. One group was etched in ca. 1757, while another was completed after 1770. See Lina Christina Frerichs, "Nouvelles sources pour la connaissance de l'activité incisoire des trois Tiepolos," *Nouvelles de l'estampe* 4 (1971): 213–228 and Aldo Rizzi, *The Etchings of the Tiepolos* (London: Phaidon, 1971), 344. The series was first published in 1773–74; a second edition appeared in 1775.

119 George Knox, *Domenico Tiepolo: Raccolta di Teste, 1770–1970* (Udine: Electa Editrice, 1970).

120 "Se potesse uscire dal sepolcro il Rembrandt et Gio: Benedetto Castiglione, bacciebbere chi Li ha fatte" in Lina Christina Frerichs, "Mariette et les eaux-fortes des Tiepolo," *Gazette des Beaux-Arts* 78 (October 1971): 242.

121 Rizzi, *The Etchings of the Tiepolos*, 19.

122 Perrin Stein, *Artists and Amateurs: Etching in Eighteenth-Century France* (New York: Metropolitan Museum of Art, 2013), esp. the essay "Echoes of Rembrandt and Castiglione: Etching as Appropriation," 157–158.

123 Stein, "Echoes of Rembrandt and Castiglione," 157.

124 Ibid., 160–161.

125 Marie-Félice Pérez, *L'œuvre gravé de Jean-Jacques de Boissieu, 1736–1810* (Geneva: Cabinet des estampes, 1994), 118–119, cat. no. 49; Stein, "Echoes of Rembrandt and Castiglione," 161.

126 Pierre Rosenberg, *Fragonard* (New York: Metropolitan Museum of Art, 1988), 154–157, nos. 67–70, and Victor I. Carlson and John Ittman, eds., *Regency to Empire: French Printmaking 1715–1814* (Minneapolis, MN: Minneapolis Institute of Arts, 1984), 152–155, cat. no. 47.

127 Stein, "Echoes of Rembrandt and Castiglione," 158, 160, 164, 167.

128 Ibid., 164.

129 Rosenberg, *Fragonard*, 155.

130 Stein, "Echoes of Rembrandt and Castiglione," 161, 163.

131 John Wilton-Ely, *Giovanni Battista Piranesi: The Complete Etchings*, vol. 1 (San Francisco: Alan Wofsy, 1994), 1–3.

132 These include the *Prima Parte di Architetture e Prospettive* (1743), the *Grotteschi* (1747), and the first edition of *Invenzioni capric di Carceri* (1749–50). See Andrew Robison, *Piranesi: Early Architectural Fantasies: a Catalogue Raisonné of the Etchings* (Washington, DC: National Gallery of Art, 1986), 65, 115, 139.
133 Heather Hyde Minor and Carolyn Yerkes, *Piranesi Unbound* (Princeton, NJ: Princeton University Press, 2020), 5–6.
134 Gilbert Erouart and Monique Mosser, "À propos de la 'Notice historique sur la vie et les ouvrages de J-B Piranesi': origine et fortune d'une biographie," in *Piranèse et les Français*, ed. Georges Brunel (Rome: Edizioni dell'Elefante, 1978), 231–232.
135 Minor and Yerkes, *Piranesi Unbound*, 6.
136 John Wilton-Ely, "Amazing and Ingenious Fancies: Piranesi and the Adam Brothers," in *The Serpent and the Stylus: Essays on G. B. Piranesi*, ed. Mario Bevilacqua, Heather Hyde Minor, and Fabio Barry (Ann Arbor: University of Michigan Press, 2006), 213–237.
137 A. A. Tait, "Robert Adam and John Clerk of Eldin," *Master Drawings* 16, no. 1 (Spring 1978): 53–57, 109–111.
138 On Sandby's role in introducing aquatint to Britain, see Rena Hoisington, *Aquatint: From Its Origins to Goya* (Princeton, NJ: Princeton University Press, 2021), 86–105. Sandby was not the first British printmaker to use aquatint and was sworn to secrecy once he learned the process, refusing to divulge the recipe to Clerk.
139 Geoffrey Bertram, *The Etchings of John Clerk of Eldin* (Thurloxton: Enterprise Editions, 2012), 11.
140 Ibid., 12–13.
141 Ibid., 103–175; B9 and B12 after Claude Lorrain.
142 Ibid., 25.
143 First invented in 1642, mezzotint was particularly useful for reproducing paintings: Stijnman, *Engraving and Etching*, 184–191; Hoisington, *Aquatint*.
144 Theo Laurentius and J. W. Niemeijer, *Cornelis Ploos van Amstel 1726–1798: Kunstverzamelaar en prentuitgever*, trans. Patricia Wardle (Assen: Van Gorcum, 1980); and Elmer Eusman, "Ploos van Amstel's Mark," *Print Quarterly* 17, no. 3 (September 2000): 248–261.
145 Jaap Bolten, *Abraham Bloemaert, c. 1565–1651: The Drawings* (Leiden: J. Bolten, 2007), cat. no. 212.
146 Laurentius and Niemeijer, *Cornelis Ploos van Amstel*, 310. His whole art collection was much larger and included seven portfolios of Rembrandt prints.
147 On the *recueil* and related publications, see Griffiths, *The Print Before Photography*, 176–177, 315–317.
148 Timothy Clayton, *The English Print: 1688–1802* (New Haven, CT: Yale University Press, 1997), xii–xiii, 23; David Alexander, "Kauffman and the Print Market in Eighteenth-Century England" in *Angelica Kauffman: A Continental Artist in Georgian England*, ed. Wendy Wassyng Roworth (London: Reaktion, 1992), 141.
149 Bettina Baumgärtel, Alison Gallup, and Bronwen Saunders, *Angelica Kauffman* (Munich: Hirmer, 2020).
150 See Bettina Baumgärtel et al., *Angelika Kauffmann* (Ostfildern-Ruit: Hatje, 1998), 115 for an overview of her development as a printmaker and Boydell's additions to her plates and 436–437 for a list of all Kauffmann's prints.
151 Baumgärtel, *Angelika Kauffmann* (1998), 267, 408–409.
152 Tobias G. Natter, "Angelica Kauffman: A Chronology," in *Angelica Kauffman: A Woman of Immense Talent* (Ostfildern: Hatje Cantz, 2007), 277.
153 Alexander, "Kauffman and the Print Market," 141; see 179–189 for a list of 311 prints after Kauffmann published in England before 1810.
154 Malaise Forbes Adam and Mary Mauchline, "Kauffman's Decorative Work," in *Angelica Kauffman: A Continental Artist in Georgian England*, 113–40, esp. 120–140; Clayton, *The English Print*, 268, 272, 279.
155 Chrétien worked with Edmé Quenedey until 1789, then with Jean Fouquet and Jean Simon Fournier. For a partial catalogue, see René Hennequin, *Les portraits au physionotrace* (Troyes: J.-L. Paton, 1932); on the process with an illustration of the device, see Gisèle Freund, *Photography & Society* (Boston: David R. Godine, 1980), 8, 13–18.
156 *Inventaire du fonds français, graveurs du XVIIIe siècle* (Paris: Bibliothèque nationale, 1940), vol. 4, 494.
157 Ibid., 495.
158 Clayton, *The English Print*, xii.

159 Diana Donald, *The Age of Caricature: Satirical Prints in the Reign of George III* (New Haven, CT: Yale University Press, 1996).

160 Mary Dorothy George, *Catalogue of Political and Personal Satires Preserved in the Department of Prints and Drawings in the British Museum, 1771–1783* (London: British Museum, 1935), vol. 5, 723, cat. no. 6251.

161 Nicholas K. Robinson, *Edmund Burke: A Life in Caricature* (New Haven, CT: Yale University Press, 1996), 7–8.

162 George, *Political and Personal Satires*, cat. no. 6251; Robinson argues that this characterization is unfair because Burke used his position to root out corruption; *Edmund Burke*, 52.

163 Donald, *The Age of Caricature*, 15; Vic Gatrell, *City of Laughter: Sex and Satire in Eighteenth-Century London* (New York: Walker and Company, 2006), 9–12, 486–489; Andrew Benjamin Bricker, *Libel and Lampoon: Satire in the Courts 1670–1792* (Oxford: Oxford University Press, 2022), 209–233.

164 Griffiths, *The Print Before Photography*, 490–491.

165 Howard P. Vincent, *Daumier and His World* (Evanston, IL: Northwestern University Press, 1968) on Daumier and lithography in Paris, 8–9; on his punishment, 29; see Dieter and Linda Noack, *The Daumier Register* for a complete catalogue: www.daumier-register.org.

166 Bruce Laughton, *Honoré Daumier* (New Haven, CT: Yale University Press, 1996), 6–19; Kristen L. Spangenberg, ed., *Six Centuries of Master Prints: Treasures from the Herbert Greer French Collection* (Cincinnati, OH: Cincinnati Art Museum, 1993), 263–264, cat. no. 122 and 271–272, cat. no. 130.

167 Peter Ward, *The Clean Body: A Modern History* (Montreal and Kingston: McGill-Queen's University Press, 2019), 44.

168 Ibid., 43–44.

169 Bernard Huin, "L'imagerie à Épinal," in *Images d'Épinal* (Québec: Musée du Québec, 1995), 33–34.

170 Denis Martin, "L'Imagerie d'Épinal; bref historique d'un entreprise" in *Images d'Épinal*, 57, 59.

171 Huin, "L'imagerie à Épinal," 43. Épinal prints were also exported to North America; Denis Martin, "Avant-propos," in *Images d'Épinal*, 22–28.

172 Martin, "L'Imagerie d'Épinal," 54.

173 Martha Tedeschi, "The New Language of Etching in Nineteenth-Century England," in *The "Writing" of Modern Life: the Etching Revival in France, Britain, and the U.S., 1850–1940* (Chicago: Smart Museum of Art, 2008), 25–37; Emma Chambers, *An Indolent and Blundering Art? The Etching Revival and the Redefinition of Etching in England 1838–1892* (Aldershot: Ashgate, 1999).

174 Richard S. Schneiderman, *A Catalogue Raisonné of the Prints of Sir Francis Seymour Haden* (London: Robin Garton, 1983), 28–29, 423. Haden is discussed extensively in Chambers, *An Indolent and Blundering Art.*

175 On Whistler and Haden, Schneiderman, *Francis Seymour Haden*, 25.

176 Ibid., 27.

177 For the quote, Francis Seymour Haden, "On the Revival of Mezzotint as a Painter's Art," *Harper's Magazine*, LXX (1885): 234; on mezzotint sketching: 238. Haden reports that his attempts to produce mezzotints with copperplates en plein air were unsuccessful.

178 Jay McKean Fisher, "Historical Perspective," in Jay McKean Fisher and Colles Baxter, *Félix Buhot, Peintre-Graveur: Prints, Drawings, and Paintings* (Baltimore: Baltimore Museum of Art, 1983), 33.

179 On Buhot's techniques, see Colles Baxter, "Painting on Copper: Félix Buhot's Approach to Etching," in *Félix Buhot, Peintre-Graveur: Prints, Drawings, and Paintings*, 39–52; and Gregory Jecmen, *The Prints of Felix Buhot: Impressions of City and Sea* (Washington, DC: National Gallery of Art, 2005), 4.

180 On Buhot's use of photography, see Baxter, "Painting on Copper," 43–45.

181 For the watercolor, see André Fontaine, *Félix Buhot: Peintre-Graveur 1847–1898* (Paris: Editions Jafont, 1982), facing 148; on the techniques, Gustave Bourcard and James Goodfriend, *Félix Buhot: catalogue descriptif de son œuvre gravé* (New York: M. Gordon, 1979), 108–110, cat. no. 165; and Fisher and Baxter, *Félix Buhot*, 116–117.

182 Phillip Dennis Cate, "Felix Buhot & Japonisme," *The Print Collector's Newsletter* 6, no. 3 (July–August 1975): 64–67; Colles Baxter, "Some Notes on Margins:

Formats, Sources, Meanings," in *Félix Buhot, Peintre-Graveur: Prints, Drawings, and Paintings*, 53–56.

183 Colta Feller Ives, *The Great Wave: The Influence of Japanese Woodcuts on French Prints* (New York: Metropolitan Museum of Art, 1974). On Delcourt, see Jacquelynn Bass and Richard S. Field, *The Artistic Revival of the Woodcut in France, 1850–1900* (Ann Arbor: University of Michigan Art Museum, 1984), 123.

184 Janine Bailly-Herzberg and Michel Melot, *Dictionnaire de l'estampe en France: 1830–1950* (Paris: Arts et metiers graphiques, 1985), 355. This distribution model proved popular through the mid-twentieth century, with such iterations in the United States as Associated American Artists, an organization that sold prints by mail order in editions of 250 or more.

185 "Ich soll das Leiden der Menschen . . . aussprechen" in Käthe Kollwitz, *Die Tagebücher, 1908–1943* (Munich: btb, 2012), 499, January 5, 1920.

186 Alexandra von dem Knesebeck, *Käthe Kollwitz: Werkverzeichnis der Graphik. Band I & II* (Bern: Kornfeld, 2002); *Käthe Kollwitz: Prints, Process, Politics*, ed. Louis Marchesano (Los Angeles: Getty Research Institute, 2020).

187 See "Leo Steinberg and His Library of Prints," 14 on this relationship.

188 On the theme of *Lustmord* (sexual murder or sexual violence) in Expressionist art of the period, see Starr Figura, *German Expressionism: The Graphic Impulse* (New York: Museum of Modern Art, 2011), 192; and Beth Irwin Lewis, *George Grosz: Art and Politics in the Weimar Republic*, 2nd ed. (Princeton, NJ: Princeton University Press, 1991), 21.

189 Hanns Heinz Ewers, "The Spider," trans. Walter F. Kohn, in *Creeps by Night*, ed. Dashiell Hammett (New York: Belmont Books, 1961), 143–185; Alexander Dückers, *George Grosz: Das Druckgraphische Werk/The Graphic Work*, trans. Steven Connell (San Francisco: Alan Wofsy Fine Arts, 1996), 274–275, cat. no. E12 II.

190 Ibid., 127.

191 On the production of his monotypes, see Jay McKean Fisher, *Matisse as Printmaker: Works from the Pierre and Tana Matisse Foundation* (New York: American Federation of Arts, 2009), 40.

192 Marguerite Duthuit-Matisse, Claude Duthuit, and Françoise Garnaud, *Henri Matisse: Catalogue Raisonné de l'œuvre gravé* (Paris: C. Duthuit, 1983), vol. 1, xix, xxvii.

193 Margit Hahnloser, *Matisse: The Graphic Work* (New York: Rizzoli, 1988), 52.

194 Duthuit-Matisse cat. no. 374, inscribed "Pour les Prisonniers civils en Bohain-en-Vermandois," the Museum of Modern Art, 1015.2011.

195 See also John Bidwell, *Graphic Passion: Matisse and the Book Arts* (University Park, PA: Penn State University Press, 2015); Claude Duthuit and Françoise Garnaud, *Henri Matisse, Catalogue Raisonné des ouvrages illustrés* (Paris: C. Duthuit, 1987).

196 Brenda Danilowitz, *The Prints of Josef Albers: A Catalogue Raisonné 1915–1976* (New York: Hudson Hills, 2010), 18.

197 Danilowitz discusses their relationship in *The Prints of Josef Albers*, 23; Eugenia Joyce Fayen, "Ives-Sillman Publications," in *Norman Ives: Constructions and Reconstructions* (Doylestown, PA: Norman S. Ives Foundation, 2020), 290–295.

198 During this time, Ives-Sillman was also at work with Albers on his celebrated book, *The Interaction of Color*, first published in 1963; see Danilowitz, *The Prints of Josef Albers*, 23.

199 Ibid., 27.

200 Ibid., 23.

201 This poem is printed on the second title page of the *Homage to the Square: Soft Edge-Hard Edge* portfolio.

202 Kate Dempsey Martineau, *Ray Johnson: Selective Inheritance* (Oakland: University of California Press, 2018), 2. See also Johanna Gosse, "New York Correspondence School" in *Ray Johnnson c/o*, ed. Caitlin Haskell with Jordan Carter (Chicago: Art Institute of Chicago, 2021), 194–197. Dance, taught by Merce Cunningham, was an important component of the curriculum at Black Mountain College.

203 Robert Descharnes and Gilles Néret, *Salvador Dalí: The Paintings 1904–1989* (Cologne: Taschen, 2019), 402–403, cat. no. 902.

204 Ray Johnson Estate, "Timeline, 1976–1982," accessed August 16, 2022, http://www.rayjohnsonestate.com/timelines/1976-1982/.

Glossary

RELIEF PRINTS

Woodcut
A design is drawn on a hardwood block; the areas around it are then carved away, leaving the raised lines of the composition. The lines are then inked and printed. The similar technique of **metalcut** (which flourished briefly in the second half of the fifteenth century), involved the hammering and punching of designs into a metal plate; its raised surface was then inked and printed either by hand or using a mechanical press.

INTAGLIO PRINTS

Intaglio (from the Italian word for "carving") processes involve incising lines into or texturizing the printing surface, whether by hand (as in engraving, drypoint, and mezzotint) or through the use of acid (as in etching and aquatint). These processes can also be combined on the same plate.

Engraving
In contrast to the raised lines of a woodcut design, engraved lines are incised with a **burin** (a metal tool with a diamond-shaped point) into a metal plate and lie below its surface. Ink is then carefully rolled onto the plate, which is then wiped to force ink into the recessed lines, leaving the surface clean. The plate is then printed either by hand or, more commonly, using a mechanical press.

Etching
Instead of using a burin to incise lines into a metal plate, an etcher uses acid. After the plate has been covered with an acid-resistant ground, a design is drawn with a thin etching needle, thus exposing the metal plate below. When dipped into or brushed with acid, the lines of the design are bitten into the surface of the plate, which is then inked and printed in the same way as an engraving. Different tonalites can be achieved through the selective covering of some areas of the plate with ground and the reapplication of acid, which bites deeper into the exposed lines. These areas will then hold more ink and print darker.

Drypoint
This is the simplest method for producing intaglio prints. Lines are scratched directly onto the metal plate with a sharp stylus or needle and the metal scrapings on either side of the lines, known as the burr, hold a dense layer of ink that prints as a rich, velvety black. However, the fragile burr wears away so quickly that only a small number of good impressions, at most a dozen, can be taken from the plate. The remaining lines are not deeply incised, so they wear away quickly.

Aquatint

A technique intended to simulate ink wash or watercolor. Fine particles of acid-resistant material, such as powdered rosin, are attached to a printing plate by heating. The plate is then immersed in an acid bath as in the etching process; the acid eats into the metal around the particles, producing an indented granular pattern that holds enough ink to create tonal effects when printed.

Mezzotint

A technique that allows the creation of painterly prints with soft gradations of tone and rich, velvety blacks. The surface of the metal plate is roughened by a rocker, a curved metal tool with raised teeth. In order to avoid the plate printing entirely black, the printmaker creates dark and light tones by gradually rubbing down or burnishing the rough surface to various degrees of smoothness to reduce the ink-holding capacity of areas of the plate.

PLANOGRAPHIC PRINTS

Lithography

In a technique that relies on the opposition between oil and water, a composition is drawn with a greasy crayon or ink on a stone and then fixed by a chemical process. The stone (and later in the nineteenth century, a specially prepared metal plate) is then wetted, inked, and printed using a press. Since such lithographic stones and plates are highly durable, a virtually unlimited number of images can be printed.

Monotype

This is essentially a printed drawing. An image is created in ink or painted directly onto a plate (traditionally a copperplate or woodblock) and then printed in a unique impression.

Screenprint

The technique is a kind of stencil printing, using a screen made from fabric (silk or synthetic) stretched tightly over a frame. The non-printing areas on the fabric are blocked out by a stencil created by a coating or film. Ink or paint is then forced through the unblocked areas of fabric with a rubber blade, known as a squeegee, onto the paper. Multiple screens can be layered to add more areas of color.

Notes on the Catalogue

All works of art in the catalogue are from the Blanton Museum's Leo Steinberg Collection unless otherwise noted.

All measurements refer to image (plate or object) size unless otherwise noted.

ABBREVIATIONS

Adamczak Adamczak, Audrey. *Robert Nanteuil, ca. 1623–1678.* Paris: Arthena, 2011.

Andresen Andresen, Andreas. *Der deutsche Peintre-graveur, oder die deutschen Maler als Kupferstecher nach ihrem Leben und ihren Werken.* 5 vols. 1864–78. Reprint, New York: Collectors Editions, 1969.

Baer Baer, Brigitte. *Picasso, peintre-graveur. Catalogue raisonné de l'œuvre gravé et des monotypes.* 7 vols. Bern: Editions Kornfeld, 1986–96.

Barrett Barrett, Kerry. *Pieter Soutman: Life and Oeuvre.* Philadelphia: John Benjamins, 2012.

Bartsch Bartsch, Adam von. *Le Peintre graveur.* 21 vols. Leipzig: J. A. Barth, 1866–1876.

Bellini (1976) Bellini, Paolo. "Elisabetta Sirani." *Nouvelles de l'estampe* 6, no. 30 (November–December 1976): 7–12.

Bellini (1982) Bellini, Paolo. *L'Opera incisa di Giovanni Benedetto Castiglione.* Milan: Ripartizione cultura e spettacolo, 1982.

Bertram Bertram, Geoffrey. *The Etchings of John Clerk of Eldin.* Taunton: Enterprise, 2012.

Bianchi Bianchi, Silvia. "Catalogo dell'opera incisa di Nicola Beatrizet (I parte)." *Grafica d'arte* 54 (April–June 2003): 3–12.

Bloch Bloch, Georges. *Pablo Picasso: Catalogue de l'œuvre gravé et lithographié, 1904–1967.* Bern: Kornfeld und Klipstein, 1968.

Bloch II Bloch, Georges. *Pablo Picasso, tome II: Catalogue de l'œuvre gravé, 1966–1969.* Bern: Kornfeld und Klipstein, 1971.

Boorsch and Lewis Boorsch, Suzanne, Michal Lewis, and R. E. Lewis. *The Engravings of Giorgio Ghisi.* New York: Metropolitan Museum of Art, 1985.

Bourcard and Goodfriend Bourcard, Gustave, and James Goodfriend. *Félix Buhot: Catalogue descriptif de son œuvre gravé.* New York: M. Gordon, 1979.

Corlett Corlett, Mary Lee. *The Prints of Roy Lichtenstein: A Catalogue Raisonné, 1948–1997.* 2nd ed. New York: Hudson Hills, 2002.

Danilowitz Danilowitz, Brenda. *The Prints of Josef Albers: A Catalogue Raisonné, 1915–1976.* Rev. ed., New York: Hudson Hills, 2010.

Daumier Register Noack, Dieter, and Lilian Noack. *Daumier Register.* http://daumier-register.org.

DeGrazia Bohlin DeGrazia Bohlin, Diane. *Prints and Related Drawings by the Carracci Family: A Catalogue Raisonné.* Washington, DC: National Gallery of Art, 1979.

De Vesme and Massar De Vesme, Alexandre, and Phyllis Dearborn Massar. *Stefano della Bella: Catalogue Raisonné.* 2 vols. New York: Collectors' Editions, 1971.

Dückers Dückers, Alexander. *George Grosz: das druckgraphische Werk/The Graphic Work.* Translated by Steven Connell. San Francisco: Alan Wofsy Fine Arts, 1996.

Duthuit-Matisse Duthuit-Matisse, Marguerite, Claude Duthuit, and Françoise Garnaud. *Henri Matisse: Catalogue raisonné de l'œuvre gravé.* 2 vols. Paris: C. Duthuit, 1983.

Field Field, Richard S. *The Prints of Jasper Johns, 1960–1993: A Catalogue Raisonné.* West Islip, NY: Universal Limited Art Editions, 1994.

Gale *Currier & Ives: A Catalogue Raisonné.* 2 vols. Detroit, MI: Gale Research Company, 1984.

George George, Mary Dorothy, and Frederic George Stephens. *Catalogue of Political and Personal Satires Preserved in the Department of Prints and Drawings in the British Museum.* 11 vols. London: The Trustees of the British Museum, 1870–1954.

Hind Hind, Arthur M. *Giovanni Battista Piranesi: A Critical Study with a List of His Published Works and Detailed Catalogues of the Prisons and the Views of Rome.* 2nd ed. New York: Da Capo, 1967.

Hollstein Hollstein, F. W. H., et al. *Dutch & Flemish Etchings, Engravings and Woodcuts, ca. 1450–1700.* Amsterdam: Menno Hertzberger, 1949–ongoing.

Hollstein Hollstein, F. W. H., et al. *German Engravings, Etchings and Woodcuts, ca. 1400–1700.* Amsterdam: Menno Hertzberger, 1954–ongoing.

Höper Höper, Corinna, with Wolfgang Brückle and Udo Felbinger. *Raffael und die Folgen: Das Kunstwerk in Zeitaltern seiner graphischen Reproduzierbarkeit.* Ostfildern-Ruit: Hatje Cantz, 2001.

IFF–18 Roux, Marcel, et al. *Inventaire du fonds français; graveurs du dix-huitième siècle.* 15 vols. Paris: Bibliothèque nationale, 1930–1977.

IFF–19 Laran, Jean, et al. *Inventaire du fonds français après 1800.* 15 vols. Paris: Bibliothèque nationale, 1930–ongoing.

Jenkins Jenkins, Catherine. *Prints at the Court of Fontainebleau, c. 1542–47.* Studies in Prints and Printmaking 7. 3 vols. Ouderkerk aan den IJssel: Sound & Vision, 2017.

Knesebeck Knesebeck, Alexandra von dem. *Käthe Kollwitz: Werkverzeichnis der Graphik.* 2 vols. Bern: Kornfeld, 2002.

Laurentius Laurentius, Theo and Jan Wolter Niemeijer. Translated by Patricia Wardle. *Cornelis Ploos van Amstel 1726–1798: Kunstverzamelaar en prentuitgever.* Assen: Van Gorcum, 1980.

Le Blanc Le Blanc, Charles. *Manuel de l'amateur d'estampes, contenant le dictionnaire des gravures de toutes les nations.* 4 vols. Paris: E. Bouillon, 1854–1890.

Lieure Lieure, Jules. *Jacques Callot.* Paris: Editions de la Gazette des beaux-arts, 1924–1929. Reprint in 2 vols., San Francisco: Alan Wofsy Fine Arts, 1989.

Lothe Lothe, José. *L'œuvre gravé d'Abraham Bosse, graveur parisien du XVIIe siècle: Catalogue général avec les reproductions de 451 estampes.* Paris: Paris Musées, 2008.

Lumsden Lumsden, E. S. "The Etchings of John Clerk of Eldin." *The Print Collector's Quarterly* 12, no. 1 (February 1925): 15–39.

Mannocci Mannocci, Lino. *The Etchings of Claude Lorrain.* New Haven, CT: Yale University Press, 1988.

Massari (1980) Massari, Stefania. *Incisori mantovani del '500: Giovan Battista, Adamo, Diana Scultori e Giorgio Ghisi dalle collezioni del Gabinetto nazionale delle stampe e della Calcografia nazionale: Catalogo.* Rome: De Luca, 1980.

Massari (1983) Massari, Stefania. *Giulio Bonasone.* 2 vols. Rome: Quasar, 1983.

Meder Meder, Joseph. *Dürer-Katalog; ein Handbuch über Albrecht Dürers Stiche, Radierungen, Holzschnitte,* *deren Zustände, Ausgaben und Wasserzeichen.* Vienna: Gilhofer und Ranschburg, 1932.

Mussini Mussini, Massimo. *La Bibbia di Raffaello: Scienza e "Scrittura" nella stampa di riproduzioni dei secoli XVI e XVII.* Brescia: Paideia, 1979.

New Hollstein Hollstein, F. W. H., et al. *The New Hollstein: Dutch & Flemish Etchings, Engravings and Woodcuts, 1450–1700.* Roosendaal: Koninklijke van Poll in cooperation with the Rijksprentenkabinet, Rijksmuseum, 1993–ongoing.

New Hollstein Hollstein, F. W. H., et al. *The New Hollstein: German Engravings, Etchings and Woodcuts, 1400–1700.* Rotterdam: Sound & Vision Interactive, 1996–ongoing.

Pérez Pérez, Marie-Félicie, and Rainer Michael Mason. *L'œuvre gravé de Jean-Jacques de Boissieu, 1736–1810.* 2nd ed. Geneva: Cabinet des estampes, 1994.

Petitjean and Wickert Petitjean, Charles, and Charles Wickert. *Catalogue de l'œuvre gravé de Robert Nanteuil.* Paris: Loys Delteil et Maurice Le Garrec, 1925.

Pillsbury and Richards Pillsbury, Edmund P., and Louise S. Richards. *The Graphic Art of Federico Barocci: Selected Drawings and Prints.* New Haven, CT: Yale University Art Gallery, 1978.

Rizzi Rizzi, Aldo. *The Etchings of the Tiepolos.* London: Phaidon, 1971.

Robert-Dumesnil Robert-Dumesnil, Alexandre-Pierre-François. *Le peintre-graveur français, ou Catalogue raisonné des estampes gravées par les peintres et les dessinateurs de l'école française.* 11 vols. Paris: Gabriel Warée, 1835–71.

Rosand and Muraro Rosand, David, and Michelangelo Muraro. *Titian and the Venetian Woodcut.* Washington, DC: International Exhibitions Foundation, 1976.

Scorsetti Scorsetti, Monica. "Giovanni Battista de Cavalieri, catalogo delle stampe sciolte." *Grafica d'arte* 49 (January & April 2002): 4–17.

Schneiderman Schneiderman, Richard S. *A Catalogue Raisonné of the Prints of Sir Francis Seymour Haden.* London: Robin Garton, 1983.

Schoch Schoch, Rainer, Matthias Mende, and Anna Scherbaum. *Albrecht Dürer: Das druckgraphische Werk.* 3 vols. Munich: Prestel, 2001–2004.

Shoemaker Shoemaker, Innis H. *The Engravings of Marcantonio Raimondi.* Lawrence, KS: Spencer Museum of Art, 1981.

Strauss Strauss, Walter L. *The German Single-Leaf Woodcut, 1550–1600: A Pictorial Catalogue.* 3 vols. New York: Abaris Books, 1975.

Talbierska Talbierska, Jolanta. *Stefano della Bella (1610–1664): Etchings from the Collection of the Print Room of the Warsaw University Library.* Warsaw: Neriton, 2001.

TIB Bartsch, Adam von. *The Illustrated Bartsch.* Edited by Walter S. Strauss. New York: Abaris Books, 1978–ongoing.

White and Boon White, Christopher, and Karel G. Boon. *Rembrandt's Etchings: An Illustrated Critical Catalogue.* 2 vols. Amsterdam: Van Gendt, 1969.

Wildenstein Wildenstein, Georges. *Fragonard aquafortiste.* Paris: Les Beaux-Arts, 1956.

Wilton-Ely Wilton-Ely, John. *Giovanni Battista Piranesi: The Complete Etchings.* 2 vols. San Francisco: Alan Wofsy Fine Arts, 1994.

Zerner Zerner, Henri. *École de Fontainebleau: Gravures.* Paris: Arts et métiers graphiques, 1969.

This book is published in conjunction with the exhibition *After Michelangelo, Past Picasso: Leo Steinberg's Library of Prints*, presented at the Blanton Museum of Art from February 7, 2021, to May 9, 2021.

Major funding was provided by the Getty Foundation through The Paper Project, with additional support from Leslie Shaunty and Robert Topp, the Scurlock Foundation Exhibition Endowment, the IFPDA Foundation, Prudence Crowther, and Robert Dance.

Library of Congress Control Number: 2023933081
ISBN 978-1-64657-034-8

Published by the Blanton Museum of Art
200 E. Martin Luther King Jr. Blvd.
Austin, TX 78712
www.blantonmuseum.org

Available through ARTBOOK | D.A.P.
75 Broad Street, Suite 630
New York, NY 10004
www.artbook.com

Produced by Marquand Books, Seattle
www.marquandbooks.com

Edited by Catherine Bindman
Designed by Thomas Eykemans
Typeset in Minion by Brynn Warriner
Proofread by Ted Gilley
Color management by I/O Color, Seattle
Printed and bound in China by C&C Offset Printing Co.

Front cover: Giorgio Ghisi, *The Prophet Jeremiah*, after a fresco by Michelangelo, early 1570s. Engraving, 11 13/16 × 17 in. (30 × 43.2 cm). Boorsch and Lewis 48 (2002.1740)
Back cover: Jasper Johns, *Ale Cans*, 1964 (fig. 55)
Front inside cover: René Boyvin, *Echevellée et nue par nuit brune*, 1563 (pl. 12)
Back inside cover: Jan van Doetecum and Lucas van Doetecum, Plate 5 from *Oval Architectural Perspective Views for Intarsia Work*, ca. 1560–62 (pl. 13)
p. 2: Giovanni Battista Scultori, *David and Goliath*, 1540 (pl. 8)
p. 4: Unknown British Artist, *The Golden-Pippin Boys on the Branches of State*, 1783 (pl. 42)
p. 6: Albrecht Dürer, *St. Christopher Facing Right*, 1521 (pl. 5)
p. 12: Hendrick Goltzius, *The Farnese Hercules*, 1592 (fig. 3)
p. 28: Raffaello Schiaminossi, *Madonna and Child with St. Vincent and St. Cecilia*, ca. 1601 (fig. 41)
p. 58: Robert Rauschenberg, *Booster*, 1967 (fig. 59)
p. 68: Jean-Jacques de Boissieu, *Studies of Heads*, 1770 (pl. 35)